LONDON 2014

THE CITY AT A GLANCE

CW00540234

Barbican

Residential towers are built ar[ound an] arts centre in this modernist ci[ty.]
See p071

St Paul's Cathedral

The once-unmissable landmark is slowly being overshadowed by nearby developments.
St Paul's Churchyard, EC4, T 7246 8350

Millennium Bridge

Due to early teething problems when the rush-hour stomp caused it to vibrate, Norman Foster's span is dubbed the 'wobbly bridge'.

Bank of England

Sir Nikolaus Pevsner called Sir Herbert Baker's 1925 to 1939 near-obliteration of Sir John Soane's building a 'great architectural crime'.
Threadneedle Street, EC2

Tower 42

Despite being rebranded, reclad and tarted up, Richard Seifert's 1980 monolith is still known as the NatWest Tower by most locals.
25 Old Broad Street, EC2

Tate Modern

This vast modern-art museum is housed in Sir Giles Gilbert Scott's former power station.
See p010

30 St Mary Axe

The profile of this early noughties addition to the City led to its nickname, the 'Gherkin'.
See p012

Shakespeare's Globe

A 1997 recreation of the theatre demolished in 1644, the Globe is the brainchild of the American actor Sam Wanamaker.
21 New Globe Walk, SE1

INTRODUCTION
THE CHANGING FACE OF THE URBAN SCENE

Twenty years ago, London's claim to be one of the world's greatest cities was unconvincing. Now it is perhaps *the* global city. Every talented son or daughter of Europe and beyond, it seems, tries their luck here, seeing if they can make it fly. Many of them man the incredible restaurants, bars, cafés and shops that London offers. From establishment-cool Notting Hill to alternative-cool Hackney, you're as likely to hear Spanish, French or Polish as English.

However, for all its luxurious fixtures and fittings, London is not always easy to enjoy. It is tough and sprawling and inscrutable, violently fluid and fickle. It is full of cliques and protected spaces, of neighbourhoods entirely at odds with one another. But if the recession has dampened the capital's good-times vibe, it hasn't dampened it much. Regeneration is happening apace. And just as the city's focal point shifted eastwards (a pull accelerated by the 2012 Olympics) the South-East became the location of major redevelopment led by Renzo Piano's <u>Shard</u> (see p067). This is not a city that stands still, and in King's Cross and the Queen Elizabeth Olympic Park, major new districts are being created from scratch. Their aim is to be London, but better. We will see.

Today, the problem is plotting a course through it all, as London scatters its treasures far and wide, and farther and wider. We can think of no other city in the world that requires so much insider nous to navigate properly. And that is where we come in, of course.

ESSENTIAL INFO
FACTS, FIGURES AND USEFUL ADDRESSES

TOURIST OFFICE
St Paul's Churchyard, EC4
T 7332 1456
www.visitlondon.com

TRANSPORT
Heathrow transfer to Paddington
Trains depart every 15 minutes from 5.10am
to 11.45pm. The journey takes 15 minutes
www.heathrowexpress.com
Bicycles
Bikes can be hired across central London;
there is no charge for the first 30 minutes
www.tfl.gov.uk
Car hire
Avis
T 0844 581 0147
Public transport
Tube trains run from approximately
5.30am to 12.30am, Monday to Saturday;
6.30am to 12am on Sundays
www.tfl.gov.uk
Taxis
London Black Cabs
T 0795 769 6673
Travel card
A one-day zones 1-2 pass costs £8.80;
a seven-day zones 1-2 pass costs £30.40

EMERGENCY SERVICES
Emergencies
T 999
24-hour pharmacy
Zafash
233-235 Old Brompton Road, SW5
T 7373 2798

EMBASSY
US Embassy
24 Grosvenor Square, W1
T 7499 9000
london.usembassy.gov

POSTAL SERVICES
Post office
The Plaza, W1
T 0845 722 3344
Shipping
UPS
T 0845 787 7877

BOOKS
London Architecture
by Marianne Butler (Metro Publications)
The London Blue Plaque Guide
by Nick Rennison (The History Press)

WEBSITES
Art
www.ica.org.uk
Design
www.londondesignfestival.com
Newspaper
www.standard.co.uk

EVENTS
Frieze Art Fair
www.friezelondon.com
100% Design
www.100percentdesign.co.uk
Open House London
www.londonopenhouse.org

COST OF LIVING
**Taxi from Heathrow Airport
to city centre**
£55
Cappuccino
£2.50
Packet of cigarettes
£7.50
Daily newspaper
£1.20
Bottle of champagne
£70

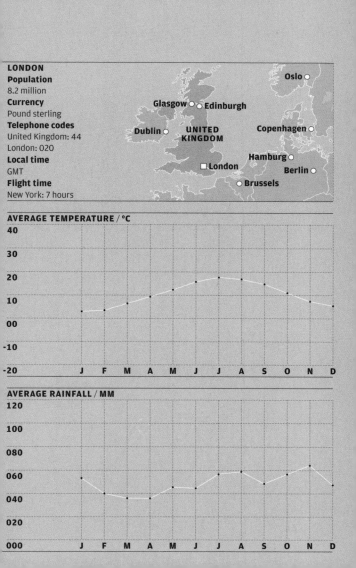

LONDON
Population
8.2 million
Currency
Pound sterling
Telephone codes
United Kingdom: 44
London: 020
Local time
GMT
Flight time
New York: 7 hours

Oslo
Glasgow Edinburgh
Dublin **UNITED KINGDOM**
Copenhagen
Hamburg
London Berlin
Brussels

AVERAGE TEMPERATURE / °C

40												
30												
20												
10												
00												
-10												
-20	J	F	M	A	M	J	J	A	S	O	N	D

AVERAGE RAINFALL / MM

120												
100												
080												
060												
040												
020												
000	J	F	M	A	M	J	J	A	S	O	N	D

NEIGHBOURHOODS

THE AREAS YOU NEED TO KNOW AND WHY

To help you navigate the city, we've chosen the most interesting districts (see below and the map inside the back cover) and colour-coded our featured venues, according to their location; those venues that are outside these areas are not coloured.

CENTRAL

London's West End is really the centre of the modern city. Bloomsbury, spiritual home of the literati, is a kind of oasis, as is Marylebone, which is now a chichi shopping destination. Soho has lost steam to Shoreditch as a nocturnal playground, but you'll still find the grandest hotels in Mayfair, including Claridge's (see p020).

NORTH

Traditionally, the hills of North London have had a more bohemian air than the West. Primrose Hill is one of the city's most desirable enclaves, Camden gets crammed with tourists, and King's Cross is undergoing an ambitious urban overhaul, with St Pancras station as its focal point.

THE CITY

This is the world's biggest financial centre, and the huge wages of the 'City boys' spill west into the top clubs and restaurants. The area is a mix of shining towers, cranes and Victorian pubs, which are largely deserted at night, although the lack of residents is now attracting hip nightspots.

SOUTH-WEST

Purest posh, this district has some of the most expensive property on the planet. You can't move for lords, ladies, oil-funded Arab royalty, Russian oligarchs and the odd Hollywood A-lister. It also houses a number of fine-dining restaurants, such as Ametsa with Arzak Instruction (see p044).

WEST

Notting Hill can feel like a fantasy land, with its pristine stucco townhouses, chic boutiques and eateries, including Dock Kitchen (see p054), and the famous and picturesque Portobello street market. The sheer pleasantness of it all can unnerve some, although tourists may believe they have found an urban idyll.

WESTMINSTER

Britain's administrative heart is the site of royal palaces and was once the seat of a globe-spanning empire. It is the country's ancient and wheezing engine room. Our tip is to visit Tate Britain (Millbank, SW1, T 7887 8888), then take a river boat to the South Bank for the most splendid of views.

EAST

After a transformation, this area dragged the epicentre of London hipness sharply eastward. In Clerkenwell, designers, architects and commercial creatives live, work and eat at venues such as St John (see p042) and Workshop Coffee Co (27 Clerkenwell Road, EC1, T 7253 5754).

SOUTH-EAST

The opening of Tate Modern (see p010) in 2000 forced Londoners to accept that Bankside was worth a look. Borough Market (8 Southwark Street, SE1, T 7407 1002) draws foodies, and evidence of Bermondsey's regeneration comes in the form of the White Cube gallery (see p037).

LANDMARKS
THE SHAPE OF THE CITY SKYLINE

It's difficult to imagine now, but 50 years ago a portrait of the London skyline was a celebration of the smaller, gentler things in life. Quaintness was the city's stock-in-trade. Until the early 1960s, the height of new buildings was prescribed, not by some far-reaching architectural masterplan but by how high a fireman's ladder could reach – about 30m, as it happened. Inevitably, this all changed later in the decade. The BT Tower (see p014), looking like a *2001: A Space Odyssey* film set *avant la lettre*, seemed to be a manifestation of an altogether better future. Today, Foster + Partners' 30 St Mary Axe (see p012) in the City holds a similarly iconic status. But the latter's role as London's totemic tower has now been taken by Renzo Piano's jaw-dropper of a glass pyramid, The Shard (see p067), just south of the Thames next to London Bridge station. Appearing in your line of sight, whichever side of the river you are on, it is impossible to ignore and hard to resist.

Trellick Tower (see p015) is a reference point in West London, and was equally controversial (JG Ballard allegedly based his novel *High-Rise*, in which tenants begin floor-on-floor warfare, on this block). Ernö Goldfinger's landmark has become a cult item, featured in pop songs and on T-shirts, and is now highly desirable real estate – the defining icon of modernism's rehabilitation and of the city's acceptance of its radically changing face.

For full addresses, see Resources.

Tate Modern

When Swiss architects Herzog & de Meuron
created a sister gallery to Tate Britain (see
p032), in a former power station in South-
East London, it seemed like utter madness.
Now, Tate Modern is a poster child for the
regenerative power of architecture, yet the
rawness of Sir Giles Gilbert Scott's building
remains the real point. An extension, also
by Herzog & de Meuron, will open in 2016.
Bankside, SE1, T 7887 8888

30 St Mary Axe

Completed in 2004, the 'Gherkin' or, more properly, 30 St Mary Axe, is still a defining marker of the City. Designed by Foster + Partners, whose team then included Ken Shuttleworth (the man behind Hong Kong's Chek Lap Kok Airport), the structure swells at its mid-point, tapering to a glass dome. The dome houses one of the world's most covetable staff canteens, part of which has been opened as a members' bar. The tower's cigar shape means that the public spaces at the base are not blighted by the street-level hurricanes produced by more traditional high-rises. Inside, it's divided into a series of coiling atriums and gardens, which work to open up the building and link the 40 floors, which are far more than a series of stacked shelves for worker ants.
30 St Mary Axe, EC3,
www.30stmaryaxe.com

Centre Point

Richard Seifert's influence on the London cityscape is unmatched (cast an eye over his 1962 Space House at 1 Kemble Street, WC2), but not always in a good way. When this office development was unveiled in 1966, it was the tallest building in London. It was also, famously, one of the most underutilised. The developer, Harry Hyams, wanted to rent the whole building to a single tenant and, as a result, it stood empty for many years. Schemes to turn it into housing have been mooted over the decades, but it seems that its legacy will be as a pointer to shoppers on Oxford Street, and to the power of the property developer's greed. On the top floors, the Paramount restaurant (T 7420 2900), and Tom Dixon-designed bar offer one of the most dramatic panoramas in the city.
101-103 New Oxford Street, WC1

BT Tower

Unusually for an instantly recognisable landmark, during the first 30 years of its existence the BT Tower (formerly known as the Post Office Tower) did not appear on any maps. As a microwave relay station for the national phone company – fabulously exotic technology for the time – it was an unlikely inclusion in the Official Secrets Act, and surely the only one with a revolving restaurant on top. But then, ever since it was officially opened in 1966 by a noted left-wing politician (Tony Benn) and the owner of a chain of holiday camps (Billy Butlin), the structure has always been a mix of contradictions. The restaurant was bombed by the IRA in 1971 and was closed in 1980, although occasionally it's used for corporate events. As a telecoms tower, the building is still in operational use.
60 Cleveland Street, W1

Trellick Tower

Ernö Goldfinger's high-rise looms over the stuccoed townhouses and chichi eateries of Ladbroke Grove, a last blast of top-quality brutalism in the UK. The architect started work on the 31-storey structure in 1969 and it was completed in 1972. The look of Trellick Tower is of a monumental concrete slab with add-ons. It is defined by a separate service tower connected to the 'living units' in the main building by concealed walkways every third floor, with a cantilevered boiler house hanging above it. The apartments themselves are huge, for social housing, and have large windows and balconies. Goldfinger took obsessive care of the details. The balconies have cedar cladding, and the windows are double-glazed and spin round for ease of cleaning.

5 Golborne Road, W10

HOTELS
WHERE TO STAY AND WHICH ROOMS TO BOOK

In The Savoy (opposite), Claridge's (see p020) and The Dorchester (Park Lane, W1, T 7629 8888), London has some of the world's most famous hotels – landlocked Titanics, all grand ballrooms and gilded doormen. The Corinthia (Whitehall Place, SW1, T 7930 8181) is a contemporary take on the grand pile, while the Café Royal (see p018), a more demi-monde destination, was rethought by David Chipperfield. The city also has several top-quality one-off townhouses, such as The Zetter (86-88 Clerkenwell Road, EC1, T 7324 4444), and Dorset Square Hotel (see p027). Terence Conran's Boundary (see p028) helped make Redchurch Street in Shoreditch a fashionable strip, and, further to the east, the Town Hall Hotel (see p030) is a beautifully executed midcentury fantasy.

London's hotel scene is set to get even hotter. A Shangri-La has opened in The Shard (see p067), and Ian Schrager and Marriott have carved out the hip London Edition (10 Berners Street, W1, T 7781 0000) from the former Berners Hotel. Meanwhile, David Collins is turning the 1922 Port of London Authority Building into 10 Trinity Square (EC3); Tom Dixon is transforming part of the PoMoish Sea Containers House into a Mondrian (20 Upper Ground, SE1); and André Balazs is converting Marylebone's old fire station. Restaurateurs Chris Corbin and Jeremy King are joining the fray too, with The Beaumont Hotel (8 Balderton Street, W1) in 2014. *For full addresses and room rates, see Resources.*

The Savoy

The renovation of this most iconic hotel (it was once run by César Ritz, with Auguste Escoffier in the kitchen) involved a £220m, three-year overhaul — surely no easy task. But interior designer Pierre-Yves Rochon and Pentagram's John Rushworth, who were charged with dusting off the Savoy's 'identity', did a respectful job, placing an emphasis on fine materials and drama only where it was needed. The cluster of in-house restaurants includes Gordon Ramsay's Savoy Grill (T 7592 1600), and the more recent Kaspar's Seafood Bar & Grill (T 7420 2111), which opened in May 2013. The gilt-edged Beaufort Bar (above) sits on the former stage where Gershwin once performed *Rhapsody in Blue*, and then, of course, there's the American Bar. *Strand, WC2, T 7836 4343, www.fairmont.com/savoy*

Café Royal
Opened in 1865, Café Royal was once
the haunt of bohemian London; Oscar
Wilde and Virginia Woolf were regulars.
Alfred and Georgi Akirov recruited
David Chipperfield to breathe new life
into the original features and create 159
rooms (Portland Junior Suite, pictured).
Six suites were sympathetically restored
by Donald Insall Associates.
68 Regent Street, W1, T 7406 3333

Claridge's

Although it may be the de facto HQ of the European aristocracy, not even a hotel of Claridge's standing can afford to rest on its laurels. All of London's great hotels have had to update to survive and none has done so as successfully as this. In 2010, Diane von Furstenberg redesigned several rooms and suites, all of which feature her trademark prints and bold colours. DVF's two-bedroom Grand Piano Suite (above), which comes with butler service, is our favourite. The public spaces, including the Foyer and Reading Room dining areas, have been restored to striking effect by New York architect Thierry Despont, and David Collins' modern art deco bar is equally attractive. And (a detail we love) the lift has its own operator and sofa.
Brook Street, W1, T 7629 8860,
www.claridges.co.uk

South Place Hotel

This is the first hotel from D&D London, the company that now runs much of what was Terence Conran's restaurant empire, and the first newly built hotel in the City for a century. It was designed by Allies & Morrison, masters of the corporate-box-with-a-twist, but the architects haven't stretched themselves that far here. The interiors are by Conran & Partners. South Place makes much play (although it is now standard) of the art scattered around the public areas and 80 rooms, such as 604 (above), although given D&D's pedigree, the hotel is really about the F&B. There are two restaurants, the seafood-centric Angler and the all-day 3 South Place Bar & Grill, and three bars. Le Chiffre is a natty games room for post-prandial playtime. *3 South Place, EC2, T 3503 0000, www.southplacehotel.com*

One Leicester Street

What was Fergus Henderson's small but lovely St John Hotel has been taken over and relaunched as One Leicester Street. Now part of Loh Lik Peng's group, Unlisted Collection, which includes the Town Hall Hotel (see p030), its essential proposition remains the same – 15 rooms (No 503, right) with an excellent bar and restaurant attached. Universal Design Studio worked on the interiors, while A Practice for Everyday Life (see p062) came up with a new identity (including hand-painted ITC Barcelona-font signage). The more serious changes are in the upper-floor bar and ground-level restaurant, which has gained a wall-length leather banquette and a Victorian awning over the terrace. Happily, Peng has retained the services of Michelin-starred Tom Harris in the kitchen.
*1 Leicester Street, WC2, T 3301 8020,
www.oneleicesterstreet.com*

Bulgari

This sparkling addition to the Bulgari chain, set in a Portland-stone block in Knightsbridge, is another (rare) new-build hotel in London. Its 85 accommodations, each designed by a team led by Antonio Citterio and Patricia Viel, feature lashings of leather, mahogany and stained oak, and all things luxe, as in the Bulgari III Suite (above). Six of the hotel's 12 floors are below ground, and its 47-seat cinema has a library of films curated by British director and producer David Puttnam. Il Ristorante, the in-house restaurant, is helmed by Robbie Pepin, who trained with Alain Ducasse. The jewel in Bulgari's new crown, though, is the two-floor spa (T 7151 1055), enhanced by a 25m pool (opposite) lined with green and gold mosaic tiles. *171 Knightsbridge, SW7, T 7151 1010, www.bulgarihotels.com/london*

ME

At the western tip of the 1920s Aldwych crescent, next to Bush House (former home of the BBC World Service), this 157-room hotel is the work of Foster + Partners, from the outer shell to the bathroom fittings. The triangular building boasts a glass and Portland-stone facade, and oriel windows with views of the Strand and Somerset House. Its centrepiece, a 10-storey atrium housing a white marble lobby, is hidden at the core of the structure. The minimal rooms, such as Aura (above), come with white leather walls and black lacquered cabinets; the penthouse Suite ME is topped by a glass cupola affording a panoramic vista. More landmark spotting, from Big Ben to Canary Wharf, can be done at the glam rooftop bar, Radio (T 7395 3440). *336-337 Strand, WC1, T 0845 601 8980, www.melia.com*

Dorset Square Hotel

Marylebone is emerging as a hospitality hotspot. And any hospitality hotspot in London has to include a Firmdale hotel. Tim and Kit Kemp's group has seven in the city, and Dorset Square is their modus operandi writ small. It has only 38 rooms spread over a townhouse that stands on the site of the first Lord's cricket ground. Petite but perfectly formed, the hotel has rooms, such as the Deluxe Garden View (above), featuring heaps of Kit Kemp's contemporary country-house furnishings and objets trouvés collected on her global travels; and the domestic-scale drawing room is decorated with fabrics produced in collaboration with designer Christopher Farr. The Potting Shed bar and restaurant places an emphasis on cosy discretion.
39-40 Dorset Square, NW1, T 7723 7874, www.firmdalehotels.com

Boundary

Launched in 2009, this hotel tickles all our fancies. It's small, with only 12 rooms and five suites, there's a great subterranean restaurant, a rooftop garden and grill, and a café/deli combo, Albion (T 7729 1051). It also has good green credentials. Each room has a designer or design movement as a theme so, among others, there's a Bauhaus Room (pictured) and an Eileen Gray Room. *2-4 Boundary Street, E2, T 7729 1051*

Town Hall Hotel
Even now, this seems an unlikely area for one of the capital's most interesting hotels. But here it is, in the Edwardian-with-art-deco-additions splendour of the former Bethnal Green Town Hall. There's so much to admire: Rare Architecture's sensitive restoration and daring extension, with its laser-cut metal skin; the mix of midcentury and bespoke furnishings; and the clever provision of rooms — the studios and one- (LG06, above and opposite), two- and three-bed suites are ideal for the creative folk who travel in packs, and the triple-height De Montfort Suite makes the most of the grand old building. And then there's Viajante (T 7871 0461), helmed by Michelin-starred chef Nuno Mendes, and its more affordable offshoot, the Corner Room. *Patriot Square, E2, T 7871 0460, www.townhallhotel.com*

24 HOURS
SEE THE BEST OF THE CITY IN JUST ONE DAY

Just a quarter of a century ago, the presentation of Carl Andre's *Equivalent VIII*, better known as 'The Bricks', at the Tate gallery, now better known as Tate Britain (Millbank, SW1, T 7887 8888), caused much gnashing of teeth in London. (The Bricks remains a byword for crowd-displeasing conceptualism.)

Since the opening of Tate Modern (see p010) in 2000, the city, and visitors to it, have embraced contemporary visual culture, and the museum has become emblematic of London's re-emergence as a global creative hub. Our day is a taste of the capital's generous spread of art and design treasures. We begin at 19 Greek Street (opposite), before heading to the renovated fashion gallery at the V&A (see p034), which holds one of the most important collections of textiles and fashion in the world. From there, we loop back to Soho's borders, to take in The Photographers' Gallery (see p036). Next, cross the river to visit the latest outpost of White Cube (see p037). As is the modern way, Jay Jopling's space is a commercial operation posing as a public resource, and doing a good job of it.

In the evening, we suggest a sortie over to Shoreditch, for drinks and dinner at The Clove Club (see p038), where chef Isaac McHale, a leading player on the East End food scene, has partnered up with DJs-turned-front-of-house-men Johnny Smith and Daniel Willis, the finance coming, in part, from a crowdfunding website. *For full addresses, see Resources.*

10.00 19 Greek Street

The brainchild of Marc Péridis of interior design agency Montage, 19 Greek Street is six floors of design set in a handsome Victorian townhouse. The first and second levels of the gallery-cum-store are devoted to Espasso, the pioneering US showroom specialising in Brazilian design from the likes of Carlos Motta ('Asturias' armchair, above right). The remainder are peppered with products that prove sustainable design doesn't have to mean a sacrifice of style. There are pieces by Nina Tolstrup ('Pallet' chair, above left), Markus Kayser and Studio Aisslinger. The gallery will also be producing its own furniture – look out for exclusive collaborations, like Tolstrup and fashion designer David David's chair (above rear). Visits are by appointment.
19 Greek Street, W1, T 7734 5594,
www.19greekstreet.com

11.30 V&A fashion gallery
6a Architects' refurbishment of the
V&A's Octagon Court has opened up one
of the museum's grandest spaces. Built
in 1909, the vast dome tops a series of
arches and alcoves. A mezzanine was
inserted in 1962 and 6a have left this in
place, reducing its impact with slender
balustrades. Their addition is three large
light rings that illuminate the dome.
Cromwell Road, SW7, T 7942 2000

14.30 The Photographers' Gallery

In 1971, in a former Lyons tea bar in Soho, Sue Davies launched the world's first independent gallery devoted to photography. Among those given their first British shows there were Juergen Teller, Andreas Gursky and Taryn Simon. Outgrowing the site, The Photographers' Gallery moved to Ramillies Street in 2008 and, in 2010, embarked on a redesign by Irish architects O'Donnell + Tuomey.

Reopened in 2012, it now contains three floors of exhibition space, including 'The Wall', which presents a rota of artists' work (Susan Sloan, above), a café, a bookshop and a print sales room. Intriguingly, the gallery is pushing for the street outside to be pedestrianised and to use the walls of other buildings as further display space. *16-18 Ramillies Street, W1, T 7087 9300, www.thephotographersgallery.org.uk*

16.00 White Cube

Jay Jopling's first White Cube gallery, which launched in 1993, was 20.5 sq m. His third, opened in 2011, is somewhat larger, at 5,400 sq m. It's a measure, literally, of how far Jopling's operation has come, but also of the degree to which the big-league art dealer has to come off as public-spirited these days. The most recent branch, a marker of Bermondsey's rebranding, has the size and ambition of a public gallery, with 'museum-quality' exhibitions, a bookshop and an auditorium. Three large spaces show the artists who White Cube represents, and three smaller areas provide a platform for younger talent. The 1970s warehouse was converted by Casper Mueller Kneer, whose adaptation of the canopy is a nod to Ed Ruscha. *144-152 Bermondsey Street, SE1, T 7930 5373, www.whitecube.com*

19.00 The Clove Club

If there is one opening that got London's food bloggerati all of a quiver, it is The Clove Club. Indeed, cynical commentators have suggested that the cooking here is designed more to be Instagrammed than eaten and savoured. Isaac McHale's dishes are certainly beautiful – as is potter Owen Wall's tableware – but they also deliver taste-wise. McHale, part of the Young Turks collective and latterly of Upstairs at The Ten Bells (T 07530 492 986) in Spitafields, serves a local, seasonal tasting menu. The restaurant is housed in Shoreditch Town Hall, an Edwardian building that is being converted into an arts complex. Working with architects Mango, the founding trio kept the interiors stark, with an open kitchen as the centre of attention. A bar area offers lighter bites that are a step up from the standard Anglo tapas.
Shoreditch Town Hall, 380 Old Street, EC1, T 7729 6496, www.thecloveclub.com

URBAN LIFE
CAFÉS, RESTAURANTS, BARS AND NIGHTCLUBS

London has a nightlife proposition to rival any city. Its dining scene is as vibrant as New York's and it boasts world-class restaurants. Indeed, some of NYC's culinary hotshots decided it was high time for a transatlantic move. Daniel Boulud opened Bar Boulud (66 Knightsbridge, SW1, T 7201 3899) and Brit April Bloomfield, who charmed Gothamites with The Spotted Pig and Breslin, is said to be looking for a venue here. But the big news is the homecoming of Keith McNally, whose launch of Balthazar (see p049) in Covent Garden has confirmed the power shift between the two cities. It's also part of a wave of bistros to have hit town, including Colbert (50-52 Sloane Square, SW1, T 7730 2804). Elsewhere, Coya (see p050), Lima (31 Rathbone Place, W1, T 3002 2640), Ceviche (17 Frith Street, W1, T 7292 2040) and Sushisamba (110 Bishopsgate, EC2, T 3640 7330) prove the Peruvian trend is still going strong.

Meanwhile, a group of young chefs is cooking up something more experimental than steak frites and salsa. Oliver Dabbous continues to make people wait (a long time) for a chance to eat at his eponymous restaurant (see p043); Tom Sellers has gone solo at Story (see p046); and Isaac McHale prevails at The Clove Club (see p038). Beagle (opposite) is leading the charge towards three-in-one venues (eating/drinking/coffee), and the tiny Happiness Forgets (8-9 Hoxton Square, N1) is winning the speakeasy wars. *For full addresses, see Resources.*

Beagle

The lower rents and spaces available in East London are allowing younger food entrepreneurs to open up and to develop new ways of doing things. Such is the case with Beagle, which operates out of three railway arches next to Hoxton station (the venue takes its name from a steam locomotive that once thundered along the North London line). It's owned by the Clancy brothers, Danny and Kieran, who made a name for themselves as DJs. And while the music is top notch, it's the food taking centre stage. Chef James Ferguson, recruited from Rochelle Canteen (T 7729 5677), emphasises local, seasonal fare. The interiors by Fabled Studio feature carefully preserved Victorian brickwork, bespoke furniture and a striking green marble bar. *397-400 Geffrye Street, E2, T 7613 2967, www.beaglelondon.co.uk*

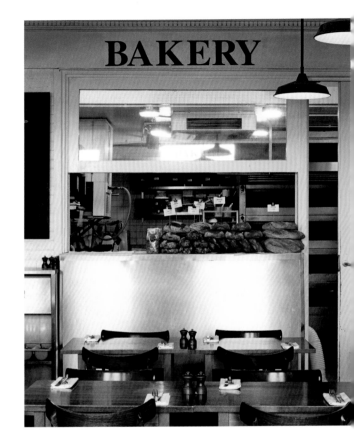

St John Bread and Wine

Fergus Henderson and Trevor Gulliver opened their Smithfield restaurant, St John (T 7251 0848), in 1994. The British menu, by Henderson (a trained architect, who cooks with a modernist clarity of purpose), has a famed emphasis on offal and is puritan in its lack of elaboration. The venue itself certainly has a white-walled seriousness about it. Having firmly established themselves among the Clerkenwell set, the pair branched out in 2003 with St John Bread and Wine. As the name quietly suggests, this space is part bakery, part wine shop, as well as an all-day restaurant, but with a far simpler menu than the mothership. Breakfast is particularly good – order the smoked Gloucester Old Spot bacon sandwich.
94-96 Commercial Street, E1, T 7251 0848, www.stjohngroup.uk.com

Dabbous

The power of Fay Maschler – the Pauline Kael of British food critics – and a Twitter frenzy have made getting a reservation here an exercise in delayed gratification (diners can face a 10-month wait). It does not hurt that chef Oliver Dabbous looks like a rock star. But it's his cooking, which has now garnered a Michelin star, that is raising temperatures. Dabbous has worked at Texture and Le Manoir aux Quat'Saisons, as well as doing stints at The Fat Duck (see p096), Noma and Hibiscus. The menu is short and the food is simple, if intensely flavoured. Brinkworth's interior design is all bare-duct functionalism, with great attention to detail. If you can't wait, snacks and cocktails are served in the basement bar, helmed by co-owner Oskar Kinberg. *39 Whitfield Street, W1, T 7323 1544, www.dabbous.co.uk*

Ametsa with Arzak Instruction

Father-and-daughter team Juan Mari and Elena Arzak arrived at Belgravia's Halkin hotel with a reputation as the champions of new Basque cooking – their Arzak restaurant in San Sebastian holds three Michelin stars. Indeed, Elena, the third generation of Arzaks to cook in the family's kitchen, may be the best female chef in the world. And although the day-to-day cooking at Ametsa (Basque for 'dream') is to be handled by Sergio Sanz, the Arzaks will make regular visits to their first international outpost. The design of Ametsa with Arzak Instruction – surely one of the oddest restaurant names in years – is the work of Ab Rogers. His new room is all spare elegance, apart from a ceiling of 7,000 spice-filled glass tubes.
The Halkin, Halkin Street, SW1,
T 7333 1234, www.ametsa.co.uk

Story

Like policemen and chancellors of the exchequer, head chefs are getting younger. Tom Sellers is still in his mid-twenties but has notched up stages with Tom Aikens, Thomas Keller and René Redzepi. Indeed, the hype surrounding Sellers meant his 2011 pop-up in Bethnal Green, Foreword, was the hottest table in town. The foodie set salivated at the idea of his permanent restaurant, and it arrived in April 2013 on the site of an old Victorian toilet block. The new, wood-clad structure is by Space Craft Architects, and the interiors courtesy of Shoreditch firm Raven. Story offers two set menus, of six and 10 courses. Both include the beef-dripping candle (served with bread), a dish that epitomises Sellers' ambitious take on British cooking.
201 Tooley Street, SE1, T 7183 2117, www.restaurant.story.co.uk

Polpo

This is the kind of bar/restaurant they do so effortlessly in Brooklyn or on the Lower East Side (bare bricks, tin ceiling, smallish square tables and no dinner reservations), but it so often feels laboured when done in London. However, Polpo has pulled the trick off so well that it's become one of the most fashionable joints in the city. The concept is a relocated *bacaro*: a Venetian bar serving Italianate tapas, installed in an 18th-century Soho house that was once home to Canaletto. Such has been its success that versions have opened in Clerkenwell (T 7250 0034) and Covent Garden (T 7836 8448). Although every second restaurant seems to serve tapas now, to our mind Polpo is up there with Morito (T 7278 7007) in terms of quality. *41 Beak Street, W1, T 7734 4479, www.polpo.co.uk*

Balthazar

Keith McNally, for so long New York's most fashionable restaurateur, has finally made the move to London (backed by Richard Caring). Like its Manhattan namesake, Balthazar is fantastic faux-brasserie – all shiny brass and red leather, mosaic tiles and Manet mirrors. Chef Robert Reid has added some Anglo elements to the menu, such as duck shepherd's pie, pork belly and black pudding hash, otherwise it's classic brasserie staples all the way. There are those who thought McNally's Pastis in New York was nothing more than a celeb-laden Café Rouge, and they may say the same about Balthazar, UK. But the food is better than that, and McNally's venues are also about service, conviviality, buzz and design that is at once hip yet comfortably familiar.
4-6 Russell Street, WC2, T 3301 1155,
www.balthazarlondon.com

Coya

Peruvian cuisine has been enjoying
a moment in London, and Coya, part
backed by Arjun Waney, is one of the
swankier options. Its design, by Richard
Saunders of Sagrada, is a mash-up of
Inca temple and elegantly distressed
Havana nightspot. Ex-Ivy chef Sanjay
Dwivedi handles the food, and the house
spins on pisco sour are very good indeed.
118 Piccadilly, W1, T 7042 7118

Experimental Cocktail Club

A rare cross-channel transfer, ECC's first outpost opened in Paris in 2007, before Romée de Goriainoff, Olivier Bon, Pierre-Charles Cros and Xavier Padovani brought the concept to London's Chinatown. The interior, by Parisian designer Dorothée Meilichzon, is in a neo-speakeasy style, all the rage in New York but slower to catch on here. There are plump love seats, a tin ceiling and a wooden bar with built-in piano. Some staff wear sleeve garters and will serve vintage spirits in vintage glasses on request. Despite being laid out over two floors, the place can cater for no more than 120 cocktail hounds, so bonhomie is guaranteed. Settle in and try a Havana: an Old Fashioned made using a cigar-infused bourbon. *13a Gerrard Street, W1, T 7434 3559, www.experimentalcocktailclublondon.com*

Pizarro

As the ex-executive chef at Brindisa in Borough Market, José Pizarro can make a legitimate claim to be the man who made Londoners tapas obsessives. We're not talking small plates or other tapas-alike innovations; and certainly not foam, mousse or other fluffed-up extractions. When Pizarro decided to go it alone, he moved only slightly east to Bermondsey Street, to open José (T 7403 4902), an authentic tapas bar with tiles, barrels, terrific wines and sherries, *croquetas*, chorizo and an unholy crush. He followed up with an eponymous restaurant, where you can sit down. There are still tiles, but also the same excellent cooking (Pizarro himself takes turns in the open kitchen), and the option of big-plate portions. *194 Bermondsey Street, SE1, T 7378 9455, www.josepizarro.com*

Dock Kitchen

Now an elder statesman of British design, Tom Dixon is on a roll. Many fashionable bars and restaurants around the world are illuminated by his designs, but he has also, almost by accident, become a successful restaurateur. Having launched as a pop-up at Dixon's Portobello Dock HQ during the 2009 London Design Festival, the Dock Kitchen remains open and is one of the city's more interesting dining rooms. Chef Stevie Parle, formerly of the River Café, is an ex-supper-clubber who has built up a steady fan club. Although Parle is fond of subcontinental cooking, here he hops between countries from course to course. The room is like an extension of Dixon's studio, a showroom with table service, but given his design nous, this is no bad thing. *342-344 Ladbroke Grove, W10, T 8962 1610, www.dockkitchen.co.uk*

Connaught Bar

Completed in 1897, the Connaught is the definition of the London luxury hotel as an urban country house. It has promised and delivered discretion and a fierce resistance to novelty. By 2004, though, the Maybourne Hotel Group (owners of Claridge's and the Berkeley), considered the Connaught a little too Wodehousian to be entirely healthy. The ensuing £70m overhaul included a complete reimagining of the property's two bars. India Mahdavi redesigned the Coburg Bar (T 7499 7070), and the heavyweight champion of bar designers, David Collins, added oodles of glamour to the Connaught Bar (above), which has a separate entrance on Mount Street. The interior cocoons you amid marble and black leather banquettes. *Carlos Place, W1, T 7314 3419, www.the-connaught.co.uk*

NOPI

In 2011, Yotam Ottolenghi, the Israeli-born chef behind an empire of deli/cafés, finally opened his first restaurant, a ground-floor dining room dressed in cleanly cut marble and brass, and a basement brasserie. Asian and Middle Eastern cuisine is served from breakfast to dinner. NOPI also boasts some of the glammest bathrooms in London.
21-22 Warwick Street, W1, T 7494 9584

L'Anima

As one rather sharp reviewer pointed out, minimalism is not easy nor cheap to pull off. It needs 'noble materials, precisely engineered', and someone who knows what they are doing. Such as architect Claudio Silvestrin, who has achieved an expensive minimalist aesthetic at L'Anima, engineering a space of cool drama with limestone floors and marble bathrooms. A glass wall separates the dining room from the bar (above), where the porphyry walls complement the white leather seats. A corridor leads to a walk-in wine cellar and a private dining room. Co-founder and chef Francesco Mazzei and his team cook impeccable, mostly southern Italian food. A new L'Anima café, also designed by Silvestrin, is slated to open in 2014.
1 Snowden Street, EC2, T 7422 7000, www.lanima.co.uk

Social Eating House

Jason Atherton is fast outgrowing the 'Gordon Ramsay acolyte' tag and is busy building his own global empire. This is his third London opening, hot on the heels of Little Social (T 7870 3730). Atherton has styled it as a contemporary bistro with Franco-speakeasy touches; the exposed-brick walls, whitewashed copper ceiling and pre-worn leather banquettes come courtesy of Russell Sage Studio. Atherton's long-time head chef, Paul Hood – here made a partner – serves crowd-pleasers such as ravioli of wild boar bolognaise, and smoked duck 'ham', egg and chips. The first-floor bar (above), unofficially dubbed the Blind Pig (slang for speakeasy), has a cocktail menu by Gareth Evans, ex of Pollen Street Social (T 7290 7600). *58 Poland Street, W1, T 7993 3251, www.socialeatinghouse.com*

Shrimpy's

This venture by David Waddington and Pablo Flack of Bistrotheque (see p062) is pulling London's fashionable to the new quarter taking shape in King's Cross. A Latin-American seafood restaurant, Shrimpy's moved into a former petrol station given a new glow by Carmody Groarke's cinematic roof signage and illuminated fibreglass walls. The kiosk has become an intimate upscale diner with wall doodles by Donald Urquhart, and head chef Kieran Barry's menu is an epicurean's pan-American dream. Given the owners' standing with London's arts, fashion and media (and occasionally cross-dressing) crowds, it is a very social space. Launched in 2012 with a two-year lifespan, it will close in December 2014. *The Filling Station, Goods Way, N1, T 8880 6111, www.shrimpys.co.uk*

INSIDER'S GUIDE
KIRSTY CARTER, GRAPHIC DESIGNER

Kirsty Carter is a director of design agency A Practice for Everyday Life (www.apracticeforeverydaylife.com), whose clients include Tate Britain (see p032) and the Barbican (see p071). She lives in Victoria Park Village, which she describes as 'East London's little secret'. Her favourite shops here include Haus (39 Morpeth Road, E9, T 7536 9291), which sells homewares, and Bottle Apostle (95 Lauriston Road, E9, T 8985 1549), 'where I can pick up good wine'.

Carter often eats out at the Corner Room (see p031), Rochelle Canteen (see p041), or One Leicester Street (see p022), where 'Tom Harris borrows from the past but uses new combinations of ingredients'. She's also a fan of The Clove Club (see p038), and Lardo (197-205 Richmond Road, E8, T 8985 2683) for its 'fabulous Italian food'. At Bistrotheque (23-27 Wadeson Street, E2, T 8983 7900), 'the upstairs bar is ideal for enjoying a cocktail with friends'. For coffee, she likes Climpson & Sons (67 Broadway Market, E8).

When shopping, Carter visits Lamb's Conduit Street. 'This is a lovely street to browse along and it has great clothes shops, like Folk (No 53, WC1, T 8616 4191) and Oliver Spencer (No 58, WC1, T 7831 3483).' Her bookshop tip is Artwords, which has branches on Broadway Market (T 7923 7507) and Rivington Street (T 7729 2000). Rough Trade East (91 Brick Lane, E1, T 7392 7788) is her one stop for 'impromptu gigs and the best records'.

For full addresses, see Resources.

ARCHITOUR

A GUIDE TO LONDON'S ICONIC BUILDINGS

When Ernö Goldfinger's 1960s cinema at Elephant and Castle was torn down in 1988, it was little lamented. In those days, London seemed to be determined only to replace its modernist heritage with anodyne office blocks, peddling nothing more interesting than 1980s aspiration. That the city largely failed in that mission is one of Europe's better-kept architectural secrets. The capital's modernist legacy is one of its least-appreciated treats.

Nowhere, except for the better stations on the Jubilee Line, can remove you so totally from the blitzed and otherwise edited mess of histories that make up the capital as the <u>Barbican</u> (see p071). Stroll along its elevated walkways and lakes set in concrete and you're in a retro futurescape – a fragment of a different city. Although the initial plans were drawn up by Chamberlin, Powell & Bon in 1955, their work was not completed until the opening of the Barbican arts complex in 1982. By then, the development looked out of date. Today, it looks like a dream.

The regeneration of King's Cross dwarfs even the ambition of the Barbican scheme. John McAslan's new concourse at <u>King's Cross station</u> (see p068) is the clearest demonstration yet of how bold and beautiful this district of the city could be. Meanwhile, in the City, <u>New Court</u> (see p066) is a graceful tower that makes much of the architecture around it look lumpen and ill-conceived. *For full addresses, see Resources.*

Economist Building

Peter and Alison Smithson were (almost) the Charles and Ray Eames of postwar Britain, being among the country's most important modernists and creators of the 'new brutalist' movement. In truth, they talked and theorised more than they built, but the Economist Building, commissioned in 1960 and completed in 1964, is their masterpiece. Actually comprising three Portland-stone towers set around a plaza in the mostly Palladian St James's, the complex had to include not only the offices of *The Economist* — as well as a penthouse for the publication's chairman Geoffrey Crowther — but a bank, shops and serviced flats for the Boodle's club next door. Their clients insisted that they build a hymn to modernity, with 'no fake antiquarianism'. And that is certainly what they delivered.
25 St James's Street, SW1

New Court

OMA's new home for Rothschild (the practice's first London building) is the most exciting addition to the 'Cityscape' in years. A 10-storey mesh cube, topped by a two-floor 'sky pavilion', it displays a lightness of touch that is missing from Norman Foster's Walbrook Building, the partly occupied metal blob that it overlooks. Nathan Mayer Rothschild first moved to the St Swithin's Lane site in 1809. This fourth headquarters of the family business, now a financial advisory company, opened its doors at the end of 2011. Given that the lane is a skinny medieval cut-through, it's hard to take in the facade at street level. What you do get is a marble forecourt and, for the first time in 200 years, views through to Christopher Wren's St Stephen Walbrook church.
New Court, St Swithin's Lane, EC4

The Shard

It can seem as if the London skyline is being devised by a seven-year-old boy, with its wheels, pyramids and rockets. Rising 310m above the low-rise Victorian red brick of Borough High Street, Renzo Piano's glazed spire is an astonishing sight. It has 72 storeys, 44 lifts and houses a Shangri-La hotel (T 3102 3704), offices, penthouses, and restaurants such as Oblix (T 7268 6700). It is not without its critics, however. It interrupts many supposedly protected views; it is, in essence, a giant glass tower when giant glass towers have a bad rap (20 per cent of the steelwork used, though, was recycled, as were 95 per cent of the other materials). Dubai-style horror or not, the structure has an elegance and ambition most locals admire. *32 London Bridge Street, SE1, www.the-shard.com*

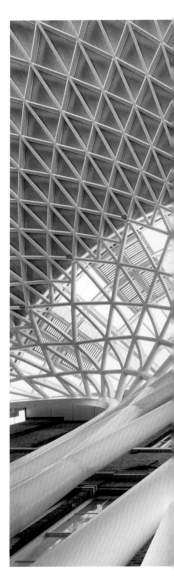

King's Cross Western Concourse
Thanks to the relocations of *The Guardian*
newspaper and Central Saint Martins art
college, the area north of King's Cross
station is starting to feel like the buzzing
new quarter that has long been promised
(even if a good deal of its 27 hectares of
brownfield land still look brown and field-
like). And the terminus itself finally looks
as if it's the anchor tenant of a lively new
'hood. From the outside, John McAslan's
Western Concourse resembles a giant
flying saucer that has crashed into the
Victorian hulk of the 1852 station. Inside,
it is a massive open dome, ascending 20m
into the air, with a span of 52m. The dome
grows out of a 16-part steel stalk, which
sprouts a latticework of branches that
plant themselves back into a plaza. There
are more than 20 shops in the concourse,
but it feels less like an upmarket mall
than neighbouring St Pancras does.
Euston Road/York Way, N1

National Theatre

This is the most visible example of heroic modernism in London. Denys Lasdun's design had to include three theatres and all sorts of backstage areas, as well as cafés, bars and foyers, yet the building remains one of the most dramatic to grace the River Thames. The interior spaces are just as impressive; the largest being the Olivier Theatre (named after the National's founder). A two-phase renovation led to the closure of the smallest theatre, the Cottesloe, which is due to reopen as the Dorfman in spring 2014; other work will continue until later in the year. The scheme includes the creation of additional public space, but the site should remain a perfect expression of Lasdun's ambition, as if he sought to make landscapes of buildings. *South Bank, SE1, T 7452 3400, www.nationaltheatre.org.uk*

Barbican

Architects Chamberlin, Powell & Bon had total control of the Barbican development, right down to the doorknobs. Eventually, it would include three towers of more than 40 storeys each, 13 terrace blocks, one seven-storey tower, a church, two schools and the Barbican Centre arts complex (in truth, something of an afterthought). The architects referenced Frank Lloyd Wright and Le Corbusier, but devised something unique, working on it from 1955 until 1982. In 2001, the concert hall was improved by Kirkegaard Associates, Caruso St John and Pentagram Architects, and Allford Hall Monaghan Morris reworked the Art Gallery in 2003. Fortuitously, where the Barbican was once a little lost in a forgotten part of town, it is now in the heart of the fashionable 'east side'.
EC2, T 7638 4141, www.barbican.org.uk

SHOPPING

THE BEST RETAIL THERAPY AND WHAT TO BUY

This city boasts two of the most innovative department stores in the world: Selfridges (400 Oxford Street, W1, T 0800 123 400) and Liberty (see p083). Nearby Bond Street may be predictable, but it's also bountiful, and Mayfair has the exciting Dover Street Market (17-18 Dover Street, W1, T 7518 0680) and Paul Smith's expanded store (9 Albemarle Street, W1, T 7493 4565), which has a new facade by 6a Architects. There's much more to the city's retail scene than this, though, from the cool boutiques of Lamb's Conduit Street, such as Darkroom (see p080), to Shoreditch's hip offerings, including menswear shop Present (140 Shoreditch High Street, E1, T 7033 0500), which has a barista. Round the corner, Jasper Morrison celebrates 'Super Normal' design (see p076), and Redchurch Street has become a retail hotspot. North of here, in Dalston, LN-CC (see p074) has reimagined the concept store as conceptual store, with an appointment-only showroom backed by an online shop to handle most of the transactions.

London is now an art-world hub, and West End galleries like White Cube (25-26 Mason's Yard, SW1, T 7930 5373), which has a branch in Bermondsey (see p037), and Hauser & Wirth (23 Savile Row, W1, T 7287 2300) lead the pack. Design galleries are moving in too. Visit Carpenters Workshop Gallery (3 Albemarle Street, W1, T 3051 5939), Fumi (opposite) and Libby Sellers (see p078).

For full addresses, see Resources.

Gallery Fumi

Tate Modern (see p010), is the world's most visited contemporary art museum, and every major international gallerist now has a presence in London. But the design gallery scene still doesn't hold a candle to that in, say, Paris. There are bright lights, though, and Fumi, set up by Valerio Capo and Sam Pratt, is one of the brightest. Launching in 2008 wasn't great timing, of course, but Fumi has weathered the economic storm, moving from its original Shoreditch home to a large, light-filled space in Hoxton. Focusing on one-off and limited-edition pieces, it has commissioned and shown works by locals Glithero, Paul Cocksedge and Max Lamb, and global names Raw Edges, Nacho Carbonell and Pieke Bergmans. Visits are by appointment. *16 Hoxton Square, N1, T 7490 2366, www.galleryfumi.com*

Late Night Chameleon Cafe

LN-CC, or Late Night Chameleon Cafe to give it its full and rather misleading title, is a new-model internet and bricks-and-mortar concept store created by British fashion dream-team John Skelton and Dan Mitchel. Both versions of the shop sell established and hard-to-find designers; books, including rarities and first editions; and top-notch audio gear, vinyl and CDs (LN-CC has even formed its own record label). The interior was conceived by set designer Gary Card, and is worth making the appointment – and the trek to Dalston, London's hipster HQ – to check out. Enter, Narnia-style, through a tunnel of branches into seven concept rooms, which include a bar. Despite the invitation-only tactic, once you are in, the welcome is warm.
18 Shacklewell Lane, E8, T 7275 7265, www.ln-cc.com

Jasper Morrison Shop

The British designer Jasper Morrison is enjoying a moment, a serious moment. After a period of time in which certain elements of the design world became overelaborate and overexcited at being told they were artists, and were paid accordingly, Morrison held steady with his quietly militant dedication to 'everyday useful objects', the 'Super Normal', as he called it. Together with Japanese designer Naoto Fukasawa, Morrison put together an exhibition of the Super Normal, and this shop, a small, unused area of his studio in Shoreditch, continues that project. It stocks his own designs, those by other members of the Super Normal crew, and further anonymous examples of the elegantly practical. Closed at weekends. *24b Kingsland Road, E2, www.jaspermorrison.com/shop*

Labour and Wait

A celebration of functional design from an age before anyone thought to fetishise functionalism, Labour and Wait was established in 2000 by designers Rachel Wythe-Moran and Simon Watkins. The duo were frustrated that the fast pace of fashion did not allow for the maturing of items into classics. In 2010, the brand moved from a rather artfully crammed store on Cheshire Street to a slightly larger space on Redchurch Street. Here, you can pick up hardware for the kitchen and garden, as well as utilitarian clothing, stationery and accessories. Standout items include the extensive selection of enamel tableware and utensils, ranging from delicate milk pans to not-so-delicate pie dishes. Closed on Mondays.
85 Redchurch Street, E2, T 7729 6253,
www.labourandwait.co.uk

Gallery Libby Sellers

At once UK design's charismatic champion and a catalytic curator-retailer, Libby Sellers promotes a generation of British and British-based designers, including Peter Marigold, Stuart Haygarth, Simon Hasan, Moritz Waldemeyer and Clarke & Reilly ('8 Chairs', above). For seven years, Sellers was senior curator at the Design Museum (T 7403 6933), putting on blockbuster-ish exhibitions and smaller shows focusing on young creatives. In 2007, she launched her own peripatetic gallery, which popped up at different locations around town (and in Europe and the US), before opening a permanent base in 2011. Experimental and ideas-driven, without taking themselves too seriously, her exhibitions question what design is for. *41-42 Berners Street, W1, T 3384 8785, www.libbysellers.com*

Charlotte Olympia

A graduate of London's Cordwainers school, Charlotte Dellal launched her first collection in 2008. The daughter of ex-model Andrea and sister of socialite Alice, her shoes are heavy on 1940s glamour with just the right amount of wit; Dellal also dresses as if she could whistle up with Humphrey Bogart. In 2010, she opened a store, Charlotte Olympia, in Mayfair. The space makes a star of the shoes, which have names like Dolly, Maxine and Ursula, and are elevated on brass stands or encased in glass cabinets. Guarded by an ornamental leopard in the window, the shop is otherwise stylishly restrained and has parquet floors and midcentury furniture. Browse the clutches and hosiery, also designed by Dellal.
56 Maddox Street, W1, T 7499 0145, www.charlotteolympia.com

Darkroom
Thanks to a highly principled landlord,
Holborn's Lamb's Conduit Street is a
shining example of fine retailing. Compact
concept store Darkroom arrived in 2009.
Mixing interior accessories and original
high-end fashion, founders and friends
Rhonda Drakeford and Lulu Roper-
Caldbeck go global to source beautiful
pieces that are unique to the shop. The
pair also peddle their own, covetable
designs, as well as hosting frequent
events to coincide with product launches,
particularly during the London Design
Festival. Darkroom is worth visiting, if
for no other reason than to check out
the immaculately styled interior. Design
team Frank were commissioned to create
bespoke furniture for the store, whereas
the statement tiled floor was hand-painted
by the talented proprietors themselves.
52 Lamb's Conduit Street, WC1, T 7831 7244,
www.darkroomlondon.com

Alexander McQueen

The late Alexander McQueen's Savile Row apprenticeship is central to his story, informing the sharp, often sculptural tailoring of his collections, so it's fitting the label should open a flagship menswear store here. It was, says creative director Sarah Burton, an ambition of McQueen's. The space, though, is more airy gallery than dark *salon privé* of the traditional tailoring house. It even has a large glass vitrine to hold artworks curated by Sadie Coles. Burton worked with David Collins on the design, which has a wit McQueen would have enjoyed. The shop also offers a tailoring service. The brand's new outlet on Dover Street (T 7318 2220), another David Collins collaboration, stocks mens and womenswear from the McQ label. *9 Savile Row, W1, T 7494 8840, www.alexandermcqueen.com*

Liberty

Renowned for its trademark prints, this London bastion has long been synonymous with luxury and international design. The Regent Street shop, stocked with decorative homewares and objets d'art from North Africa, Japan and the East, was opened in 1875 by Arthur Liberty, who did not want 'to follow existing fashions, but to create new ones'. The Tudor-style building, designed by Edwin T Hall and his son Edwin S Hall, was constructed in 1924 from the timbers of two ships. More recently, it has become a cutting-edge emporium following a strategic tune-up. The imaginative, focused buying skills of the fashion department are more akin to a sharp-minded independent than a generic, label-bagging department store. *210-220 Regent Street, W1, T 7734 1234, www.liberty.co.uk*

Mint

Established by Lina Kanafani in 1998, Mint is the kind of design store that goes far beyond the usual suspects, commissioning exclusive one-off and limited-edition products from both new and established designers, in addition to handcrafted glass, ceramics and textiles. One of the joys of Mint is Kanafani's fearlessness and aversion to the safety of quiet good taste. Mint challenges you to get to grips with the founder's selection, to take your time, and to come back once you have thought it over. It's a strategy that has paid off handsomely. Since 2009, regular Minters have had to get used to going back to the newer, larger store in the Brompton Quarter (above) and not the tiny former shop on Wigmore Street. Closed Sundays. *2 North Terrace, SW3, T 7225 2228, www.mintshop.co.uk*

Hostem

Shoreditch may have been forsaken by the hipsters, who have headed north and east for their late-night clubbing thrills, but, by day, its retail scene gets more interesting. This store presents a smart array of international labels, from Ann Demeulemeester to Visvim, and has a startlingly spare interior by rising design duo James Russell and Hannah Plumb, collectively JamesPlumb. Here, they have created hybrid pieces, reusing old furniture and materials, infusing them with wit and charm. The space is split into several areas. There's one section for menswear, above which a dedicated womenswear floor opened in 2013. As a whole, the shop seems to summon the Victorian spirits said to haunt the area.
41-43 Redchurch Street, E2, T 7739 9733, www.hostem.co.uk

Margaret Howell
A stalwart of British fashion, Margaret
Howell graduated in the late 1960s from
Goldsmiths College. She began producing
men's shirts in the 1970s, wholesaling to
future fashion giants Ralph Lauren and
Paul Smith. In 1977, in collaboration with
Joseph's Joseph Ettedgui, she opened a
store on South Molton Street. In the past
decade, she has enjoyed a renaissance
as a champion of immaculately tailored
casualwear for men and women, with an
emphasis on natural materials such as
cotton, linen and tweed, and subtle dyes
and colours. Her Wigmore Street flagship,
designed by William Russell of Pentagram,
also displays British modernist furniture,
new and vintage. She has produced several
reissues in collaboration with Anglepoise,
Ercol and Robert Welch, as well as a take
on Ernest Race's 1955 'Heron' chair.
34 Wigmore Street, W1, T 7009 9009,
www.margarethowell.co.uk

SPORTS AND SPAS
WORK OUT, CHILL OUT OR JUST WATCH

The Olympics left London with some excellent and architecturally daring sports arenas. Zaha Hadid's Aquatics Centre and Hopkins Architects' marvellous Velodrome (see p090), where Team GB showed the world a clean pair of heels, are the crown jewels of the Queen Elizabeth Olympic Park in Newham, East London. Both venues are due to open to the public in early 2014, as will new outdoor road circuits and off-road trails at Lee Valley VeloPark.

The city also boasts what Norman Foster calls the world's finest football ground: Wembley Stadium (Empire Way, HA9, T 0844 980 8001). One of London's iconic structures, it has a huge illuminated arch, and facilities that are a vast improvement on its predecessor.

Squeezing fitness into London life isn't easy, but there are fine gyms – try The Third Space (13 Sherwood Street, W1, T 7439 6333) or Matt Roberts (16 Berkeley Street, W1, T 7491 9989) – good football pitches and stylish spas, including Espa Life at Corinthia (Whitehall Place, SW1, T 7321 3050), Aman Spa (see p095) and the Cowshed treatment rooms at Shoreditch House (Ebor Street, E1, T 7739 5040). Among the city's neglected treasures are its lidos, such as London Fields Lido (London Fields West Side, E8, T 7254 9038), while the River Thames is, of course, famous for its rowing clubs. Finally, the provision of cycle lanes is getting better as the number of riders on the roads increases exponetially.

For full addresses, see Resources.

Dunhill

In 2008, Dunhill opened a retail store-cum-exclusive members' hangout in an 18th-century grand pile (very grand, as it was once the home of the Duke of Westminster) on Davies Street, just north of Berkeley Square. Our favourite feature of the house is its wonderful spa and barber's (above), which is a witty and thoroughly welcoming update of the traditional gentlemen's grooming parlour – think Geo F Trumper et al. Customers even get their own TV screen, so they can watch a movie while enjoying tonsorial attention. In addition to the wet shaves and short-back-and-sides administered here, two treatment rooms host more modern forms of pampering, including hot-stone and sports massages, and facials. Closed on Sundays.
2 Davies Street, W1, T 7853 4440,
www.dunhill.com

Velodrome

Post-Gherkin (see p012), any new London
building without right angles in all the
right places is liable to be saddled with an
affectionate (often food-based) nickname.
And so Hopkins Architects' Velodrome
was tagged the 'Pringle'. And indeed it
does resemble a Pringle crisp, its angled
wooden oval (a hyperbolic paraboloid if
you prefer) directly referencing the track
within. Fittingly, given the UK's emergence
as a cycling superpower, it was the first of
the Olympic Park stadia to be completed.
And, along with Zaha Hadid's Aquatics
Centre, it is an architectural high. (Make's
Copper Box, used for handball during the
Games, is a triumph too.) The Velodrome
is the park's most eco-conscious venue,
its red cedar bowl again referencing the
sustainably sourced pine track.
Queen Elizabeth Olympic Park, E20

Laban Building

Built for £22m, the 2002 Laban Building at Trinity Laban Conservatoire of Music and Dance is one of the largest and most expensive contemporary dance centres in the world. It was designed by Herzog & de Meuron and is, many would say, their most important contribution to London's landscape to date (even if Laban's position on a former rubbish tip in Deptford means not enough people get to see it). Conceived in collaboration with artist Michael Craig-Martin, the building is a polycarbonate-coated box that allows shadowy views of the student dancers during the day. At night, it becomes a giant lantern, lit up in lime, turquoise and magenta. The interior is no less successful, with a Pilates studio, health suite, 300-seat theatre and café.
*Creekside, SE8, T 8691 8600,
www.trinitylaban.ac.uk*

Lord's

It seems odd that the Marylebone Cricket Club, the ultra-conservative high court of English cricket, should commission such an outlandish structure. In fact, the lords of Lord's are daring patrons of innovative architecture. Witness Future Systems' Media Centre (above), finished in 1999, at roughly the same time as Nicholas Grimshaw's grandstand. The Media Centre still startles. Built using shipbuilding and aircraft technology, it was the world's first all-aluminium semi-monocoque building. And it's not often we get to say that. Its purpose is to contain all the TV, radio and press people under one roof. Raised 14m above the Compton and Edrich Stands, it looks like the sinister eye of a monstrous machine, which it kind of is. *St John's Wood Road, NW8, T 7616 8500, www.lords.org*

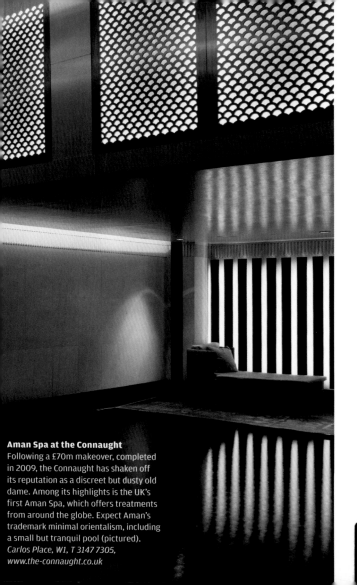

Aman Spa at the Connaught
Following a £70m makeover, completed
in 2009, the Connaught has shaken off
its reputation as a discreet but dusty old
dame. Among its highlights is the UK's
first Aman Spa, which offers treatments
from around the globe. Expect Aman's
trademark minimal orientalism, including
a small but tranquil pool (pictured).
Carlos Place, W1, T 3147 7305,
www.the-connaught.co.uk

ESCAPES

WHERE TO GO IF YOU WANT TO LEAVE TOWN

London has no Hamptons or Sitges, although the Cotswolds to the west and Norfolk to the north are weekend haunts. Both areas now have good stocks of decent delis, shops, restaurants, old pubs gone gourmet, and contemporary country hotels, such as Cowley Manor (Cowley, T 01242 870 900) and Babington House (Babington, T 01373 812 266). The Olde Bell (see p102) is less grand but just as welcome an innovation, with country-modern interiors.

The village of Bray in Berkshire has become a global gastro-resort. Here, Heston Blumenthal cooks up snail porridge, quail jelly and other classics of his notorious molecular gastronomy at three-Michelin-starred The Fat Duck (T 01628 580 333). Its near neighbour, The Waterside Inn (Ferry Road, T 01628 620 691), which also has three stars, is overseen by Alain Roux. Meanwhile, super-gallery Hauser & Wirth (see p072) plans to turn the small town of Bruton in Somerset into a major cultural draw, opening an art centre in 2014. The complex will include a restaurant, At The Farm, run by chic local inn At The Chapel (High Street, T 01749 814 070).

London's nearest major seaside resort is fashionable Brighton, just 70km away. It's full of Regency architecture, including the bizarre Royal Pavilion (Old Steine, T 01273 290 900). There are also some fine examples of modernism close to London, including De La Warr Pavilion (opposite) and The Homewood (see p100). *For full addresses, see Resources.*

De La Warr Pavilion, Bexhill-on-Sea

Completed in 1935, Erich Mendelsohn and Serge Chermayeff's De La Warr Pavilion, situated on the East Sussex coast, was the country's first modernist public building. In 1933, the competition to construct a seaside entertainment complex was announced within a couple of months of Mendelsohn arriving in England, and the German émigré, already a renowned figure in European architecture, hit the project at some speed. He created an impossibly glamorous docked-liner of a structure, with large glass windows and curving terraces, and a huge chrome-and-steel staircase. An £8m restoration project by architects John McAslan + Partners helped to re-establish the pavilion as one of southern England's most important cultural buildings. *Marina, T 01424 229 111, www.dlwp.com*

Turner Contemporary, Margate

A faded seaside town in Kent, Margate is probably now best known for its part in Tracey Emin's open wound of a life story. 'Whatever I do, part of Margate always comes with me,' she said. It seems right, then, that an art gallery is being viewed as a lever for the town's reversal of terminal decline. The Turner Contemporary, which was designed by David Chipperfield and opened in 2011, is named after Margate's other artist-in-residence, JMW Turner, who went to school here and returned often, because he loved the light (and a local hotel keeper). Chipperfield's building, a series of elegant, angular art sheds, is built on the site of the guesthouse where Turner painted, and is mostly about the wonders it plays with light on the inside. *Rendezvous, T 01843 233 000, www.turnercontemporary.org*

The Homewood, Esher
A counterpoint to Surrey's wealthy but dull stockbroker belt, The Homewood is essentially an open-plan glass-and-air take on the country house. Completed in 1938 by Patrick Gwynne, a modernist who worked alongside Wells Coates and studied the designs of Le Corbusier, the property makes use of marble, terrazzo and gold leaf to stunning effect.
Portsmouth Road, T 01372 476 424

The Olde Bell, Hurley
In some ways, The Olde Bell (10 minutes
from Henley-on-Thames) simply reflects
the boutique-ing and gastro-ising of the
traditional British coaching inn. Rooms
that were once fusty and stale-smelling
now feature walk-in monsoon showers.
But designer Ilse Crawford has managed
to assemble private and public spaces
that sit easily with the history of this
wonky Tudor building – some parts of
which date as far back as 1135. In the
dining room, banquettes are brightened
with geometric-print Welsh blankets, and
contemporary Thonet bentwood chairs
are matched with Matthew Hilton for
Ercol's birch Windsors, produced in High
Wycombe. The food, by chef Adrian Court,
which, of course, makes use of locally
sourced ingredients, is excellent.
High Street, T 01628 825 881,
www.theoldebell.co.uk

NOTES

SKETCHES AND MEMOS

RESOURCES
CITY GUIDE DIRECTORY

A

Albion 028
Boundary
2-4 Boundary Street, E2
T 7729 1051
www.albioncaff.co.uk

Alexander McQueen 082
9 Savile Row, W1
T 7494 8840
14 Dover Street, W1
T 7318 2220
www.alexandermcqueen.com

Aman Spa at the Connaught 094
Connaught
Carlos Place, W1
T 3147 7305
www.the-connaught.co.uk

Ametsa with Arzak Instruction 044
The Halkin
Halkin Street, SW1
T 7333 1234
www.ametsa.co.uk

L'Anima 058
1 Snowden Street, EC2
T 7422 7000
www.lanima.co.uk

Artwords 062
20-22 Broadway Market, E8
T 7923 7507
69 Rivington Street, EC2
T 7729 2000
www.artwords.co.uk

At The Chapel 096
High Street
Bruton
Somerset
T 01749 814 070
www.atthechapel.co.uk

B

Balthazar 049
4-6 Russell Street, WC2
T 3301 1155
www.balthazarlondon.com

Bar Boulud 040
Mandarin Oriental Hyde Park
66 Knightsbridge, SW1
T 7201 3899
www.barboulud.com/london

Barbican 071
EC2
T 7638 4141
www.barbican.org.uk

Beagle 041
397-400 Geffrye Street, E2
T 7613 2967
www.beaglelondon.co.uk

Bistrotheque 062
23-27 Wadeson Street, E2
T 8983 7900
www.bistrotheque.com

Bottle Apostle 062
95 Lauriston Road, E9
T 8985 1549
www.bottleapostle.com

BT Tower 014
60 Cleveland Street, W1

Bulgari Spa 025
Bulgari
171 Knightsbridge, SW7
T 7151 1055
www.bulgarihotels.com/london

C

Carpenters Workshop Gallery 072
3 Albemarle Street, W1
T 3051 5939
www.carpentersworkshopgallery.com

HOTELS
ADDRESSES AND ROOM RATES

Babington House 096
Room rates:
double, from £240
Babington
Somerset
T 01373 812 266
www.babingtonhouse.co.uk

The Beaumont Hotel 016
Room rates:
prices on request
8 Balderton Street, W1
www.thebeaumont.com

Boundary 028
Room rates:
double, from £205;
Bauhaus Room, from £205;
Eileen Gray Room, from £230;
Suites, from £350
2-4 Boundary Street, E2
T 7729 1051
www.theboundary.co.uk

Bulgari 024
Room rates:
double, from £440;
Bulgari III Suite, £8,500
171 Knightsbridge, SW7
T 7151 1010
www.bulgarihotels.com/london

Café Royal 018
Room rates:
double, from £400;
Portland Junior Suite, £610
68 Regent Street, W1
T 7406 3333
www.hotelcaferoyal.com

Claridge's 020
Room rates:
double, from £390;
Grand Piano Suite, from £7,800
Brook Street, W1
T 7629 8860
www.claridges.co.uk

Corinthia 016
Room rates:
double, from £360
Whitehall Place, SW1
T 7930 8181
www.corinthia.com

Cowley Manor 096
Room rates:
double, from £185
Cowley
Gloucestershire
T 01242 870 900
www.cowleymanor.com

The Dorchester 016
Room rates:
double, from £510
Park Lane, W1
T 7629 8888
www.thedorchester.com

Dorset Square Hotel 027
Room rates:
double, from £260;
Deluxe Garden View Room, £375
39-40 Dorset Square, NW1
T 7723 7874
www.firmdalehotels.com

The London Edition 016
Room rates:
prices on request
10 Berners Street, W1
T 7781 0000
www.editionhotels.com

ME 026
Room rates:
double, from £410;
Aura, from £410;
Suite ME, £3,820
336-337 Strand, WC1
T 0845 601 8980
www.melia.com

Mondrian 016
Room rates:
prices on request
20 Upper Ground, SE1
www.mondrianlondon.com

The Olde Bell 102
Room rates:
double, from £95
High Street
Hurley
Berkshire
T 01628 825 881
www.theoldebell.co.uk

One Leicester Street 022
Room rates:
double, from £175;
Room 503, £210
1 Leicester Street, WC2
T 3301 8020
www.oneleicesterstreet.com

The Savoy 017
Room rates:
double, from £450
Strand, WC2
T 7836 4343
www.fairmont.com/savoy

Shangri-La 067
Room rates:
prices on request
The Shard
32 London Bridge Street, SE1
T 3102 3704
www.shangri-la.com/london

South Place Hotel 021
Room rates:
double, from £210;
Room 604, £480
3 South Place, EC2
T 3503 0000
www.southplacehotel.com

10 Trinity Square 016
Room rates:
prices on request
10 Trinity Square, EC3
www.10trinitysquare.com

Town Hall Hotel 030
Room rates:
double, from £300;
Studio, £380;
One-bedroom Suite, £400;
Two-bedroom Suite, £470;
Three-bedroom Suite, from £495
De Montfort Suite, £3,000
Patriot Square, E2
T 7871 0460
www.townhallhotel.com

The Zetter 016
Room rates:
double, from £235
St John's Square
86-88 Clerkenwell Road, EC1
T 7324 4444
www.thezetter.com

WALLPAPER* CITY GUIDES

Executive Editor
Rachael Moloney

Author
Nick Compton

Art Director
Loran Stosskopf
Art Editor
Eriko Shimazaki
Designer
Mayumi Hashimoto
Map Illustrator
Russell Bell

Photography Editor
Elisa Merlo
Assistant Photography Editor
Nabil Butt

Chief Sub-Editor
Nick Mee
Sub-Editor
Farah Shafiq

Editorial Assistant
Emma Harrison

Intern
Phil James

**Wallpaper* Group
Editor-in-Chief**
Tony Chambers
Publishing Director
Gord Ray
Managing Editor
Oliver Adamson

First published 2006
Revised and updated
2007, 2009, 2010, 2011
and 2013

All prices are correct at
the time of going to press,
but are subject to change.

Printed in China

PHAIDON

Phaidon Press Limited
Regent's Wharf
All Saints Street
London N1 9PA

Phaidon Press Inc
180 Varick Street
New York, NY 10014

Phaidon® is a registered
trademark of Phaidon
Press Limited

www.phaidon.com

A CIP Catalogue record for
this book is available from
the British Library.

ISBN 978 0 7148 6629 1

PHOTOGRAPHERS

Richard Bryant/Arcaid
Turner Contemporary,
pp098-099

Emma Blau
Trellick Tower, p015

Joakim Blockstrom
Dabbous, p043

Michael Bodiam
Café Royal, pp018-019

Theo Cook
Centre Point, p013
BT Tower, p014
St John Bread and
Wine, p042

Jason Hawkes
London city view,
inside front cover

Hufton + Crow
King's Cross Western
Concourse, pp068-069

Martin Jordan
Laban Building, p092

Jamie McGregor Smith
South Place Hotel, p021
Bulgari, p024, p025
ME, p026
Town Hall
Hotel, p030, p031

19 Greek Street, p033
The Photographers'
Gallery, p036
The Clove Club, pp038-039
Beagle, p041
Ametsa with Arzak
Instruction, pp044-045
Story, p046, p047
Balthazar, p049
Coya, pp050-051
Experimental Cocktail
Club, p052
Pizarro, p053
NOPI, pp056-057
Social Eating House, p059
Shrimpy's, p060, p061
Kirsty Carter, p063
New Court, p066
The Shard, p067
Gallery Fumi, p073
Gallery Libby Sellers, p078
Alexander McQueen, p082

Dennis Gilbert/NTPL
The Homewood, pp100-101

Chris Parker
De La Warr Pavilion, p097

Simon Phipps
Economist Building, p065

Christoffer Rudquist
30 St Mary Axe, p012
Claridge's, p020
Boundary, pp028-029
Polpo, p048
Dock Kitchen, p054
Connaught Bar, p055
L'Anima, p058
Barbican, p071
Jasper Morrison
Shop, p076
Labour and Wait, p077
Charlotte Olympia, p079
Darkroom, pp080-081
Liberty, p083
Mint, p084
Hostem, p085
Margaret Howell,
pp086-087
Dunhill, p089
Aman Spa at the
Connaught, pp094-095

6a Architects
V&A fashion
gallery, pp034-035

Clare Skinner
Lord's, p093

Edmund Sumner
Velodrome, pp090-091

LONDON
A COLOUR-CODED GUIDE TO THE HOT 'HOODS

CENTRAL
The bustling commerce of the West End is leavened by Bloomsbury's cultured calm

NORTH
King's Cross might be arriving, but glorious, laidback Primrose Hill is already there

THE CITY
By day, the increasingly high-rise centre of the financial world; by night, largely deserted

SOUTH-WEST
If you're looking to snare a Russian oligarch or an Arab prince, start your search here

WEST
Stucco central, this is what first-time visitors expect to find everywhere in the city, sadly

WESTMINSTER
To dodge the coach-party crowds, get in, get a glimpse of the urban gothic, then get out

EAST
The locus of capital cool has been steadily shifting this way for more than a decade

SOUTH-EAST
One of the fastest-changing areas of London is heading upwards at a dizzying rate

For a full description of each neighbourhood, see the Introduction.
Featured venues are colour-coded, according to the district in which they are located.

MEDICAL
Pulse-racing passion

Father For The Midwife's Twins
Fiona McArthur

Reunited With The Children's Doc
Susan Carlisle

MILLS & BOON

Father For The Midwife's Twins
Fiona McArthur

MILLS & BOON

Fiona McArthur is an Australian midwife who lives in the country and loves to dream. Writing medical romance gives Fiona the chance to write about all the wonderful aspects of romance, adventure, medicine and the midwifery she feels so passionate about. When she's not catching babies, Fiona and her husband, Ian, are off to meet new people, see new places and have wonderful adventures. Drop in and say hi at Fiona's website, fionamcarthurauthor.com.

Visit the Author Profile page at
millsandboon.com.au for more titles.

Dear Reader,

I do hope you enjoy *Father for the Midwife's Twins*.

The twins are so cute but such a lot of work. One of the most amusing parts of writing this book was finding that Lisandra spent a lot of time caring for her babies, as any mother of twins would, and like Lisandra, we both had to find the time to fall in love. A bit like giving a heroine really long hair and you spend a lot of the book brushing and tying it back.

But I wanted that first scene I saw in my mind— Malachi being there in her moment of greatest need.

Lisandra's so capable and independent, and Malachi is such an intense, brooding soul with so much to offer if he could just relax and enjoy life! It had to be a slow-burn and awakening type of love.

I had so much fun as Lisandra coaxed Malachi to show his long-buried sense of humour. It really was an emotional journey for both of them, and I hope you laugh and cry with them as much as I did as they all become a wonderful family.

With warmest good wishes,

Fi xx

DEDICATION

Dedicated to Loretta.

You're a magnificent mother. I'm in awe.
xx The MIL.

PROLOGUE

THE BRIGHT SUNSHINE slipped behind a heavy
cloud as Lisandra Calhoun climbed awkwardly from the taxi at her almost-in-laws'
house not far from Coolangatta airport. Small
splats of rain had begun to fall with increas-
ing force and she didn't have an umbrella. Or
a free hand to hold one.

That was okay. It was only water. And she
was here.

She'd sent her flight numbers and hoped
Josie and Clint would meet her at the airport
but they hadn't made it to the terminal by
the time she'd picked up her luggage. Josie
had said they would. She'd sounded so excited on the phone when they'd arranged for
Lisandra to come as soon as she started maternity leave, even before her new house was
ready. She'd tried to call but there'd been no
answer. Must have been a mix-up, Lisan-

dra had thought—they happened—so she'd caught a taxi.

The flight up from Melbourne had been smooth enough but being seven months pregnant with twins made it awkward and uncomfortable. And she'd been tense with nerves and exhaustion despite the idea of flying from the cold of Victoria up to tropical Queensland. Packing up your life took a toll, though in the end she'd left nearly everything behind to start fresh in the small semi-detached house she'd put a deposit on that was close to Richard's parents. It was a doll of a house, she'd snatched it up as soon as it listed, and despite the long settlement date it had felt right. And there was very little else for sale in the current market.

After the last horrific six months, all she wanted was a safe and secure place for her babies. Despite leaving her Melbourne friends behind, it would be good to be near the only other family her babies would have, and Lisandra would be away from all the bittersweet memories she and Richard had rose-coloured their distant lives with.

At their son's funeral six months ago, a ghastly blur in Lisandra's memory, Richard's mother had said Lisandra should move north, let her help with the baby, and stay with them until she found a place in the Gold Coast. And that had been before Lisandra discovered she was pregnant with Richard's twins and the Smythes would be double grandparents.

She had wanted a change, she thought, as an uneasy foreboding dripped along with the rain down her neck, but she climbed the front steps, dragging her suitcase in noisy bumps upwards. Richard's mother had invited her to come. Had urged her. Lisandra pushed back the disquiet.

It was the right thing to do. Everywhere at home had reminded her of the man she'd lost so painfully, so harshly and horrifically, just a month before their wedding.

Beginning maternity leave had meant sitting at home alone, missing Richard, cradling her bulging belly and waiting for labour to arrive.

No, it felt right to ensure her children knew their grandparents, from the beginning.

Josie would help her settle into her new home when it happened and the boys would know more family than they would have if they'd stayed in Melbourne.

The frosted-glass-panelled door swung open and the sweet face of Richard's mother peered out. Lisandra felt hot tears sting behind her eyes, but she forced them back and smiled. Warm relief eased the cold dampness soaking her neck and shoulders from the rain. She'd lost her parents as a seven-year-old and this woman reminded her of the grandmother who had always been a loving haven for her. 'Josie.' The word puffed out in a little huff of relief.

Josie didn't say anything, instead she glanced over her shoulder back into the house and chewed her lip. 'Lisandra. My dear.' Her hand opened and closed as if she wanted to reach out and couldn't. 'I'm so, so sorry.' She didn't open the door wider.

The rain grew heavier and, even though Lisandra stood under the porch eaves, bouncing water droplets splashed against her legs and soaked her shoes and ankles. It felt as if a yawning chasm had cracked open in a tectonic shift under her feet. Lisandra forced a smile. 'Can I come in?'

The large figure of Richard's father appeared at the door in such a swirl of dark emotion, both Josie and Lisandra stepped back. Josie twisted her hands and disappeared from view, murmuring, 'I'm so glad the cab waited.'

All Lisandra could see then was the twisted

face of Clint Smythe and the wild, frightening grief in the older man's eyes.

'Go away. Get out of my sight. I told Josie, no.'

Lisandra felt the words slap against her. 'What?'

'It's your fault we lost our son. You should have saved him. Your fault.'

The storm of words hit her, like hail, like the lash of rain against her back. She stared aghast into the hard, unyielding, twisted face of Richard's father and knew she'd made a mistake. A huge one. She moistened her suddenly dry lips and tried to make her brain work. 'You're wrong. I tried everything. The paramedics tried.'

'We don't want you.'

She heard Josie gasp and plead behind him but Richard's father went on.

'Get off our property and take your spawn with you. They're not our Richard's babies and you're not foisting them on us.'

CHAPTER ONE

Malachi

'MALACHI MADDEN, YOU are always cancelling dinner. I speak to your secretary on the phone more than I speak to you.' As he listened, Malachi realised he was coming to dislike mobile phones intensely, or at least when Grace rang to complain.

From the fourth floor of The Kirra Beach Maternity Hospital, Dr Madden stared through his office window out over the soothing waves. 'It's a category two emergency caesarean section, Grace.' Which meant he had fifteen minutes to be there.

A hundred metres out from the shore, kite surfers skipped on their boards like bright butterflies from wave to wave with their wind-filled sails. He wondered what that would feel like to be skimming emerald waves in the wind. Maybe one day, but he knew that scenario looked unlikely.

'Not good enough.' Grace's voice penetrated his distraction with her indignation. 'Your patients always come before me.'

'Well, yes.' *Duh.* 'And patients will be waiting until after I'm finished and that will make me later. What would you like me to do?'

An odd noise came through the phone. Could be the sound of gnashing teeth, Malachi guessed. She did that. Funny the things you learnt about people when you became more intimate with them. He'd thought he and Grace were a good idea, mutually low maintenance, when she'd suggested it. His grandmother had seemed moderately excited, but he suspected that was because she'd given up on the idea that he'd organise his own love life.

He imagined she'd hoped Grace would make an excellent doctor's wife. She wouldn't. He knew that now. As did Grace. All they had to do was stop pretending this relationship was going to work. It wasn't Grace's fault—he knew he wasn't husband, let alone father, material, and she had mentioned she wanted children.

Finally, Grace ground out, 'If you want this

to work you will have to try harder. Get someone else to do the caesarean and share a meal
with me on time at least once a week.' Words
cold and determined. A finality creeping into
her voice. He'd heard that tone before, from
girlfriends past.

Get someone else to do the operation? For
a patient he'd seen all through her pregnancy?
Now something unexpected like an emergency caesarean had arrived and she wanted
him to walk away from the mother?

It would be a late night. Unless he was mistaken, Grace was saying choose her over his
patients. As well as skip the caesarean for the
sake of their relationship.

And here was the answer. 'I can't do that.'

He heard her hiss at his words.

Technically there were half a dozen other
obstetricians in the hospital who had asked
him to do something similar for them, which
he had, but Malachi didn't work like that.

'Then I can't do you,' Grace snapped.
'That's three dinner engagements in the last
week. And four last week.'

Malachi wondered who made dinner engagements through the week anyway.

A hint of sadness laced her voice. Only a
touch. Mostly, it was annoyance. 'Our farce of
a relationship is over. Have your housekeeper

pack anything I've left in your flat and I'll arrange to have it picked up.' The call ended.

There was definite relief in the breath he let out.

This was why he didn't do relationships. He was hopeless at them but at the same time he didn't understand how Grace could ask him to hand over one of his clients in her moment of need.

Malachi's brows furrowed as he slipped his mobile phone into his trouser pocket. His father had told him never to ruin the line of the jacket with objects in pockets. As that was one of the few times the old man had actually given him calm advice, he took it on board. His father had been a very, very busy cardiac surgeon. And deeply disappointed in his mild-mannered son.

He pushed his office door wider and stepped into the empty reception area of his office. 'Looks like we'll be running sixty minutes late for the afternoon appointments, Ginny.'

'Yes, Doctor.' His office manager, Ginny, thin, freckled, and happily married, nodded her head.

'I'll come straight back here after Theatre. Please apologise to those waiting.'

Ginny's eyes held warmth and sympathy. 'I will.'

She did apologise really well. Ginny had enough practice apologising for his absence when he was called away to emergencies. She'd probably slip a protein drink onto his desk when he came back, too, because Ginny noticed when he didn't eat. He should give her a rise. He'd get her to arrange it.

Normally, he'd jog up the stairs to Theatres and slip in that way but suddenly he felt weary. Bone weary.

Malachi rolled his tight shoulders and rubbed the dull ache lodged behind the bridge of his nose. Tired. Instead of the stairs he pressed the button for the middle lift. It was coming up and would be quicker.

Of course he felt tired. He'd been up for a breech delivery at three this morning and the Wilson baby's foetal heart rate aberration had given everyone a scare, but it had settled down. At least they'd avoided that caesarean unnecessarily, but he'd had to stay for the birth to make sure, which meant he hadn't made it home before six a.m. And today had been busy all day.

Must be getting old because five years ago he could have done three all-nighters in a row with only a couple of naps. He didn't know why he was surprised that Grace had severed their trial relationship—his father had never been able to maintain a liaison beyond a couple of months, not even the one with Malachi's mother.

Lucky he wasn't planning on kids and having someone rely on him to turn up for parent-teacher night because he'd be hopeless at it.

The lift doors opened and, oddly, the lift bounced a little as it stopped. The inside floor wasn't quite level with the white tiling he stood on. He hesitated. Maybe he wouldn't catch the lift?

He glanced into the small, suspended cubicle. Only one passenger, a blonde woman, and, judging by the voluminous sea-green dress she wore, her pregnancy was advanced. He smiled at her, not really seeing her face, mentally acknowledged the dilemma—he couldn't quite step back and leave her to the odd lift, so he stepped in boldly. Go him. Idiot.

She'd pressed five, the button was the only one glowing, an appointment with an obstetrician obviously, so he'd get out there too and hike up the rest of the stairs.

The lift doors closed and the lift began to jerkily ascend. Malachi put his hand out to the rail at his side and gripped it. Handrails were not something he usually touched, germs and all that, but the cool steel restored his balance.

Up for a few seconds more and the lift

shuddered, bounced once and stopped. It didn't start again. Stuck.

His gaze flicked to the woman across the small space.

'We're okay.' His most composed voice. He looked at the panel and pressed the button again for five. Nothing happened. He tried G for ground. Again nothing. Malachi opened the small door that held the emergency telephone and dialled for the switchboard.

'This is Dr Madden.' His voice unruffled. Matter-of-fact. Yet with authority because he wanted action. 'The central lift has stopped between floors four and five. Please have someone come and release us as quickly as possible. Thank you.' He put the phone back into its cubbyhole and swung the little door shut.

He took out his mobile phone and speed-dialled the operating theatres. 'This is Dr Madden. I'm due in Theatre Three, in five minutes. At the moment, I'm stuck in the middle lift, which seems jammed between floors four and five. I'm sure they'll get us out soon but perhaps a contingency plan for another surgeon for the caesarean might be in order.' He listened. 'Yes. I'll come up as soon as I'm free.'

Malachi slipped the phone back into his pocket and smiled at the woman again.

He held out his hand. 'I'm Malachi.' She didn't answer and he took more notice. She was breathing heavily and holding onto the rail on her side of the lift so tight her knuckles bleached white. Actually, her fingers looked bloodless.

She didn't offer her hand and he realised she had her other palm cupping her belly over her pubic bone. He'd always being quick on the uptake. 'Claustrophobic or in labour?' he asked, his voice gently enquiring. His refrain for life. Even in the face of a screaming woman or an irate bully of a cardiac surgeon. Keep everything composed.

'Not claustrophobic.'

The other then. Labour. Oh. Not too far in labour, he hoped. 'First baby?' They always took longer. Still calm. Feel the serenity.

'Yes.'

He let his breath out but it caught again when she said, 'Twins.'

'Twins.' His brows crept up. Glanced again at the roomy frock. Could be quite far along, too. 'Congratulations. Probably best you don't have them in the lift.' Argh. He couldn't believe he just said that!

She narrowed her eyes at him and he finally

noticed her face. Fine bone structure, a pink bow of a mouth and big eyes the exact colour of the ocean outside his office window. Gorgeous shade. A deep turquoise with flecks of deeper navy. Beautiful eyes.

He was staring. 'Sorry,' he said and blinked to break the spell. 'Stupid thing to say.' And think. 'Lack of sleep, rushing and getting caught in the lift must have scrambled my brains.'

She blew a breath out and he twigged she'd been deep-breathing for a while. 'Regular, painful contractions?'

Her lovely face grimaced as another contraction rolled through her. Gritted out, 'Yes.'

How long had they been here? He glanced at his watch? Less than five minutes. 'How often?'

She didn't answer and he realised she couldn't because she was breathing through the pain in her uterus. Finally, she said, 'Every two minutes.'

Not good. Best to get the information before the next contraction. 'For how long? Who's here with you? And when are you due?'

'The last half an hour.' She looked away. 'Nobody. And not for three weeks.' She sucked in a new breath and he guessed he had about sixtyish seconds to work out what else he needed to know.

He could ask, who should be here with you? Who can I call? Who is your doctor? But she sucked in a gulp and gasped.

Fluid, pink tinged and flecked with white, obviously amniotic in origin, splashed with spectacular force onto the tiled floor of the lift and up the walls in a dramatic wave.

CHAPTER TWO

Lisandra

LISANDRA CALHOUN GASPED. It felt as if someone had just stuck a crochet hook between her
legs and pulled out her bladder.

Except it wasn't an incontinence problem,
it was an Oh-my-heaven-my-babies-are-com-
ing problem. And it was all the fault of the
idiot who said she shouldn't have the babies
in the lift.

Slowly, gingerly, hanging onto the steel rail
with both hands, she eased herself closer to
the floor of the lift and crouched.

The floor looked clean, but couldn't possibly be clean, considering all the shoes that
would have walked all over it. A floor that
was now puddled with amniotic fluid, flecks
of white vernix and tiny stray lanugo baby
hairs. A lift floor where it looked as if, felt
as if, she just might birth when all she'd ever

wanted in life was to create a safe world for her babies. This was not safe!

'Are you okay?' A voice intruded on her panicked introspection. He was crouching down beside her. Shiny shoes and grey suit-trouser legs.

The idiot. She didn't even look at him. 'Of course, I'm not okay.' At least he was a doctor. She'd read about women who birthed their babies by themselves in small places. She hadn't read about anyone having twins in a lift, single-handed, so she'd probably need him.

The idiot rose out of sight and strode back to the telephone cubby and lifted the receiver. 'Escalate the speed of our removal from the lift. There is a woman in labour about to have twins. Get hospital maintenance. They can liaise with the lift company by phone. I want those doors open now.' He put the receiver down.

For some reason the contractions seemed to have paused—hopefully not because she was about to go into second stage and push her premature babies out into this two-metre-by-two-metre marble box.

But, from her half a dozen years as a midwife in birthing suite, she suspected that was a possibility. Transition anxiety. Which could also explain her crabbiness against Dr Malachi Madden. Funny, she remembered his name. Not high on her worry list.

'Sorry.' Her fingers jiggled—great, now she had the shakes—and her voice wobbled as hormones surged. 'I think that was transition.'

'You've done antenatal classes.' He looked vaguely relieved. And unhappy at the same time. Intelligent, dark hazel eyes assessed her. 'You're feeling pressure?'

'Not y...' *No, no, no.* The surge gripped her lower body in an iron fist and squeezed. She grunted. Guttural. Primal. Yanked her dress up and frantically tried to remove her granny pants. Thank goodness for granny pants, she thought wildly as they stretched under her fingers.

Big, gentle hands reached down, holding both of her arms to steady her as she wriggled so, so awkwardly out of her bottom half of underwear. 'Maybe stand when you can,' he said. 'Do the knicker removal properly or they'll trip you up later.'

So, when that urge finished, he hauled her to her feet. She leant on his rock-solid arm and stepped out of her granny pants. If she could care she'd think they'd look so forlorn and embarrassing there on the floor—but she couldn't care. The next pain was coming.

His hand left her for a moment and she desperately missed his support but he was shrugging off his jacket. Tucked it between her feet on the floor and took her arm again.

Ah, she had a clean piece of floor. Thank you. But she didn't have the breath to say it out loud. She leaned into him as the expulsive contraction built.

'Did you want to squat or kneel?'

'Wait.' One word was all she could do. 'Oh!'

She felt something shift down below. And then finally the pressure eased away again yet didn't leave completely. 'I'll squat.' She used to squat as a kid for hours at the waterhole, watching the fish, back on her grandparents' farm before Nan and Pop died. Her safe haven from the world. She wished she were there now.

Malachi said, 'We should get out of the lift soon—but little babies, if they come, they'll need to stay warm. I'll take my shirt off if they birth, not till they arrive, so the material stays warm.'

He was unbuttoning his shirt with one hand. Dextrous. Nice fingers. Strong hands. She was insane thinking of that.

Her babies. They'd be premature, susceptible to cold, and this was a cold, air-conditioned lift, with a marble floor. And a man's warm jacket. Her babies needed to be warm.

Best place to warm a baby was on the mother's skin. 'We can pull my dress off over my head. Pat them over with the bodice that's still dry. I can pull them onto my skin if their umbilical cords are long enough to reach my belly. Put your shirt over the top. K…k…keep them warm.' He looked at her strangely. 'I'm a midwife,' she said her shakes finally settling. 'Five years in birthing. Skin to skin is my bread and butter.'

He smiled into her eyes. His dark swampy green and so very compassionate. 'I'm sure you're a wonderful midwife. You'll be an even more wonderful mother.'

The crazy, spinning world of baby drama stopped for a brief, brilliantly lit, kindness-filled, nanosecond. He meant that. If those words weren't the most beautiful thing anyone had said to her in the last month, she didn't know what was. Good somebody had faith.

A deep, dragging, pulling pain gripped her again and she squeezed his hand as she tried to blow out. No breath-holding. No screaming. Steady slow inbreath and ease that breath out.

'You can do this,' he said quietly with absolute conviction. Yes, she could. But she appreciated the vote of confidence.

There was a thump on the closed doors and they both jumped. The lift jerked. Bounced.

Their eyes met. 'I've got you,' he said and indeed his hand had an excellent grip on hers.

'Let's hope we don't go down together, then,' she muttered and pushed again. There was no stopping this little red wagon her babies were riding on.

On the outside of her very internal world, the lift went up and not down, and when the doors opened, someone rattled a wheelchair in.

Malachi's strong arms scooped her up as if she weighed nothing like a woman pregnant with twins, but she was too busy in her own world to admire his strength. The downward, incredibly powerful urge was on her again.

'Great time to pant if you can,' Malachi said quietly into her ear, his warm breathy tone just for her. She clung to that sanity of connection in a swirling world as the wheelchair spun. 'Just give me one minute and we'll have you somewhere private and safe,' he said.

No. She couldn't. Just one minute was something she didn't think she had.

Gripping the arms of the chair as they sped along, Lisandra jammed her thighs and her mouth as she tried to hold herself together. They were rolling along the corridor at a brisk pace with a small band of noisy people behind her that she couldn't see.

The urge built. She blew breath between pursed lips. Her belly shoved.

A door opened in front of them and she was whisked through but it was too late.

'Now,' she said just as they pulled up beside a bed and she pushed.

'Perfect. You're so clever.' In the distance she could hear Malachi's gentle tones. In that moment of craziness, she clung to that voice.

'Beautiful,' he said as she pushed and then suddenly there was the sound she'd been waiting months for, a crying baby, and a sudden exquisite relief flowed over her in a breath— but that was all the breath she was given.

There wasn't time to relax.

'Now. Again,' she said just as Malachi's arms scooped around her body and softly settled her onto the bed, which she had to admit was easier than arching back and lifting her bottom in a wheelchair. She landed just as the next overpowering surge overcame her.

'I've got you. You're all safe. Let it happen.' Malachi's voice. Malachi's arms. Malachi's hands.

Until a second baby's cry filled the room and she sobbed out the relief at the sound and another sob at the sudden, poignant, emptiness inside her.

So, in the end, Lisandra didn't have the babies in the lift.

Malachi caught them both, smiling up at her after each one, and the babies both screwed their faces and screamed as if someone had taken their favourite toy. And then he disappeared.

Sitting up in the deserted birthing unit an hour later, the staff having rushed off to another emergency, Lisandra blinked around at the tidied room.

At one stage here, the place had looked as if it had been ransacked. Everyone had dashed about expecting the worst-case scenario. She'd given them the best-case scenario—nice, simple, headfirst deliveries for both boys like two tiny seals following each other down a slippery slope.

Who knew she'd be Mother Earth?

Which was lucky because, the twins coming three weeks early, the settlement for her little house wasn't for another fortnight and the contingency plan—Richard's parents' hospitality—had crashed and burned in the worst possible way.

So, she needed to be grateful, because a caesarean section or a horror tear during the births would have slowed her down considerably. Thank you, Malachi Madden, whom she hadn't seen since the births and didn't expect to see again.

After the rushing and the drama had died down a nice young doctor had introduced himself as Dr Cohen, the original OBGYN she'd booked in to see, and said that he would be looking after her.

Thank you, universe, for putting my unflappable Dr Malachi Madden in the lift with me. She'd been relying on the universe a lot, to look after her when Richard's heart had stopped so suddenly, four weeks before their wedding and with their pregnancy just known.

The universe that had helped her find temporary accommodation and kindness with a house-sitting company after Richard's previously delightful parents piled blame on her for not caring well enough for their precious son.

That little flat with the low-maintenance cat she was minding for the travelling owner meant she hadn't been eating too much into her maternity leave pay and the little she made from her online midwifery advice presence.

Sadly, bad luck had found her again. The owner had broken her leg on a ski slope and would arrive home tomorrow. There was no way she could stay in a one-room flat with an invalid, a cat, and two new babies.

Lisandra's new plan would have to be move to a house-share or similar while she waited for settlement and the previous owners of her new home to vacate.

Well... The babies were here. Safely—that was the most important thing. Though, with those moments of sheer terror in a lift before Malachi had stepped in, it had been a close call.

The fact that poor Richard had missed out on all of this made her heart ache. Everything would have been so different if he'd been here with her, but fate had cut him from her life and she would just have to shelve her own heartbreak and do the best that she could with his children.

She wasn't doing so hot with that.

She'd thought moving here had been the best for the children. Just went to show how wrong she could be.

If only she and Richard had had more time, had had the chance of marriage and life to-gether so his father couldn't have disputed her babies were a part of their family, but it wasn't to be. Less than a year together and Richard was gone. Even now, his face in her mind had grown misty without his photo by her bed—but that was only because she had so much else to think about. Once she had her house she'd put his framed face there for recognition in the boys' room and in her own.

All she wanted at this moment was a safe world for her babies. She suspected she'd have to cast herself on the chest of the first social worker the hospital offered to help find a stop-gap until that new home was ready.

CHAPTER THREE

Malachi

MALACHI KEPT SEEING her eyes. Deep pools like the ocean that he could plunge into—if only he had the time. Which he didn't. He'd never been at ease with women. Even the ones who fancied him and put in all the work. He couldn't even keep a convenient woman like Grace happy.

But there was something about Lisandra Calhoun that pierced him all the way to his heart. Stopped his heart. And his brain, apparently, because he was so not the man she needed in her life.

Plus, Lisandra had babies. Babies who deserved a father. A huge fail with him; he hadn't had that training, so it was fortunate for them they weren't his.

Straight after Lisandra's births when the team had taken over, he'd dropped his soaked,

bundled jacket someone had given him in a
bag off to Ginny, changed shirts and slipped
off to the operating theatre to check the
mother and baby up there were happy. When
he'd apologised for his no show that family's
sympathy for his ordeal had made him embarrassed. And thoughtful. Ordeal?

Lisandra hadn't been an ordeal—she'd been
a delight. His jacket was sorry, but he had
no regret he'd stepped into that wonky lift,
though he'd be taking the stairs from now on.

Imagine if she'd been there alone? The
thought made him uneasy. Someone should
have been with her. She'd said no one was
with her but her family should have arrived
by now. They'd probably be with her right at
this moment.

It had all been just a crazy slice of time
where the skills he was passionate about had
been useful and appreciated.

With the precipitous babies born so healthy
he'd been elated and possibly more relieved
than he normally allowed himself to feel.
He'd checked with the paediatrician a couple
of times when they'd crossed paths, and both
boys were with the mother—no need for special care nursery so far—but they were being
watched carefully.

He wondered if he should ask his paedia-

trician friend, Simon, to come in for a second
opinion? Shook his head. No, everything was
fine with the babies. Hopefully everything
was fine with their mother.

Lisandra, who would probably be wrapped
in her family's celebrations, should be wearily
happy. He hoped so.

It had been a long day for both of them and
was nearing eight p.m. now.

Visitors would be leaving.

She'd probably be asleep.

Though, with new twins, he suspected he'd
get more sleep than her in the next couple
of months. He'd just drop into the midwifes'
station and ask how she progressed before he
went home.

The midwife smiled at him as he ap-
proached the desk. He'd met her a few times.
Molly—he'd always been good with names.
'Quick check on Lisandra Calhoun?'

'Lisandra? She's great.' Molly scanned the
chart. 'I'm not looking after her this shift,
but we all know her. She does an online blog
that's super popular with antenatal mums.'

Did she now? Different. And one she could
add to after today's experience. 'Has she any
visitors with her at the moment?'

The midwife looked at him with an ear-
nest expression on her round face. Almost

pleading. 'No. she's had none except the social worker. Did you know her fiancé died at
the beginning of the pregnancy?'

He knew nothing bar Lisandra's name, par-
ity and delivery date, but he didn't say that.
He shook his head.

Thinking that if he didn't say anything, she
might go on.

Obligingly, her voice lowered to barely a
whisper. 'His parents cut her off—no family support—so if you could suggest to Dr
Cohen to keep her in a couple of extra days
that might help her get sorted.'

Cut her off? Someone was being horrid to
the courageous woman in the lift? That wasn't
right. He narrowed his eyes. 'Is she awake?'

The midwife nodded. 'Yes. This way. The
boys are feeding.'

Molly knocked on a door and pushed it
open. All of the rooms on this floor were single, which was good.

It would be hard to keep two babies quiet
in a shared ward. He was peculiarly satisfied
that Lisandra had comfort and good care, but
he didn't follow down that path of reasoning
about why that pleased him.

Another midwife sat on the edge of the
bed—he knew her, Ris—patting the back
of one of the babies. The other newborn lay

tucked under Lisandra's arm at the breast and seemed to be alert and happy. Not acting prem at all.

'Here's Dr Madden to see you, Lisandra.'

'Hello there,' Malachi said, feeling too much a fraud as a visiting doctor. 'Just a social call before I went home.'

'How lovely.' Her smile warmed and she did look pleased to see him. Some of his awkwardness eased.

Ris stood. 'If it's social we'll give you privacy.' She smiled politely and handed Malachi the infant she'd been patting, which he took because he was fine with them at newborn stage.

As both midwives left, Lisandra called out, 'Thanks, Ris.' Ris smiled and shut the door. Malachi could feel the awkwardness creep over him again.

Funny how he never felt awkward with his patients, but Lisandra wasn't his patient, even though he'd been there for her. Which made him wonder at himself for so adamantly ensuring that the box stating which doctor she was under the care of had been ticked with Dr Cohen, not him.

'How are you?' he said.

At the same time she said, 'Thank you.'

They both stopped and she laughed.

He waved her on. 'Ladies first.'

Her striking blue eyes shone like sequins in a shimmering sea. Suspiciously shiny. Was she crying? Or had she been? The thought pierced him.

'If I'm going first, then, I need to say thank you.' She waved her free hand. She paused as if trying to think of the words until she finally shrugged, smiled and said, 'You are the best person to be stuck in a lift with when in labour.'

Her voice sounded falsely jolly. To him, anyway. But none of his business. None, except it made him sad. 'My absolute pleasure.' He meant it. She looked like a bruised angel with the shadows under her eyes and he wanted to gather her up, hug her to him and protect her. And that wouldn't be happening any time soon. What was he thinking? She'd recently lost the babies' father and been traumatised by a precipitate twin birth. And he was a disaster as a hero. Remaining right where he was, he said instead, 'Do you have names for the boys?'

'Not yet.' She looked at the cots with a soft smile. At the moment, I'm calling them B1 and B2.'

Ah. This he understood. '*Bananas in Pyjamas*.' One of his clients had a toddler with two curved dolls and he'd explained the yellow TV characters to him. 'I'm sure more names will come to you.'

She chewed her lip. 'I'm sorry about your jacket.'

He drew his brows together until the thought processed and he remembered the floor of the lift. He waved his hand. 'Good we didn't need it. My secretary sorted that. She's excellent at sorting everything.' Speaking of sorting. He remembered Molly's request. 'You know you can stay as long as you like, here? We can always extend your stay until you're ready to go home.'

Her corn-coloured hair swung as she disagreed. 'Two weeks? I don't think so.'

And there was the prompt. 'Why two weeks?'

She gestured vaguely to the window. 'The little house I'm buying doesn't settle until then. They extended the settlement since I paid the deposit. I hope the sellers aren't wavering.'

'They're probably looking for their own place. Where are you living now?'

'I've been house-sitting a one-bedroom flat. Watering the plants.'

He watched her frown and chew her lip. Surely damaging that petal-pink skin, and he wanted to say, 'Don't do that,' as her teeth chewed down on the soft flesh.

'I've heard of house-sitting,' he offered while his mind tried to imagine her alone in a flat carrying a watering can, but it sounded strenuous for a heavily pregnant woman.

She nodded. 'I was minding the cat, too, but the poor owner's been injured and is coming back now so I'll have to go. It won't hold two babies and the noise they'll make.'

'One bedroom? No. I don't think so.'

'Maybe a hotel for a fortnight if the social worker can't find anywhere else.'

'No family?' It was a reasonable question. Anyone would ask that. Wouldn't they? Now he second-guessed himself. She really did throw him off kilter.

Quietly she answered, 'No family.' She glanced at her mobile phone. 'Can't even ring friends. Mobile phone's dead. No charger. I didn't bring my hospital bag.'

He had the craziest urge to say, I have an apartment that's empty ninety per cent of the time. It has everything. But, of course, he didn't. She'd be embarrassed.

Instead, he stood. 'I'm sorry,' he said again. Useless. 'Stay as long as you like. I'll have a word to Dr Cohen.' He offered her the baby that had gone to sleep in his arms.

She tilted her head at the two tiny beds

on wheels as she lifted the second baby and draped him over her shoulder to burp. 'Would you put B1 in the cot, please? It's easier to have one at a time.'

'I'll bet,' he murmured. Lord, he couldn't imagine how crazy it would get. His world was all for handing them over once they'd arrived. He really had little experience of day-to-day baby care.

He smiled and did as asked, constantly expecting the baby to wake and scream. Inexplicably, the newborn didn't, so he wrapped it in the muslin and tucked it into the cot in the same way he'd watched countless midwives do over the last ten years.

The child stayed asleep. How about that? His hand rested briefly on the little mound of baby and lifted to salute her.

'You were amazing, today, Lisandra.' He smiled and as he walked to the door he said softly under his breath, 'I imagine you're amazing every day.' He turned back. 'Goodnight. I hope you get some sleep.'

'Thank you.' She looked at the corridor past the door and then back at him. 'Will you come tomorrow?'

'If you'd like me to. Of course. But late. To check all is well.' Malachi forced himself to walk away.

* * *

The next evening, this time before seven p.m., not quite as crazy a day for him, he knocked on the door of Lisandra's room and she called, 'Come in.'

She'd intruded on his thoughts many times during the hours since he'd last seen her. And again, at lunch, when he'd bought and brought her a magazine and a cordless phone charger he'd seen in the hospital shop.

She'd taken both gifts without any false protestations. Appreciative but calm. 'Can I pay you the cost?'

'No.'

To his relief she'd just nodded. 'Then, thank you. Wonderful.' The smile she'd given him had made him want to run out and buy six more of each for her, but he'd inclined his head instead.

Now he saw the charger and phone were connected so she'd used it. 'Chargers never go astray.'

'Such a thoughtful gift. And I hated asking the midwives if they'd take my phone and charge it for me.'

He'd thought that, too. Thought about everything. 'You strike me as a person who likes to be independent.'

She furrowed her brows at him but some-how, no idea how, he suspected she was amused. 'You sure that's not just because I'm sitting here alone?'

It was a good question, but no, he doubted he was wrong. Sometimes he read women wrong, look at Grace, but not Lisandra. She'd tell it straight. 'I'm sure.' He said it with con-viction.

She smiled. A smile that could energise an army so he felt as if he'd just had a vitamin boost. 'You're a nice man, Dr Madden.'

Dr Madden. Let's not go there. 'Not your doctor, your friend from an extraordinary event, and I introduced myself in the lift as Malachi. You should use it.'

He sat in the visitor's chair. 'How was your day? Did the boys give you a run for your money?'

'Oh, yes. We've had our moments of un-usual interest, but I expected that. I sleep when they do.'

Of course she would, which was probably why she looked pale but lovely and not totally washed out. 'You do strike me as a sensible woman.'

Her brows pretended shock again. 'How can you say that? We met with me giving birth in a lift.'

'Ah, but you didn't. You sensibly waited for the birthing room.'

She laughed. 'You're an intelligent man, I can see that.'

'So. They. Say.' He pretended to be ponderous then peered at the babies. 'Have you named them?'

Her shoulders drooped just a little. 'No. Any suggestions?'

He shrugged. 'You could call this one Mal and that one Kai?'

Lisandra snorted. 'What unusual names.'

'But such intelligent names.'

She snorted again, such a funny, cute noise, and they smiled at each other. 'You have a dry sense of humour, don't you?'

'Possibly. Or so all my exes say.' He shrugged. 'Which means I can be a little blunt. I hope you don't mind?'

'Honesty is all I want.'

'Good. Then Molly mentioned your babies' father died unexpectedly. I'm sorry. That must be hard.'

'Yes.' She lifted her lovely chin. 'But even more difficult when I've moved two states thinking his parents wanted the babies near.'

'And they don't?'

Her eyes met his and he could see the hurt, confusion, and, even more sadly, embarrassment as well. 'I thought so. Or I think their grandmother would have made us welcome. But something changed. Accumulated grief, a mental health issue, I'm not sure what happened. But their grandfather basically showed me the door and denied my fiancé was the father.' The words had thickened towards the end. Serious hurt. He wanted to hug her, again, what was with that? He also wanted to snarl at the in-laws.

She said, 'Richard was a beautiful man. I don't understand how his father can be so cruel.'

Malachi would like to have a word with Richard's father. Instead, he said, 'Loss does strange things to people.'

He certainly knew that. His father had become more driven and even colder after Malachi's mother died. 'But you shouldn't be the one to suffer.' There was absolutely no excuse to make her suffer more. 'What about Richard's mother? You say she might have welcomed you?'

A small, delicate shrug, which reminded him she'd had the hugest thirty-six hours and he should leave her to sleep.

Lisandra said after a moment, 'I don't think she has the choice. She texted me to apologise and hoped I found happiness. Asked me not

to call. I think that means I can text. I sent her
a photo of the boys but didn't ring.'

'Sad.' He agreed. 'But that doesn't help you.
Still leaves you out on your own?'

'I'll manage until the house comes through.
And I have an online advice business for new
mums that will keep me going financially
until I go back to work. I do have contacts
for work up here.'

'I'm sure you will achieve all you wish. But
not yet. Stay and get a routine with the boys.'
He thought about the paediatrician and looked
more closely at B1. Touched his tiny nose and
it turned a pale orange under his finger. 'This
young man looks a little yellow.'

'He's sleepier today, too. Hopefully he
won't need phototherapy.'

'Probably will. It might take a few days but
thirty-seven weeks, a twin, showing yellow
already, jaundice is likely.'

'Thanks, Dr Blunt.' But she was smiling,
shaking her head ruefully at him. 'Do your
patients cry often?'

'Not usually. But then we know each other
well by the time they have their baby. They
know I'll be there for them.'

'I'm sure you are.'

'I'm here for you, too, Lisandra. I hope you
don't mind, but I've asked my secretary to

phone your room tomorrow morning. To see if you need anything from the shops. She can pick requests up on her way to work and drop in before she comes to the office. Of course, if you don't answer your phone, she understands you'll be sleeping, but you can text her any needs.' He put a card down on the bedside table. 'Ginny is the kindest person I know and wants to do this. She'll drop by in the morning, anyway, briefly, to introduce herself.'

He stood. Suddenly awkward again. 'Let me know if there's anything else I can do for you. Did someone bring in your suitcase?'

'Molly brought it this morning. The midwives are lovely.'

'They're looking after you. I'm glad.' He moved towards the door. 'Goodnight, Lisandra.'

'Goodnight, Malachi.' He smiled and walked down the corridor towards the stairs. She'd called him Malachi. That made him feel surprisingly good.

CHAPTER FOUR

Lisandra. A week later. Still in hospital.

LISANDRA TOUCHED HER WATCH. Five-thirty. Malachi would be here in an hour or two.

The twins were a week old and as long as she kept their feeds almost simultaneous, she managed enough sleep to feel human, keep herself bathed, and eat. It had been challenging, even with the help of the midwives, but she'd known it would be. But there was delight in the dark blue stares of her boys as they watched her and gratitude in her heart for the precious gifts she'd been given. And sanity in Malachi's and Ginny's visits.

There'd also been a brief 'thank you' text from Josie and a request for more photos when she wasn't busy.

Lisandra was always busy. Luckily B2 was a patient baby and waited with eyes open until his brother was sorted after the feed before having his own bottom changed and being resettled to his cot.

For the last two nights she'd been itching to be out in the world, settling into her new home, finding a routine, reaching for some kind of new normal. But she had to be patient—while being a patient—which was driving her mad.

On the upside she collected amusing incidents for Malachi through the day to share when he arrived but she suspected, with real regret, the tentative friendship that had grown between them might end when she left.

Not that she had time to think about male friends with the boys taking up all of her attention, but she would miss his short and amusing evening visits.

On her first day, she hadn't foreseen visitors over the weekend but he'd arrived at seven p.m. on Saturday and stayed the hour.
On the Sunday night the clock read just before nine, so she hadn't expected him, and she'd been a little emotional with both boys awake and unhappy. Emotional because she'd been tired, not because Malachi hadn't come. Not that.

But when his face appeared around the door she felt as if a load had lifted from her shoulders. Surely coincidence. Again, he'd brought a small gift. A perfect apple and a bottle of exotic flavoured mineral water. Even better, he reached for a grizzling B2 and scooped him up.

She tried for a light voice but her throat felt clogged with tears. 'In the nick of time. He was just about to do his nana.'

Malachi studied her face seriously but his tone stayed light. 'Being B2 that would have been impressive.'

She chuffed a small, unexpected laugh and it felt good. Great even. He was such a life-saver when she needed him—though this was down the smaller end of the scale, she supposed, from looking after her in a lift and in labour.

'Having a cranky baby night?'

'Yes.' She swallowed back the prickling in her throat again. Hormones. It was just hormones and that prevailing tiredness all mothers suffered from. 'B1 is not feeding and they're talking about phototherapy again for his jaundice if his levels go higher.' He'd already had three days of it.

'Better to get it over with,' he said prosaically, and she pretended to frown at him.

'Nice unvarnished truth, thank you.'

'I'll never profess to have the qualities of a good father...' There was something faintly wistful in that statement and it stuck to her thoughts like a grassy thorn to a sock while he went on. 'But I do know my jaundiced babies. This little man will need more phototherapy.'

She believed him. And the way B1 struggled to stay awake for the last feed she was almost ready herself. She watched him with her baby as that first part of his statement niggled. 'Why do you think you wouldn't have the qualities of a good father? You handle these two with skill and assurance.'

'My lifestyle. I'm not present enough for a family. Not my forte.' He waved it away. 'I'll stick with being a busy professional.'

'You're a wonderful doctor, you'd be a wonderful father.'

He frowned at her. As if too polite to disagree but totally doing so. 'I studied from the best to be a doctor...' Then he cut the sentence off and turned to put B2 back in the cot.

There was something here that made her want him to face her, to see what he was thinking if possible, but his shoulders were taut and when he turned his face showed aloof politeness. Not an expression she'd seen before but it said leave well enough alone. Sadly, she didn't. Instead she risked driving him away.

'What do you think makes a good father?'

Black brows rose. 'I have no idea.' He gestured to the cot. 'B2 seems settled. I hope you get some sleep. You look tired. I'll see you tomorrow.'

And with that unflattering, though sincere, comment, he left.

On the Monday Ginny had brought an apple and two blue hand-embroidered face washers, a friendly face after only a few days, something she'd sorely needed, along with more baby wipes.

B1 had become jaundiced again as Malachi had predicted but the staff returned the portable biliblanket to wrap him, which meant he didn't have to go under the phototherapy lights in a cot away from her. Her firstborn just lived in his bright-lights-on-the-inside blanket with his eye covers on and slowly recovered. He'd glowed in the corner of the room like a little blue glow-worm but today they'd removed the covering.

So much better than when babies were taken away from their mother to the nursery with overhead lights, she'd thought. B2, the bigger of the two, had avoided the jaundice and both boys were feeding well today.

It was funny how the naming was becoming such a huge dilemma. Malachi had begun bringing two silly names on a folded paper, like Conan and Igor, Panda and Pluto, and even Brick and Diggory. He'd left the papers unopened for her to smile over once he'd gone.

Today was Thursday, she'd finally settled on the boys' names, and they even felt right. That was exciting.

But she was waiting for Malachi. She wanted him to be the first to know. First to hear her decision.

When her phone rang, the ringtone had been turned so soft she barely heard it, but she scrambled to answer. A tiny hope inside wondered if Richard's mother had changed her mind and was coming to visit. Or perhaps it was Ginny with her nightly call. Ginny rang twice a day now. But no, a private number.

Before she could pick it up the call ended after only three rings and she had no way of calling back. Spam, of course. Until the text came in from Beach Realty.

Her heart sank.

Miss Calhoun. It is with regret we inform you that the owner has decided to withdraw his house from sale and your deposit will be returned to you within fourteen days. If something similar comes up we'll contact you.

No. *No.* That was it. All her plans. Her few things in storage. She looked at the time. Pulled the realty number from her contacts and dialled. A recorded message to say they were closed. She doubted the timing was a co-incidence. They were avoiding her. The hoops she'd gone through to secure the loan—something she would have much more difficulty accessing now she was on maternity leave and no current employment—had been mammoth and the thought of doing it all again felt daunting, but she would have to try. Tomorrow. Or the next day. Before she left here, that was for sure.

Her breath hissed out and she stared at the two cots with sleeping babies. All she'd wanted was a safe and stable place for her babies.

The phone in her hand rang again. This time it really was Malachi's secretary. 'Hello, Ginny.' Lisandra's voice sounded shaken, which she was, but suddenly it was too hard not to choke up.

'You okay, Lisandra?'

'Not really.'

'I'm on my way home. Want me to come up and visit?'

'I'll be fine.'

'Of course, you are.' Agreeing. 'But I'll be there in two minutes just to listen.' The phone clicked off.

And that was how Malachi found them half an hour later. Ginny handing tissues to Lisandra and her face a blotchy mess.

Ginny stood when he came in and Lisandra could see the secretary looked relieved. He'd been getting earlier every night since Sunday, she realised. Which was probably just luck but still nice. She sniffed and tried to blot her face.

'I'm glad you're here,' she heard Ginny say, her voice calm. 'Lisandra's new home fell through. The owner withdrew it from sale. Tell her not to worry. I'll get onto finding at least a rental tomorrow when all the real estates are open.'

Malachi's face creased with concern as he stepped closer and touched her arm. 'I'm sorry that's happened to you.' He looked at Ginny. 'That would be excellent.'

'She needs to leave the hospital as well,' Ginny said. 'I was thinking holiday accommodation with washers and driers, and a view to feed babies by, while I work it out.'

Malachi smiled at his secretary and then at Lisandra. 'See. I told you she was good at sorting. Do you have a favourite beach along here?'

Her head spun as she tried to keep up with the conversation. 'I like Kirra. It's quieter than Coolangatta but Coolie is lovely too.' Why hadn't she thought of that? So much easier than a hotel with no facilities in the rooms. Expensive, not as much as a hotel though, and she had savings. Plus, an urgent need right now to get settled. Get her bearings. Start to believe, again, that everything wasn't so bad. She let her shoulders ease back a couple of notches.

'Why not take the loft at my place?' Malachi's words dropped into the silence. 'It's self-contained, soundproof, and you can lock the door between the two sections. Easy.'

Ginny and Lisandra offered him matching stunned faces. 'What?' He frowned at them. 'Just until Ginny sorts you a rental. Seems silly to move until you've found the right place. Even though the loft is part of my apartment I have separate rooms downstairs.'

Lisandra's brain froze. No. Despite how fast a solution to her problem, she couldn't. He didn't know her. Though he had helped her remove her granny pants in extremis, a voice inside whispered. 'No. I couldn't.'

He turned his attention to Ginny. 'It's empty. I trust her. And she's homeless.'

She and Ginny both winced at that. Captain Blunt. Well, she guessed she was, though she didn't like hearing it out loud. But he was right. And there was a gift horse called Malachi staring her in the face. Literally.

Staring into her totally red eyes. 'I want you happy and not weeping with worry.' He shrugged. 'You said all you want is a safe and secure place. I'm not going to throw you out when the boys cry. And it has state-of-the-art security. It's empty. Save the rent for the new place when it comes up.'

His phone beeped and he pulled it out. 'Birthing Unit needs me. Have to go.' He walked back out of the door.

Both she and Ginny stared after him.

'That's Dr Madden for you.' Ginny shook her head fondly. 'He lives at Kirra. It's a two-storey apartment, and the self-contained loft that used to be his father's bolthole to practise his violin is standing empty. There's two bedrooms up there and three downstairs. And Malachi is barely home. That's what Grace said.'

'Grace?'

'Grace was his lady friend. She broke it off

last week. He wouldn't mind me telling you.' She looked at Lisandra's face. 'Don't worry. Neither of them was sorry.'

'I can't move in with him.'

'You're not. It's a separate loft. I've only been there once but I'm pretty sure there was a mini laundry and kitchenette up there as well. The keyed lift opens on that floor, too. Which makes it easy for prams.'

Lisandra put her head in her hands and mumbled, 'How do I say no to all that?'

'You don't.'

When she surfaced Ginny was holding out her hand as if she had all the good reasons in the palm of it. 'Malachi is good people.' She turned up the other hand. 'I think you're good people, too.' She moved both hands like weighing scales. 'He needs a friend. A friend who's a woman would be even better. He doesn't have any that I know of. Lots of acquaintances but he buries himself in work.'

'A friend?'

'Yes. A low-maintenance one—not like Grace.'

'A low-maintenance new mum with twins,' Lisandra said dryly.

Ginny clenched her fist as if catching all those good reasons inside her palm. 'You're emotionally low maintenance. Look at you. You refuse to stay down every time fate tests you.'

'I cried when you came.'

'And then you started working out what to do.' She gestured to the empty doorway Malachi had disappeared through. 'That man is one of the kindest men I know. Despite his sometimes abrupt manner.'

'Like saying I'm homeless.'

Ginny winced again. 'Yep. Like that.' A thoughtful expression crossed Ginny's face. 'He's been less obsessed this week. You and the boys are good for him. He told me once he's never having kids because he can't give them what a father should. So maybe he can learn about himself from you while you're there. Something you can give back to him that he wouldn't get otherwise.'

She couldn't do this. 'It feels so awkward.' She barely knew him. 'He's too generous. I have to pay my way.'

'He won't take it.' Ginny shrugged. 'Just be yourself. Bank what you would have paid for rent and if you ever want to pay him one day—' she shrugged again '—you'll feel like you can. But I'd be keeping it to add to your deposit on a house. He doesn't need the money and would be offended if you offered.' She rolled her eyes theatrically. 'He'd make me figure out something to escape the hassle.'

Despite herself, Lisandra laughed. Then sobered. 'Should I do this?' It was more to herself than Ginny, but the answer came from the other woman.

'Mad if you don't. How about I sort it all for tomorrow after five-thirty? I'll tell my family to buy take-out for dinner on Malachi, and we'll do a girl power move-in.'

CHAPTER FIVE

Malachi

MALACHI SUPPOSED HE'D been pretty high-handed about the suggestion, and probably shouldn't have said Lisandra was homeless, but she was. This was the perfect answer. That said, he'd been happy when the summons from the birthing unit came, so the women could chat about it.

He had full faith in Ginny's good sense and that she'd share it with Lisandra.

With no more waiting for her house there was no reason for Lisandra to stay in hospital. At his home, they didn't need to cross paths if she didn't want to.

Plus, he'd be happy if he knew she was safe upstairs. He had no concerns she'd be a horror tenant nor he a bad landlord.

He'd barely gone upstairs since his father left the place to him in his will so he wouldn't miss it. The old man had soundproofed the loft for violin practice, so he wouldn't even hear the boys if the doors were all shut.

Grace had suggested he renovate, move upstairs and entertain more downstairs, but he'd said he was fine without the entertainment. And hadn't that worked out well? He doubted Grace would have been as welcoming to Lisandra moving in if they were still an item.

All in all, he'd made a lucky escape from a not very convenient relationship there. Though, he probably needed to hint to his grandmother that a woman was moving in and it wasn't Grace. The thought made him smile. She'd be happy for all the wrong reasons but having the one woman he really did care about happy was always good.

By the time he made it back to Lisandra's room it was almost eight p.m. and Ginny had gone. His new tenant-to-be was tucking the boys back into their beds.

He came to stand beside her at the cots looking down at the infants. B2 rolled his eyes and grimaced. He'd probably cry in a minute with wind. 'So? Have you decided if you and the boys will move in upstairs?' He was hoping the conversation wouldn't be awkward.

He should have known better. Lisandra had sorted her thoughts by now.

She snorted. 'You left at a good time. Ginny and I worked it out. Your offer is too good to refuse.' She raised her brows at him. 'Apparently your secretary is going to charge you for take-out for her family and help me move tomorrow afternoon after she finishes work.'

Ah. Good news indeed. 'Excellent.' He tapped the nearest cot gently. 'So, what happened today?'

'Today, I decided on their names.'

Malachi straightened. That was good news. He'd seen the indecision had bothered her but it was something she had to come to on her own. 'Tell me.'

'Bennett and Bastian. B1 will be Bastian and B2 will be Bennett. Alphabetical precedence in age.'

His eyes lit up. 'I like that thought process.'

Malachi repeated the names. 'I like the names. Very masculine and individual. Better than Mal and Kai.'

'I was thinking of those for their middle names.'

She was joking, he thought, but it was a nice story. 'BMC and BKC. That works.' He studied her face. 'Are you ready to leave hospital?' She still looked tired but he could detect that brittle edge women got when they stayed longer than they wanted. He saw that in his work. A lot. Especially when he needed to keep mums in for a complication. Weighing up the medical barrier to discharge with the mother's need to go home and nest.

'Very.'

'Excellent. My housekeeper will put sheets on the bed and stock the cupboards with basics. When you're ready you can order online shopping and they'll deliver anything Mrs Harris hasn't supplied. That's what I do if I want something in. Bachelor perks.'

She lifted her chin and met his eyes. He saw sympathy, thankfully not pity, though he gave Lisandra credit for good sense. 'I'm sorry. Ginny said your relationship ended last week.'

'It was fledgling. Grace and I are both much happier apart.' Her eyes were truly a beautiful shade of blue-green. 'I'm not husband material and it was useful to have that confirmed.'

She frowned at him. 'Perhaps Grace wasn't the right woman for you?'

He shook his head. Shifting uneasily to-

wards the door. 'I prefer to be single. Goodnight, Lisandra. Congratulations on the boys'
names.'

'Thank you. Goodnight, Malachi.'

CHAPTER SIX

Lisandra

LISANDRA WATCHED HIM GO. Strong shoulders back, head high, powerful legs creating distance between them. He didn't hurry but he moved like an athlete down the hall and didn't look back. Not that he ever did. Always focussed on the next objective was Malachi.

Ginny said he achieved twice as much as other doctors in the hospital and never said no to a request for help.

Lisandra had discovered he didn't like to talk about his personal world but was happy to dissect hers. So, unless he was making personal comments, she'd keep it general, but if he was being personal... She'd ask.

That would be the only way she'd find out what made this man tick. He was turning out to be fascinating, but difficult to understand. She was still pondering his idea that he wouldn't make a good father. How much of that was because of his career? What would he even give as his reasons? Maybe he had a ridiculously idealised view of family life—the Hollywood version—home every night at five p.m. Dad was there to play cricket or footy on the weekend, to pick you up from school when you were sick, fun and present and full of dad jokes.

She tried to remember doing things with her father but could only remember him coming home from work and sitting down to tea. There'd been jokes and smiles and she remembered her parents as happy—before they were gone for ever on her seventh birthday. Anyway, now Malachi had stated he wasn't husband material either.

But not any of her business, she reminded herself.

Which was fine.

He would be her landlord. One that wasn't taking any money, which rankled, but she'd do as Ginny suggested and meticulously hoard the payments until she had a chance to pay him back. She had funds.

Obviously, he did too. What sort of apartment had a separate, lockable loft? She suspected it was a very nice one but when she did find a place of her own to rent or hopefully buy, she would move out quickly even if it wasn't as flash as Malachi's.

She needed to consider her little family's long-term future. Malachi might not think he was husband material but he'd find a wife one day and that wife sure as eggs wouldn't want a single woman with twins living upstairs.

And for Lisandra, with twin babies who needed a lot of care, there would be years before any man would be thinking about chatting her up. She wouldn't have the time anyway. In that way both she and Malachi were alike.

When Ris came in to see if she needed anything for the night, Lisandra shared the good news she was finally going home. Tomorrow evening. She'd have to get the address off Ginny for the discharge papers, but she wasn't mentioning to the staff it was Malachi's loft. No offence to dear Ris, but she'd worked in hospitals. He didn't need that sort of rumour running down the halls and seeping like legionnaires' disease through the air conditioners as hot gossip to make people stare at him.

Her staying under his roof was appreciated. It required discretion. And was temporary.

The next evening as Lisandra waited for Ginny to arrive, she'd already taken her few things down to the car park of the hospital and brought back the two little carry seats. One of the things she had achieved in the week before the boys were born had been to have the infant car capsules for the babies installed. Thank goodness for that.

Since last night, online, she'd ordered a twin pram and two porta cots plus all the necessary paraphernalia that went with setting up a baby nursery. All flat-packed and click and collect. All dying to be picked up and assembled. Though she was a little daunted at the idea of assembling furniture and prams between feeds.

She'd planned to collect the purchases on discharge, since she drove an SUV with plenty of hatchback storage area, but this morning Malachi's extremely efficient secretary had suggested she had them delivered. The unopened packages, Ginny assured her, would be waiting for her inside her flat, thanks to the presence of Malachi's housekeeper.

In fact, Lisandra should have her current leftover possessions at the house-sitting flat collected by a courier and delivered. It was only clothes and a suitcase with the baby things she'd begun to gather and her unfortunate hostess had been happy to prepare what was left for the courier. They could pick up her few boxes in storage as well. It wouldn't cost much and save her the hassle.

Lisandra had to admit, after another long day of feeding and caring for the boys, the idea of navigating armfuls of parcels would have been daunting, let alone transferring them from the car park to the unit once they arrived. And to have her few things packed and delivered was just too easy. Bless the woman's brilliance.

A butterfly buzz of excitement fluttered under her ribcage at the thought of having her own space to create the nursery she'd been dying to establish since she'd arrived from Melbourne. She'd refused to buy much until she had her own house, had brought little up the coast as the transfer costs were more expensive than buying new.

But, thanks to Malachi, now she had a short-term haven to relax and nurture her sons. A place of no judgement by others and she could heal from the hurt and distress that had been dealt out by Richard's father.

She still believed the babies' grandmother would one day defy her husband and turn up. So far, she'd only sent one photo of the boys on the day they were born but would send another today. Intending, unless she was asked to stop, to send one a week for the first four weeks and, if she still had no reply, then one a month for the first year. It broke her heart she didn't have a photo of Richard as a baby so she could compare with the boys. But she suspected Josie was suffering, too. When she was out and about, she'd make two matching baby photo albums—and keep one for Richard's mother. Perhaps one day she would hear from her.

For now, she had her new life to get on with. She wouldn't be lonely. Malachi would drop in after work every now and then to catch up with the latest news of the babies. But even if he didn't, she knew downstairs, or with Ginny's contact number, someone cared about them, and would be there in an emergency. There was a lot of peace in that thought and she would be grateful to Malachi Madden and his secretary for ever for that gift.

Ginny arrived and suddenly, in a flurry of goodbyes to the staff, she was in the lift with Bennett and Bastian and Ginny. Going home with twins.

In the same lift they'd nearly arrived in.

Funny how the memory didn't bother her. She and Malachi had managed. She'd apparently been sensible, as Malachi said, but the maintenance people getting the doors open had allowed that boon.

Holding one baby capsule and her hand-bag, she looked at the corner where a week ago Malachi had laid down his suit jacket and crouched beside her.

Lisandra's lips twitched and she shook her head with a smile at the memory. She almost wished he'd been there to meet her eyes and share the moment. But that was silly. He probably thought of it as a disaster that hadn't quite happened.

Once the boys' capsules were loaded into their safety-locked cradles, she followed Ginny's car in her own to the boom gate. Lisandra slipped into the fast-moving traffic for the first time in a week and she had a sudden crazy feeling of panic.

What if she had an accident with the boys in the car?

What if she died suddenly as their dad had and the boys were left alone in the unit?

Lisandra crushed the feeling down. She would manage. She would manage it all. But for the moment, Ginny and Malachi were there. She had friends. She and the boys weren't alone. That fact was priceless.

The indicator light from the car ahead brought her back to the present and she followed Ginny left down another boom-gated car-park ramp. She tapped the electronic key card she'd been given to keep the boom gate up.

Ginny had told her Malachi had two car-parking spaces and Ginny would park in the visitor's parking. Ginny stopped and indicated a parking spot directly opposite the lift doors next to a long, low black sports car with chrome spoked wheels. She'd never been a car buff but it looked fast and expensive and she'd have to be very careful when she opened her doors not to scratch it.

She'd certainly moved into a privileged position and even though she hadn't had time to look at the outside of the building very much, she'd seen the beach opposite, and the cars surrounding her looked like a private school of automobiles.

She shrugged and tried not to be excited. This was lovely holiday accommodation until she found her for-ever home for the boys. But very nice for a brief sojourn.

When she opened her car door Malachi stood with his back against the sports car next to her. She blinked. 'Malachi?'

'I finished early. I thought I'd come and see how you settle in.'

'Oh. Thank you.' A well of delight and happiness surged up her chest and into her smile. 'How lovely.'

His eyes widened, and the smile he gave her back held a tinge of shyness. 'I'm glad. Though I can't guarantee I won't get called away, so we'll still ask Ginny to stay. I was thinking about the parcels Ginny mentioned and I've always loved assembly puzzles. Maybe I can help?'

'Excellent,' she said, trying to damp down her pleasure. 'I dislike building them intensely.'

When they were standing in the lift with Ginny, nobody spoke as the floor lights blinked past and Lisandra thought about that day a week ago when she met the man standing so still and tall beside her.

He held Bastian's carry cot. 'Were you nervous getting back in a lift?' He must have been thinking of it too.

Lisandra smiled. 'No. And it was the same lift.'

'Oh, my heaven, I never thought of that.' Ginny looked horrified she hadn't been supportive. She turned her head and stared at Malachi as if surprised he had.

Why was Ginny surprised? Malachi was always thoughtful. Lisandra shook her head. 'I have no bad memories from that day. Once

Malachi stepped in I knew I had help even if I did have the babies. When it jammed—' she shrugged '—he was so calm about ordering them to get us out I knew he had that part under control.'

'Glad I fooled you, then,' Malachi said dryly.

She grinned at him. 'And he didn't seem fazed when my waters broke all over the floor.'

Ginny made a strangled hiccough of a noise. 'He doesn't get fazed.' Ginny looked at her boss fondly. 'A furrowed brow is all you'll get as he works on the solution.'

They both looked at Malachi, who shrugged. 'No idea what you two are going on about.'

Lisandra smiled again. Said softly to Ginny, 'Yes. I was lucky he stepped in.'

'Maybe you both were,' Ginny said even more quietly as the lift doors opened right at the last number, but Lisandra stared at Malachi with wide eyes. 'Do you have the penthouse?'

Malachi shrugged. 'Inherited from my father. I enjoy the view.'

'I thought you knew that.' Ginny grinned. 'Penthouses are the only apartments I know with lofts. Just enjoy it.'

Her cheeks had grown hot at the idea of the

luxury, but she suspected she would 'enjoy' living here indeed.

Lisandra looked down at Bennett in his little capsule. Sang very softly to him about going on a summer holiday. Ginny laughed. Malachi looked intrigued and she stopped in embarrassment. Then she looked at the small entry and closed loft door.

She turned to Malachi. 'Would you like to show me?'

He gestured with his hand inviting her to precede him and they stepped out into a foyer each carrying a car-seat capsule with the boys asleep. Bonus, right there. Much more fun when the babies weren't screaming.

He swiped the door lock. 'The lift to here isn't accessible to floors below mine, unless somebody has our code on their card. People such as maintenance and reception do. I'll keep mine in case of emergencies but won't use it without your permission.'

'Thank you.' What else could she say? Especially in view of her earlier dire thoughts, it was good he had the back-up access.

The door swung open and white marble tiles flowed from the front door through the serene lounge area to the narrow, wrap-around balcony. Straight ahead blue waves and blue sky stretched across the Tasman Sea, technically all the way to New Zealand.

Loft? It looked like an enormous open-plan house on the top of the world. 'So much bigger,' she murmured. Good grief, she'd arrived at the Taj Mahal.

Malachi made a small, pleased sound, as if happy she liked it. She raised her brows at him. Who wouldn't? 'Downstairs is much larger and there's a small private pool.' His tone was amused. 'The boys might be a bit young for that, but you're welcome to use it.'

No way in heck was she sauntering through his house to get to his pool.

As if he'd read her thoughts, he said quietly, 'There's a spiral staircase off your veranda down to the pool.'

She raised her brows. Snorted. Couldn't help herself. 'Of course, there is.'

He looked pleased. 'You find it over the top, too?'

She laughed. So, it seemed extravagant to him as well? That was interesting. 'Yes, Malachi. But wonderful.' More seriously, 'Thank you for trusting us into your home. I won't take advantage of your kindness.'

'I know that.' He shrugged. 'Nobody else uses it. And that's your internal stairway down to my apartment if you need me in an emergency. The lock is push button and on your side. Of course, I have a key, but won't use it unless you need me to.'

If she locked herself out? Or in an emergency? She prayed that would never be required and turned away from the thought of something so bad she'd run to Malachi. She turned her face to the room.

Thick blue rugs lay between two long white leather sofas, with blue shell-embroidered cushions and white occasional tables and lamps. Not cluttered, but soothing and seamless leading to open floor-to-ceiling doors and the narrow wrap-around balcony twelve floors from the ground. Thankfully, glass enclosed the drop from over waist height. Not that she'd still be here when the boys were crawling, but still. That was some drop.

They stepped in further and he pointed to a white door to the left. 'Butler's pantry in there with sink, coffee machine, small stove and microwave.'

Then to another door next to it. 'Guest bathroom and laundry. The boys' room, and your room at the far left with en-suite bathroom.

Malachi crossed the wide living area to the external glass doors and opened them to the gentle ocean breeze carrying the tang of salt, and the sound of distant waves and seagulls. Lisandra put her carry cot down and followed him.

The bay curved away in both directions, left to Surfers Paradise in the distance and right, back towards Coolangatta and the Tweed, though she couldn't see around the headland. Curving footpaths butted the beach and swept under trees and palms in both directions. Utopia for anyone...let alone a new mother with twins. 'Plenty of places to push a pram down there,' she said.

'Are you going to have the boys in with you tonight or in their own room?' Malachi asked.

'I think I'll keep them with me for now, until I'm used to sleeping here. But I can't wait to set up their things.'

'Let's do that, then.' His eyes gleamed. 'If I start with the pram assembly you could put them there for the night and just push them around the loft.'

She looked at this tall, gorgeous, generous man offering his time, a precious commodity he didn't have much of, with such enthusiasm. 'Are you a thwarted engineer?'

'Apparently,' he said over his shoulder as he headed to the butler's pantry. 'There should be a knife in here to open the tape.'

She exchanged looks with Ginny, who

shrugged. 'I hate assembling,' she said, and gestured to the suitcase.

Lisandra nodded. 'Me, too.'

Two hours later Lisandra stood beside Ginny waiting for the lift. Her new friend had been busy. She'd sorted the boys' new clothes, wraps and cot sheets and washed them in the pure soap she'd brought for just that purpose. Those that could be whirled inside the clothes dryer in the guest bathroom were either dry or still doing so and those that couldn't stand the heat had been stretched on the clothes-drying rack that pulled out from the bathroom wall.

Ginny screwed her face. 'You sure you don't want me to stay until all the clothes are dry? I can fold them and put them away in the wardrobe.'

Lisandra shook her head. 'You've done enough. Took the biggest load off me while I've just sat on the lounge and fed the boys. The least I can do is fold some clothes.'

Ginny looked back in towards the boys' room. 'It's all worked out really well.' Her gaze travelled over the pram that sat next to the lounge with the two boys asleep in it. 'So good Malachi managed as much as he did before he left.'

Malachi had assembled the pram, while

Lisandra fed the boys, and Ginny made it up for them to sleep in. Malachi took himself into the bedroom to assemble the change table and the portable cots. Five minutes after he was done his phone rang and he left to return to the hospital.

All around her those two wonderful people had unpacked and sorted for her and by the time she'd resettled the boys after the feed—everything was done.

Thank you.' Lisandra leaned forward and hugged her. 'You're a champion, Ginny.'

'You'll be busy enough while you ease these boys into a routine. I think you're the champion. Having one baby at a time was hard enough for me, and the last was sixteen years ago—I still remember the exhaustion. Watching you juggle the two of them fills me with awe.'

'Thanks to you and Malachi I don't have anything else to do. I've been given a beautiful place to stay and now you've organised everything else. I'm feeling very spoiled.'

'You sure you don't want me to make you some food before I go?'

Lisandra shook her head. 'Go home to your family. The boys are asleep. It's my first night with them and I'm excited. I'll just have something simple.'

The lift arrived and Lisandra waved at her new friend as the doors shut.

And then she was alone. Just her and the boys in their new home. Suddenly the space was silent except for the swish of the waves in the distance and the traffic far below.

When she stepped out onto the balcony the crescent moon hung over the ocean leaving a trail of sparkling light across the waves. Across the bay, the night-lit buildings of Surfers Paradise twinkled in the distance.

She walked to the end where the small, gated spiral staircase led down to the floor below. She could just see the edges of the pool with the blue of the water lights glowing under the surface.

She turned and walked back to the other end of the balcony and stared out along the beach far below. It was going to be very hard to return to ground level once this little holiday was over.

That was what it was, though, a holiday for her and the boys to get used to each other. She was blessed at the opportunity and wasn't in a position to be squeamish over the favour she'd been given as a gift beyond expectation. Somehow, she'd figure out how to repay Malachi, but for tonight she'd just soak it in.

CHAPTER SEVEN

Malachi

ON SATURDAY MORNING before Malachi's alarm went off, he lay on his back smiling at the ceiling, still enjoying that pleasure of accomplishment from yesterday. Lisandra and her babies were settled upstairs. Strange how good that made him feel.

He hadn't heard any noise at all and hoped Lisandra realised that she didn't have to worry about disturbing him. Next time he saw her he'd remind her of that.

The alarm beeped quietly and he rose, dressed, and left to jog along the shoreline from headland to headland, the best part of living at the beach, and even if some mornings he was called out, that only made the dawns he did see more satisfying.

Grace had not been an early riser and hadn't appreciated him disturbing her as he dressed for his run. All in all, life was so much simpler and more pleasant without Grace, which reminded him he needed to let his grandmother know he was not headed for a long-term relationship.

He'd been a fool to expect any relationship to not be a rolling disaster—but the few times he'd suggested it might not be working Grace had managed to reassure him until he'd been distracted by work. Luckily, even work had finally exasperated Grace.

Today, he'd invite his grandmother over and break the news. If it all worked out she could meet Lisandra and the twins before she formed the wrong idea.

Malachi had only been back from his run for half an hour when his doorbell rang.

When he swung open the door he was expecting Lisandra, actually, hoping for Lisandra, as only one other person had a key to his level, but it was a tall, grim-visaged woman, who lifted her chin at him. He should never have given Gran a key, but they'd both agreed asking Reception to be allowed to visit her own grandson was unacceptable. But she always knocked.

Busted. Too late. Millicent Charles, his mother's mother, stood almost to Malachi's height. His gran had never suffered fools and he'd been a clown not keeping her up to date. She didn't intimidate him, the thought made him smile, but he indulged her because she deserved some indulgence from someone and he was all she had.

'Grace tells me your relationship has ceased to be—just over a week ago.' She looked him up and down. Not impressed, her narrowed eyes said.

'Please come in, Gran.'

'Thank you,' her cultured voice clipped as she swept past. Seemed he had some explaining to do. His mouth kinked up. He loved her very much, but she would be cross.

More proof of her displeasure came his way. 'One would have thought one's grandson would have mentioned that fact.'

'Grace didn't appreciate my current workload.'

'What woman would?'

Lisandra didn't seem to mind. 'My apologies. I intended to invite you for lunch to speak to you today.'

'Too late. I'm here. You could make me coffee if you're not dashing out.'

'Love to.' He held up his hands peaceably. 'I'm not going anywhere.'

'Unless your silly phone rings.' His grand-mother knew him well.

'My phone is quite clever but I'm not on call either,' he said mildly. 'Would you like something from the patisserie?'

'A dreadful frozen something?'

'Fresh this morning after my run.'

Millicent appeared slightly mollified. 'I might.' She glanced towards the balcony. 'I'll sit out on the deck and wait for you. I always did appreciate this view.'

Malachi cast his own look towards the wide-open space of the outdoor entertainment area. All he needed now was Lisandra to be spotted upstairs by his grandmother before he could ease into the fact that he had a stranger and her newborn twins living above him.

Of course, it was his house, he could invite whom he wished, but he didn't like to upset Gran or give her the wrong idea. She had that dicky heart and was the one person who had loved him unconditionally when his world fell apart. He knew she wanted him to be happy but he didn't need her assuming Lisandra was his new girlfriend. She'd be embarrassed at her mistake. To make his guilt worse, Ginny had reminded him twice yesterday to ring his grandmother, but both times he'd been called away before acting on her advice.

Last night, it had been too late coming home from the hospital after his call back, and he'd been busy enjoying that warm sense of accomplishment thinking of Lisandra relaxed and happy with her babies. He'd had an amusing time assembling the pram, the change table and setting up the little portable cots. The uninhabited loft had taken on a heart and soul that had been dreadfully lacking in the space before.

He'd known it was too late to go up and see them then but knowing she'd been up there with her babies had left him strangely content.

Now he had to explain that to his favourite, and only, relative without sounding like an idiot hoodwinked by a beautiful woman. He knew it wasn't so. And when his grandmother actually met Lisandra, she would know the same. Still. A difficult conversation that didn't need an interruption by a crying baby above.

Which was exactly what the distinctive newborn wail drifting in through the open doors provided. His lips twitched. Oh, dear.

Malachi put his head down, smiling, and prepared his grandmother's latte the way she liked it and then his own long black coffee. Next, he placed a pastry on each of two small bone-china plates along with paper napkins. A skill she'd insisted he learn when he'd spent his weekends with her in his teens. She'd grumble about the lack of linen but he expected there would be more to discuss than that.

Everything went on the tray and he carried it out to the long outdoor table under the shaded area. He didn't glance up.

When he was seated and the tray had been distributed, he said, 'In more news...'

'You have a woman living upstairs with a baby?' his grandmother said dryly.

'Yes. Lisandra Calhoun. With newborn twins, actually. I'm sure you'll like her.'

For once it seemed Malachi had silenced even his grandmother. He let the pause linger as she assimilated his words for just the right amount of time before she could assemble a question.

'We've become friends and the house she was buying fell through so I offered her the loft.' He shrugged. 'Basically, I'm her landlord.'

There. That sounded very reasonable and sensible. She couldn't have any problem with that.

'So, you are charging her rent?'

Malachi frowned. He didn't need money. 'No.' He lifted his brows. 'Why would I?'

'It's what landlords do.' Millicent sipped her latte.

'Not this one.'

'I see,' his grandmother said.

'I'm glad,' he said and smiled at her. There you go then. All done. 'How have you been, Gran?'

'Oh, no, you don't, Malachi Madden. I want to hear the rest of the story.' She lifted her own chin.

'No more to tell.' He shrugged. 'Lisandra was looking for a place to rent short term and upstairs was empty.'

'I heard that bit,' Millicent murmured, her tone deceptively soft. 'I want to hear the section about where you met her and why have I never heard of this friend before.' She pressed her pastry with one manicured fingernail and, apparently satisfied, lifted it, pausing before it reached her lips. 'And, how it is that you trust her to move into your life like this.' Her gaze drilled into his and behind the imperiousness he saw concern. For him. Real worry. No need for that.

Somehow, he deduced the fact that saying he'd known Lisandra for only a week wouldn't go over well. Malachi thought about what he wanted to tell his grandmother and what he didn't. He thought about how much she'd been there for him in the times when no one else had been and the fact that he knew she cared for him very much. This consideration was followed by his natural aversion to raised voices.

'I like Lisandra better than Grace.'

'I'm not sure that's a compliment,' Millicent said, 'since I didn't like Grace.'

He blinked. 'You never said.' And if she had, maybe he would have put that with his own doubts and bailed much earlier. 'I thought you liked her.'

'I was happy you were in a relationship. Not so much with Grace. I could see Grace was more of a casual partner and I accepted her assurance that if you did eventually become a couple she'd be securing an heir for the future. There will be a fortune you and I will leave behind.'

'Oh.' Grace had mentioned children.

'Is this woman going to step into her shoes?'

'No.' The word came out more forcibly than he intended. 'Lisandra is a friend.' Surprisingly, that too was true. 'A good friend.' Or at least he hoped so. 'There are no ulterior motives for Lisandra being upstairs and she will go when she's ready.'

He picked up his own pastry. 'Perhaps now, we could go back to my original question—

how are you, Gran?' He opened his mouth and took a big, it-would-take-a-very-long-time-to-chew bite.

'I'm well.' In the distance a baby cried again and Millicent glanced up, but of course the shade sail blocked her view. 'How is she managing with twins on her own?'

Eventually he swallowed. 'Well. She is a very sensible woman. And a midwife, so she has skills.'

'And will I meet her?'

Malachi gave up. The sooner the better probably.

'I have no idea how her day is progressing, but I can certainly phone her and ask if she would like to join us.'

CHAPTER EIGHT

Lisandra

LISANDRA'S PHONE RANG as she pushed the pram towards the butler's pantry. If she had only two small coffees a day, it didn't seem to disturb the boys and she'd been dying to try out the new coffee machine in the nook.

Sometimes, over the last week, there'd been a few times when she'd felt everything was out of control but now moving into Malachi's loft she had a stable base to build on. So it wasn't surprising she felt more in control.

She didn't recognise the number. Which explained the question in her voice when she said, 'Lisandra?'

'Good morning. It's Malachi.' The usual calm thrum of basso she'd grown to admire so much made her smile. Gave her a little thrill, actually. Something she hadn't expected to happen—was she that kind of fool? Hadn't she had enough heartbreak?

Here she was, excited because he'd phoned, though perhaps it was just because she didn't have his number, the emergency thing had worried her. That was the only reason.

Really? Mmm-hmm? Liar.

That thought swiftly followed by a stab of guilt that Richard, someone she'd loved so much that they'd been set to marry and spend their lives together, had been dead less than a year—and here she couldn't deny she felt drawn to a man she barely knew. Kindness. It was only the kindness. But she suspected she was lying to herself.

'You still there?' His deep voice bringing her back to the present.

'Oh, yes, sorry.'

He asked, 'How are you?'

'Human. Thank you. And happy waking up in this lovely place, Malachi. I hope you weren't too late home?'

'Not long after ten.' She could almost see the shrug. The man worked ridiculous hours but it was none of her business.

'How are the boys?'

'Good. Seems they enjoy sleeping in the pram. I've just popped them back in. I was looking at your new coffee machine, considering giving it a go.'

'Perfect timing. Would you consider pushing the pram into the lift and I'll make you one down here? My grandmother has popped in and would love to meet you.'

His grandmother. Oh, I'm sure she would, Lisandra thought with an uneasy wince as her neck tightened. She couldn't help thinking of Richard's father's horrid accusations. What would Malachi's grandmother think? Or say?

When she didn't answer immediately, he said, 'Or you can leave it and join us for lunch if that works. Or another day. No pressure.'

No pressure. Right. If she'd been Malachi's grandmother, she'd be wanting to know who the bird upstairs with the babies was, too.

Lisandra glanced down at her new stretch jeans and button-up shirt, which, she had to admit, she'd put on in case Malachi dropped in. 'Meeting your grandmother, as well as coffee I don't have to make, sounds perfect. Give me five minutes and I'll be at your door with my pram. We can hope they sleep.'

'Perfect. Sorry about the short notice.'

'That's fine. Good practice.'

'I have pastries from the patisserie.'

Just what she needed. 'The last thing I need with twin baby fat.' Then felt like an idiot because she imagined he'd heard that many times before in his job.

'Good,' he said, and she wasn't sure if he meant because he got to eat all the pastries or because she was coming, but she could hear the smile in his voice. Then the call ended abruptly in a typically Malachi way and she slipped the phone into her pocket.

'Bye,' she said to the closed connection.

Lisandra backed out of the pantry and glanced at the boys both sleeping. One little capsule in front of the other with Bastian's higher at the back and his brother's closer to her. She appreciated the design because she could see both their faces. 'Our first excursion in your new pram coming up,' she said to the sleeping babies. She spun and hurried into her bedroom to brush on a touch of lip gloss and sweep a comb through her hair. Before the boys woke.

Her clothes would be fine for his grandmother, she decided. It would be worse to dress up for coffee when everyone knew she'd planned to be at home.

She had nothing to be nervous about but that didn't stop the wriggling in her belly and the slight increase in the rate of her breathing.

If Malachi's grandmother was anything like him, she'd be very proper and straightforward.

And perhaps silently horrified at her grandson's philanthropy.

Oh, well, no use worrying about something before it happened. At least he hadn't brought his visitor up here in the middle of a feed.

Two minutes later, waiting for the lift doors to open, she couldn't decide if she wanted to push in frontways with the pram or back in for a smooth exit. Backing in seemed the most sensible thing, especially when the lift was empty, so she tried that. All new adventures she had in store.

When the lift stopped one floor down, Malachi's door had been chocked open. He must have been listening for the ding of her arrival, because he appeared almost immediately.

'Hello.' His dark hazel eyes were warm and welcoming, and she felt her own mood lift. 'How are you managing with the pram?'

'It's a work in progress.'

'Excellent.' An appreciative smile this time. 'Good we don't have steps to traverse.'

'True story.' When she stepped into his apartment it seemed to stretch twice as far as hers, probably because the sea air flowed seamlessly through open sliding doors to the wide terrace instead of a narrow balcony. The same white marble expanse, more white and blue accents, on a much grander scale, with a wall-length television screen and a small, curved bar with stools. An eye-boggling array of spirits that could have stocked a wild west saloon made her blink and she looked at Malachi.

He must have been watching her face because he nodded. 'My father's bar. Seemed a shame to toss them. I rarely drink.'

He wouldn't have opportunity, which was why she'd been surprised. He'd always be climbing into the car on his way to the hospital.

'Your home is beautiful.' She gestured at the enormous room that seemed to stretch in all directions.

'It's too big for one man. Push the boys over near the lounge. We'll hear them from there.'

Once she'd done that, and the brakes were on, he gestured her out of the doors. 'Come through and meet my grandmother, Millicent.' There was an underlying gentle pride when he said grandmother, and she could see he was fond of her. That was sweet. 'She and your coffee are waiting.'

She smiled at him. 'I look forward to meeting her.' And she actually did look forward to learning more about his family.

A tall woman, possibly early eighties, stepped away from the balcony rail she held

and turned their way. Not quite as tall as Malachi, wearing silk jade trousers and a paler
green, almost white sleeveless tunic, the silk
pantsuit softly draping her reed-thin body.
Her make-up glowed with perfection and her
short, curly, snow-white hair sat artfully tou-
sled. Her smile appeared pleasant but inscrutable.

'Gran, I'd like you to meet Lisandra Calhoun. Lisandra, my grandmother, Millicent
Charles.' So, probably his mother's mother.

Lisandra smiled. 'It's lovely to meet you,
Mrs Charles.'

The actually quite scary lady smiled back.
'Likewise. And, please, call me Millicent.'

'Thank you.'

She inclined her head towards the pram
through the doors. 'Malachi says you have
twins. What did you call them?'

Lisandra glanced at Malachi and then back
towards the still silent pram. Their eyes met
and the history of the names flashed between
them. 'Bastian and Bennett.' She didn't add
the Mal and Kai that sat in the middle of their
monikers.

'Bastian and Bennett Calhoun.' Millicent's
amusement flowed to her eyes, which had
warmed to the same hazel as Malachi's. 'Two
very auspicious names.'

'Yes,' Lisandra said. 'They are. Would you
like to see them? They're asleep, which in
these early days is a bonus.'

'Of course.' So, they all trooped in and
looked down at the sleeping babies. Bastian
wrinkled his nose with a dream and Bennett
pursed his lips and made a kissing noise. She
adored them both so much it was almost overwhelming. When she looked up Malachi was
watching her with an intense scrutiny and
something that looked almost like wonder.

He said quietly, 'I think they've changed
and grown in just one day. Are you getting
sleep?'

'I wouldn't be surprised if they've grown.
As for sleep…' she shrugged '…enough.'

When she looked towards Millicent she was
watching both of them, not the babies. 'Very
handsome young men. I think they look a little like you.' Her gaze swung away from the
pram. 'They're a credit to you. I can see you're
an organised mother. Before they wake up
you deserve one of Malachi's excellent coffees.' She smiled and turned to go back towards the terrace.

Once they were all seated again at the glass
table Lisandra sipped her latte and sank back
in her seat. Oh, my goodness, she'd needed

that coffee. She smiled at Millicent. 'You're right. Malachi makes excellent coffee.'

'You must be very busy up there.' The older woman raised her eyes to the ceiling.

'I'm rushing a little too much if I want to get something done, at the moment.' She shrugged. 'Like heading to the shower. I need to achieve that while they're asleep.' She shook her head. 'It's as if one senses the other is awake and doesn't want to miss out on anything.'

'That sounds like children, men in general, really,' Millicent said dryly, 'but tell me...' She paused, and Lisandra knew what was coming. Just knew. 'Where did you meet Malachi?'

And how much did she tell? 'In the hospital,' she said.

'Of course,' Malachi broke in, 'Lisandra was not my patient.'

His grandmother glanced at him. 'Of course, my darling, you are nothing if not professional.'

And Lisandra wondered why she hadn't thought of that complication. Had Malachi left himself open to censure?

'We met in the lift.' Lisandra glanced across at the man who had been there for one of her more terrifying moments.

His eyes were on her, warm and there was amusement crinkled in the corners. When she looked away, and back at his grandmother's face, she appeared intent on them both.

'I was already in the lift, Malachi stepped in, and the lift jammed. My waters broke. It was messy.'

Millicent's eyes went wide. 'Disconcerting,' she said. 'How many people were in the lift?'

'Just the two of us. Malachi remained completely calm.'

As for the idea there could have been others? Not a pleasant thought. 'I hadn't really thought about others. I guess I was lucky.' She couldn't imagine a whole roomful of people with damp shoes and she winced at Malachi.

'Not really worth thinking about.' He waved his hand. 'So best not to.'

She shook her head at his practical statement.

Millicent raised her brows. 'Did you have the babies in the lift?'

'No. Despite the fact the lift stayed jammed. We were rescued in time.'

'I told you she was a sensible woman.'

'You did. This does become more and more interesting,' his grandmother said as she lifted her cup and peered at them over the top of the rim. Her eyes sparkled. 'Please go on.'

'It was a very close thing.' She glanced at the man beside her and he was watching her. His face calm and difficult to read. 'Malachi did a Sir Walter Raleigh for me in case they were born.'

She saw his lips twitch and smiled back. Millicent narrowed her eyes as she thought about that. Turned to her grandson. 'You put your suit jacket on the floor?' Malachi shrugged and his grandmother laughed. 'Terrifying, I'm sure, but it is a little like a soap opera.'

'Except they forced the doors open and we made it to the birthing suite in time.'

'Most fortuitous,' Malachi said.

'Malachi caught Bastian, who was born in the wheelchair, and Bennett was born on the bed less than a minute later.'

'She was amazing,' said Malachi. 'Composed throughout.'

Lisandra pretended to shake her head in mock disapproval. 'And then you disappeared.'

'People were looking after you.' He lifted his chin. 'I was due in Theatre.'

'I'm teasing you.' He was just that little bit more serious than expected sometimes. 'I was in good hands.'

Their eyes met and his were slightly narrowed. 'Yes. You were.'

The cup in his grandmother's hand returned to the saucer with a gentle rattle. 'So, you only just met. No previous acquaintance?'

'None.' Lisandra looked at her. 'But very glad we did meet.' Malachi smiled at her.

'How did you end up here?'

'Gran.' Malachi's voice held disapproval, but Lisandra wanted no misunderstandings.

'When Malachi visited me that same evening, he discovered I had no family. When, a week later, my accommodation fell through, he offered his loft, until the wonderful Ginny could find me a new lease. They both helped me move in last night until Malachi was called back to the hospital.'

Millicent looked thoughtfully approving, which was not what Lisandra had expected. 'Ginny is a magician.' There was no malice or innuendo in her words. 'And Malachi has always been concerned for others. Malachi is rarely here. I can see the sense of the idea.'

A single low wail came from the lounge room and Lisandra put down her cup.

Malachi put out his hand. 'I'll get him. Finish your coffee.'

She sank back into her chair as Malachi strode into the house.

Millicent blinked her wide eyes. 'I suppose he must be good with babies, with his profession,' she said, 'but I've never seen him with one.'

'He's had a bit of practice over the last week,' Lisandra said. 'He came every evening before he went home and was often handed a baby by the midwives when he arrived.'

'Did you think it was odd that he visited when he wasn't your specialist?'

'No. We shared an intense few minutes and trust was established.' She shrugged. 'His were very short visits. I looked forward to both Malachi and Ginny dropping in. They were the only ones apart from the midwives.'

Millicent's brows drew together. 'Where is your family? Your friends?'

'No family. My midwifery friends are in Melbourne. I was invited by the baby's grandparents to visit, when their father first died, so his parents could know their grandchildren. By the time I arrived that welcome had been rescinded. It was a shock. I hadn't expected his father to blame me for something beyond my control, but he did. Richard's mother has little choice, I think. I have savings, but, as we had been living together for less than a year, I'm on my own with the boys.' And it shouldn't still hurt but it did.

Millicent said, 'Grief does odd things to people. I'm sorry that happened to you.'

Malachi had said something very similar. Which made her wonder if something had occurred in their family.

Malachi strolled back into the room with Bastian looking comfortable in the crook of his arm. It was funny how she could tell the boys apart even though they looked so similar. More of an expression than different facial features, which was also odd considering the boys were so young. Bastian yawned in the big man's hold.

Millicent watched her grandson with an amused glint in her eye. 'I despaired that he would ever have a child but maybe there's hope for him yet.'

'Talking about me, not to me, Gran?'

'Of course, darling, you know I like to do that.'

Lisandra hid her smile and finished the dregs in her cup. 'Here. I'll take him.' She reached up and Malachi placed her son in her arms. 'He might sit for a few moments more before the noise escalates.'

As the transfer completed another low complaint came from inside the apartment. Malachi's lips twitched and he turned and went back into the room to retrieve the one left behind.

'I see what you mean about them being

aware of each other and missing out,' Millicent said. 'May I hold this one?'

Lisandra stood up. Juggling the baby as she rose. 'Normally I'd say yes. It's been lovely to meet you, Millicent, but I think I'll take the boys back upstairs to change and settle them.'

'Of course. Thank you for coming down to meet me on such short notice.'

Lisandra smiled and Malachi returned with Bennett. 'I'm going back upstairs while the complaints are low-key. I've decided to put them back in the pram and leave while I'm ahead.'

'Would you like a hand?'

'I'll be fine, thank you. If you could hold the front door when we get there, that would be great.' She slid Bastian into his pram bed and then took Bennett to do the same. Over her shoulder she said, 'I left the main doors open upstairs so I could get in easy when I came back.'

'Excellent idea.' Malachi moved to the door to open the way for her. He slid the chock under the wood and pressed the lift button.

'I think I'll reverse in. It worked well last time.' Lisandra made a wide circle in the roomy foyer. Malachi shook his head in appreciation as she manhandled the long pram. 'You're doing so well.'

Lisandra smiled. 'You sound like a midwife more than the obstetrician.'

He screwed his face. 'Heaven forbid.'

Did Malachi just make a joke? She grinned at him. 'You wish.'

He smiled back at her. 'Sometimes.' The lift arrived and she reversed in. 'Have a good day.'

'You, too. Thanks for the opportunity to meet your grandmother.' She watched him nod as the doors closed. And no doubt that would be the last she saw of Malachi for the weekend.

CHAPTER NINE

Malachi

AS THE LIFT doors closed Malachi turned back to his apartment. He nearly bumped into his grandmother standing just inside the front door. She tilted her chin at him as if waiting to pounce. His lips twitched again. Oh, dear. He knew that look.

'Your Lisandra seems a commendable woman.'

'She's not my Lisandra.' Cold reason was the only way to divert her when she was in this mood. 'But yes, I believe her to be admirable,' Malachi said as he closed the door behind his back. 'I'm glad you think so, too.'

'Better than social-climbing Grace, anyway. You do still need a wife.'

Lisandra a wife? He hadn't thought of that. Especially after the disaster of Grace, but the unexpected beauty in that idea rocked him.

And that sort of dreaming, him being a husband and father to the twins, was way out of the realms of possibility. Not a response he wanted to share with his grandmother. Because that could never happen. He would not do to Lisandra what his father had done to his mother. Diversion. Quick. 'I imagine Grace would dispute that label.'

Wherever she tried to lead the discussion he held up his hand and she subsided. He was not going down that path. Certainly not at his grandmother's bidding. 'I believe I'm not looking for a wife, thank you, Gran.'

She waved her manicured fingers at him. 'You like Lisandra.' A statement of fact, apparently, by her tone. 'Why else would you offer her your loft?'

He couldn't explain why. He just knew he wanted to help her. Wanted her safe up there. He lifted his chin. '*Altruism* is a word.'

'Pfft.' Said with a derisive flick of her fingers. '*Oblivious* is also a word and that's what you'd normally be to a woman you met at the hospital.'

His grandmother sat herself comfortably on the lounge and crossed her elegant legs as if settling in for an extended discussion. 'There was something about this particular woman that shook you out of your normal state—no world except work—and made you step out of character.'

She leaned forward and gestured to the seat opposite. 'I want to know what it was.'

With a sigh, he sat as well. He might as well humour her, but he didn't agree with what she was saying. 'Both Ginny and I wanted to help a woman who didn't deserve the unfair misfortunes that had come her way.'

'Mmm-hmm.' He mistrusted that look of mischief in his grandmother's eye. She leaned further forward her gaze fixed on his face as if searching for some hidden mark. 'Do you fancy her?'

Who wouldn't? She was gorgeous. He studied his fingernails. 'The poor woman is a single mother of newborn twins.'

His grandmother sat back as if satisfied. 'And thanks to you there was no disaster at their birth. She has to feel relieved that she met you?'

'I hope so.' He did hope so. Sincerely.

His gran smiled. 'I believe she looks more at ease in your company than Grace.'

They needed to steer away from these discussions. 'Lunch?'

Her brows rose along with her hands. 'At least Lisandra appears even-tempered.'

Lisandra was extremely even-tempered.

Admirably so. Amazing, but he needed to stop comparing her. 'Enough about my new tenant. Where would you like to go for lunch? I hear there's an excellent seafood restaurant just opened in Coolangatta. They're offering lobster mornay. I know that's your favourite.'

Three hours later, once Millicent had driven herself home, Malachi drifted around the apartment and almost wished his phone would ring.

No. Not work. Work wouldn't do it for him today. And since when was that the case? Since his improbable but delightful friendship with the woman upstairs whom he'd known for a week. He was mad.

He couldn't hear any noises from above, but he wondered if Lisandra had the urge to be outside as much as he did.

Perhaps she felt tentative in case there was a problem getting the pram across the road? If so, Malachi's help could solve that problem.

He pulled his phone and texted to her number.

Would you like company to take the boys for a walk? Just in case you need an extra pair of hands. M.

The answer flew back gratifyingly fast.

I'd just been thinking that. Perfect. What time? Now would be good!

She'd probably just fed her babies and tucked them into the pram to sleep. Strolling with happy babies would be so much more relaxing.

Within a minute he'd ascended one floor, knocked and could hear her coming to open the door. His pulse rate rose and he realised he looked forward to seeing her even though it had been just a few hours. His grandmother's words drifted back. *You do still need a wife.* Sadly, and he could admit that much with regret, that scenario was not something he would afflict Lisandra with.

The door opened and she smiled at him as if he was the one person she most hoped to see. Of course. He was the only one with a key, he reminded himself. No big shock.

'Great idea to get out,' she said.

Was it? Pleasure expanded inside him. Excellent. 'Are you ready?'

'Yes.' So, she had needed to get out. Of course, she did. She'd been in hospital for more than seven days. He felt like patting himself on the back.

She went on, 'Apart from the drive here yesterday, it feels like I've been inside for weeks.'

'Not quite.' He smiled at the exaggeration. 'But the day does look pleasant on the paths.'

She glanced at the pram. 'I've been nervous to actually push the stroller into the world on my own for the first excursion.'

'Time for an adventure, then.' He gestured to the wheels. 'Can I try to reverse into the lift?' She made it look easy and he wondered if it really was.

'Sure. I'll grab my hat and cross-body bag.' Which she did while he manoeuvred the long pram and in less than a minute they were in the lift with two babies going down to the ground level. Everything seemed to happen fast when Lisandra was around.

'My grandmother was impressed with the way you handle the boys. Though...' he remembered how Lisandra had arrived at his door with her babies perfectly settled and her face serene '... I'm not surprised she was impressed.' He couldn't remember when he'd last admired a woman so much.

Her eyes widened. 'Why on earth...?'

'You were splendid.'

The dazzling smile she flashed seemed to

flow through him from top to toe. A shock of pleasure.

'Splendid is such an old-fashioned word,' she replied softly. 'But a lovely compliment. Thank you.'

He wasn't finished. 'You were also decisive when you decided to go home. All things my grandmother admires.'

She blinked at him as if she couldn't understand why he would be delighted. Good grief. She had no idea how wonderful she was.

'Thank you, Malachi. For everything.'

'What for?' Now he was the one honestly puzzled.

'Your confusion says a lot for your innate generosity. It would be too easy to abuse your trust. I'm determined not to.'

'I still don't understand.'

She waved her hand encompassing the flats above them and the world outside as the doors opened. 'For the use of your loft in my hour of need. For your friendship and kindness, like coming with me now.'

He lifted one hand from the stroller to brush the comment away. 'I'm selfish. I want people to think I'm clever enough to have twins and a beautiful woman on my arm.' The truth in the statement startled him. Where the heck had that come from? He didn't have time for a woman on his arm. Yet he'd made time for Lisandra. He thought about that. Shied away. Remembered his own childhood when his father was never there.

He did not have the skills to be a father to one baby—let alone twins.

'You're teasing again.' She smiled back at him. 'You're much less serious out of work.'

'I was serious.' But he smiled when he said it. She made him smile. She made the sun shine brighter and he let his misgivings slide away just for today.

They slipped out onto the footpath, which thankfully was deserted on their side of the street as he worked out how to steer the long pram. He aimed for the pedestrian crossing.

She pointed to the pram. 'I need to do this to make sure it's safe for me to be in charge of an expedition.'

He stopped and stepped back at once. 'Of course, sorry, I forgot. Though I do have great faith in your abilities.'

'Thanks for that,' she murmured with a shake of her head. 'Let's see if it's true.'

Once across the busy road—she seemed to find getting on and off the kerb not too bad— Lisandra pushed the pram along the tree-shaded path. He walked beside her. Strange how pleasant it was just walking along with

Lisandra and her boys asleep, the breeze blowing, and the world passing them safely to the side. People on bikes and skateboards and motorised scooters zipped past.

He stood to the right between her and the path traffic, ensuring she wouldn't be bumped.

To her left, waves crashed onto the shore and seagulls squawked and winged in arcs of white against the blue of sky and gold of the sand.

She sighed, her face happy. 'It's beautiful, today.'

He realised she made it beautiful for him. He took a deep breath and let it out. Sea and salt and a tendril of Lisandra's scent like a drug slowing him down to have time to enjoy. 'I'm glad you think so. This is very pleasant. I don't often go out in the afternoons, just early mornings for a run.'

She glanced at him. Apparently liking what she saw because she said, 'I must watch out for you. Nothing nicer than watching a strong, athletic man run past.' She winked and it was his turn to shake his head at her.

She thought he was strong and athletic? 'Now you're teasing me.'

'A little.' Her eyes were full of mischief and his heart gave another of those odd gallops of pleasure.

A huge red kite with trailing board rider zipped by on the waves out from the shore. She laughed as the rider bumped off one wave and skipped onto the next. 'I'd love to try wave-surfing with those kites.'

He'd often thought so but doubted he would ever actually try. 'It looks like it requires some skill.'

'But fun.' She grinned across at him and he smiled back. 'Maybe one day my boys will try it.'

She was so brave. Her boys would be too. 'I don't doubt it.' But not him. He'd be at work. Not doing dad things. Whatever they were. But the future man she should choose for the boys' father, he would know how to teach his boys about life and love. And sail boarding.

For Malachi there was always work.

CHAPTER TEN

Lisandra

LISANDRA WATCHED THE unexpected animation she'd enjoyed so much disappear from Malachi's face. What did she say? Before she could ask, Bastian wailed, and she stopped the pram to lift him from his capsule. 'Do you have wind, my baby?'

Malachi stopped as well. 'Probably. Do you want me to take him or push the pram?'

She gestured to a vacant bench. 'Let's sit there overlooking the water. I can sort his request and enjoy the view. No doubt his brother will ask to be lifted as well.'

Malachi pushed the pram over the bumpy grass to stop beside the bench. Of course, Bennett grizzled and moaned when the motion ceased. 'Is your brother getting all the attention and you are not?' He glanced at Lisandra. 'May I lift him?'

It wasn't necessary but she really liked the way he asked before he reached for the boys. 'Go for it. Thank you.'

Malachi sat beside her, his big arms and solid thighs close to hers, giving off heat though they weren't actually touching—the subtle brush of closeness. He held Bennett in the crook of his arm just as Bastian let out an impressive burp. 'Good grief. Such a big noise for a small gentleman.'

And that was why Malachi charmed her. He projected the busy Gold Coast specialist, the decisive obstetrician and senior consultant but at heart he was such an old-fashioned guy brimming with kindness. Between them, he and Ginny had restored her shattered faith in the human race.

She lay Bastian in the crease between her legs and held out her hands. 'Give him to me and if you could take this one now, we can almost move on. Tuck him back into his capsule if you can without him complaining. I'll see if I can get his brother to do the same. That might give us another half-hour of walking before we need to go back.'

Ten minutes later and between the two of them they resettled the boys in the pram and pushed forward along the wide sweep of path that reached out around the headland towards

Coolangatta. The waves crashed beside them, surfboards and riders skimmed along the bigger waves, and seagulls wheeled.

'This is glorious. It feels so good to get out.' Even she could hear that enormous relief in the words. Not very flattering considering the boon she'd been given with her accommodation.

She turned to look at him. 'Not that I'm not living the dream inside your gorgeous loft.'

Malachi laughed. Not something he did often and the flash of teeth made him even more handsome. 'I understand what you're saying. No offence taken.' His understanding warmed the cold parts left from her loss and Richard's parents' rejection. She really needed to move on from letting others bring down her mood.

'Thank you.'

'I do wish you'd stop saying that.' She felt his gaze on her as she steered the long pram. 'Twins on your own is a very big responsibility. I'm just helping a little where I can. I'm not really putting myself out. But I do wonder if perhaps you could use more consistent help.'

She snorted. As if that were an option. She joked, 'Are you moving in with me?'

He blinked and then laughed again. Such

a fabulous deep, basso laugh. 'Technically...'
He let the sentence trail off.

'What?'

'You moved in with me.'

She shook her head at her own mental slowness. 'I asked for that.'

'You did.' They smiled at each other and Bastian whimpered. Malachi looked thoughtfully down at the grimacing infant. 'Are we going back?'

'Best to quit while we're ahead.' She checked the path for a gap in traffic and swung the pram in a wide circle until they were heading the other way. In fact, she was tired as well, and the pram had morphed to heavy.

'May I push for a while?' And there it was. His awareness of her. His watchful care and attention to her needs. Even Richard hadn't been that observant.

'Thank you. Suddenly, I am flagging a bit.'

He stepped in behind her, put his arms on her waist and shifted her sideways. His hands were warm and strong and very gentle. She resisted the urge to lean back into him but that wasn't their relationship. He was her friend, not her lover. What a ridiculous thought. The last thing she needed was a lover. But if she ever had one again... He would be like Malachi.

'You expect too much of yourself.' He took control of the push bar.

She lifted her chin. 'I'm not a wilting flower.'

He smiled. 'Just a little. Just at this moment.' And the words were all the more sweet because she knew it wasn't his default to tease. Trying hard to be amusing for her. She wanted to hug him. And thank him again but he'd asked her not to. She'd have to figure out some way of showing him just how much his kindness meant to her.

Once back in the loft she pushed the boys' pram into their bedroom and swung the door to leaving only a crack. 'Would you like a coffee? You could show me how to use that machine.'

'Excellent idea.' But when he shifted his wide shoulders and solid chest into the small narrow room she knew it would be difficult. They'd have to squish up together in the tiny butler's pantry to have the coffee lesson. His breadth and long arms and her tucked in beside him would be very, very cosy.

She saw Malachi glance left and right in the small space and raise his brows. 'Not much room. Perhaps I'll just make you a coffee and the next time you come down to my apartment I can show you then. We have the same machine.'

She tried not to sag with relief. 'A fine resolution to the problem.' Now *she* sounded old-fashioned, which made her lips twitch. 'I could get spoiled with all this attention.'

A sharp cry drifted from the boys' room. 'I doubt it,' Malachi said dryly and watched her walk away.

By the time she returned a steaming latte rested beside the chair she favoured and Malachi sat opposite with his own cup. When she eased down they raised their small mugs together in unison and sipped. Perfect. Of course. The man's brew was barista quality.

He said, 'Do you feel you need anything else? Something that would make it easier to manage?'

'I have everything I need. Thank you.'

He waved his hand in complaint.

She lifted her mug. 'I have to be polite.'

Malachi smiled. 'You don't have to be anything. This is your home until you choose to leave.'

She bit back another thank you. 'It will get easier as the boys get older and I establish a routine.'

He sat opposite her. One elegant leg crossed, relaxed, more relaxed than she could remember seeing him, with an odd smile in his eyes. 'How do you see that routine?'

She waved her hand dismissively. 'Seriously?'

'Yes. Seriously.' He was watching her face as if it was a pastime he could really enjoy. Just friends. That was all they were. Nothing more.

She pushed past that ridiculous thought. 'Something like...feed, breakfast, feed, walk with pram, feed, nap.' She stopped and his eyes were twinkling.

'Please go on,' he said. 'This is riveting.'

She laughed. 'Where was I?'

'Nap,' he said, 'and I'm very pleased to hear you do plan one.'

'I plan two. They're very short naps.' She shook her head at him paying enough attention to be able to answer her rhetorical question.

He waved her on. 'Please. Give me the rest.'

'More?'

A decisive nod. 'More.'

She pretended to tick them off her fingers. 'Feed, lunch, feed, nap, online shop, clean, business time, then feed and bathing the boys.' Inclined her head sagely as if imparting a great secret. 'Bathing being a very busy time. Feed, dinner, sleep.'

His mouth curved. 'Sounds like a demanding day.'

'It does.' She shrugged. 'But that's what routines with breastfed twins are. Luckily, it comes with smiles and coos, and magic moments too precious to miss.'

His face turned serious. 'I can see that. I'm going to miss it all while I'm at work.'

'I know. Please don't feel left out. We'll be thinking of you as we watch the waves.' This conversation was crazy. Silly. Fun.

'You won't have time.'

She smiled and didn't say anything else. Just sighed back in her seat, sipped her coffee, and savoured this delightful adult company for the time she had.

'Would you like to go to lunch next Saturday?' His offer surprised her.

She huffed out a small laugh. 'Where can we take a pram that's nearly two metres long?'

'Good point. Would you like to have lunch with me next Saturday and we'll order in? There's a new seafood restaurant that I'm sure I could persuade to provide takeaway.'

'That does sound much easier. Aren't you on call next weekend?'

'No. I declined. I haven't had a weekend off hospital call for six months and I've called in some favours for the next four weeks. Apart from my own patients, of course.'

He declined? She'd have to ask Ginny how often that happened.

He sipped his coffee with obvious relish. 'And I'm quite enjoying the difference.'

She huffed again. 'I don't see how you can be. You brought your work to your place when you invited the boys and me into your home.'

'You and your small family are not work. Or in my home. And on that note, I don't want to outstay my welcome—so I'll leave you.'

He stood. 'Thank you for your hospitality, Lisandra.' He paused. 'A favour?'

'Of course.'

'When I'm home early—I'll text you if it's before six—could you let me know when the bath-time shenanigans are about to start and maybe I could help?'

'He said that?' Ginny's voice held astonishment. It was Monday night and Ginny had phoned and reminded Lisandra she'd said she would drop in after work Mondays and Wednesdays.

Lisandra was very glad to open the door to her as she hadn't spoken to any adults since Malachi on Saturday.

'I hope you're going to let him help,' Ginny

added. 'Malachi needs to understand he deserves a life of his own, not just to be on call for everybody else.'

Lisandra spread her hands out in disbelief. 'I don't think him helping me bath the boys is a favour to him.'

Ginny bustled in and placed a small, vigorous-looking African violet on the kitchen bench. 'You need flowers in here.' She turned back to Lisandra. 'As far as I'm concerned, you're giving a gift by showing him there's more to life than being at the beck and call of a hospital service.'

That didn't make sense, or not in the context of him coming here to help her with the babies. 'Malachi loves his job. He wants to be there for his patients.'

'Yes, but the hospital takes advantage of him and most of the other doctors do as well. He's the go-to doctor for their social lives and all the patients on the floor. It will run him into the ground if something or someone doesn't make him change.'

'At least he's not doing every weekend on call this month.'

'That's why I brought you the violet. To say thank you.'

Lisandra stepped forward and hugged Ginny. 'You're a doll. I don't deserve it, but

I love it. I love the fact that you worry about Malachi. And in the short time that I've been here we have smiled a lot over the babies. So maybe we're not too much of a burden so far.'

'Have you met Millicent yet?' Ginny whispered.

Lisandra laughed. 'Yes. I met his grandmother. The first morning after I arrived.'

'How was she?'

'Fine.'

'She must have liked you. If she didn't you would have known. She was scathing about Grace.'

CHAPTER ELEVEN

Malachi

TO HIS SURPRISE, and not a little machination on Ginny's part, Malachi managed to make the boys' bath time for Tuesday and Wednesday nights for the first week. It could have possibly been a world record for him to leave work in the daylight two days in a row.

At the actual events he had been a tad ham-fisted at drying wet babies and easing small feet into trouser legs, but he was getting the hang of it. All he knew was that he enjoyed every second and Lisandra seemed glad of his assistance.

Then all of a sudden it was Saturday again and he was off work and he had a date with Lisandra for takeaway lunch. He'd been looking forward to it all week.

Lisandra had suggested fish and chips, but

he'd requested the pleasure of her company at one p.m. downstairs for a sumptuous banquet, 'so don't eat much for breakfast'.

She'd laughed and agreed to be on time with the pram, and he'd set the table outside on his patio, with crystal and non-alcoholic wine prepared to spoil a woman who deserved a little fuss.

Keen for something special, Malachi was now on his way to collect a seafood smorgasbord from his new favourite restaurant, where, if he hadn't given them a very generous tip, they would still be grumbling about the idea of takeaway.

He'd called it a banquet for a private party and they'd grudgingly accepted the order.

Ten minutes later, soup tureens and foil-covered platters nestled in the front seat and on the floor of his convertible, Malachi carefully drove back to the apartments.

Thank goodness the lifts weren't busy, he thought as he juggled his loads, and hoped the boys would be settled and sanguine while he and Lisandra feasted.

Fifteen minutes later she knocked at the door and just before he opened it, his phone rang.

Torn between answering the door and the

phone he did both, regretting the false start to what was supposed to be a perfect day.

'Come in,' he said. 'Sorry...' He was gesturing to the phone and saying, 'Dr Madden?'

And that was when it all went wrong. He watched as Lisandra smiled and sailed past with the pram, parking the boys in the same spot as last week, and stepping out onto the outdoor area and his laden table.

He watched her turn back with an appreciative smile just as the words sank in. *Urgent. Worrying foetal heart sounds. His very stressed IVF patient.* He knew he had to go.

'I'm on my way,' he said, and sighed for all of them. Lisandra, of course, waved him away.

'Go. We'll do dinner,' she said. And he felt as if a load had shifted off him.

He didn't make dinner, more like late supper, and he ate upstairs in Lisandra's loft. She'd already had hers at his insistence, but it was still special. She'd sorted it all, his table cleared, everything packaged and carefully managed to preserve the food. It had been delicious, but it had brought home all the reasons he could never be a person a woman and her children could rely on.

* * *

Malachi made bath time twice through the next week. Three the next and four the following week. The boys were seven weeks old now.

On that Saturday evening, the thirty-seventh day that Lisandra had lived above his apartment, Malachi arrived with boxes of pizza—an idea he'd thought might make Lisandra smile—which he left in the kitchen nook for reheating.

Her happy hello of welcome made the last couple of hours of fast work worthwhile as they bathed the boys, smiling at the infant antics and working in unison. After that first week beside the mini tub he had it down pat. Lisandra was sure and speedy while he took a while to work out how to keep the young fellows happy as he dried and dressed them. But it was an easy skill to learn when you were used to babies.

In the beginning while Malachi dried Bastian she'd finished the second bath and redressed her wriggling baby. But, she assured him, his help cut her bath times in half while keeping the boys happy.

By now, he'd almost reached her speed.

'It's amazing how much you've improved

my day without the stress of upset babies at night.'

'By the end of the day you must be tired.'

'A bit. But I bet two months ago you wouldn't have thought you'd be undressing babies before dinner on weekday nights.'

No. He hadn't. 'True.' Not even close. Two months ago he'd dreaded going home to Grace complaining how he couldn't leave the hospital before midnight. He'd actually managed four early nights this week to help Lisandra. Funny that. 'There is an unexpected delight in watching babies as they grow past the hospital stage.'

But he doubted that was his motivating factor. The motivation stood beside him deftly soothing infants. Her hair loose, her face flushed and a beam in her eyes every time he looked at her. She was like a happy flower making him smile.

'I guess doctors are like midwives,' Lisandra said. 'The parents usually go home by day two or three and we don't see their babies again until six weeks.'

'Exactly. We miss out on all this.' He waved his hand at the bath and the splashing baby.

She lifted Bastian out and passed her eldest son into the waiting towel and took the newly undressed Bennett and lowered him in the water.

Malachi squeezed the towel around his little charge and opened it to dab the creases under his arms. Bastian took that chance to unerringly aim a powerful pee stream into the centre of Malachi's shirt.

Lisandra laughed. 'Ha. The big smart doctor was too slow to shut the towel.'

'Hey. Don't shoot the help,' he said to the baby. He pretended to glare at Lisandra. 'And you shouldn't laugh.'

'No. I shouldn't. But it's funny.'

He smiled at her and she smiled back and for several long seconds their gazes met and held. Her eyes were magical grotto pools of blue amusement, and he had to fight the urge to lean forward and take her cheek in his hand. He wanted to move his face towards hers and touch her lips with his. His brain was hinting at things she wasn't ready for, and slowly the laughter in her eyes fell away as she watched him.

Stop, his brain chanted. He had no right. Would never be the person she needed. The father her boys needed.

Malachi looked down at Bastian. 'Let's get you dressed.' He glanced her way without meeting her eyes. 'If you want to top up the boys with a feed I'll put the pizzas in the oven to reheat.'

'Can we sit outside on the veranda?' Head down, he listened hard but couldn't hear any strain in her voice. Just him, then, feeling the need and the angst and the want.

He glanced towards the little balcony. 'We could. Why don't you bring the pram and I can meet you down at my place? I'll reheat the pizzas down there.' He gestured to his damp chest. 'I can change shirts and set the table while you feed and settle them in the pram. There's more room on my deck.'

She slipped Bennett into the pram and took Bastian from him. He'd nearly eased all of the baby's long legs into the pyjama bag. 'Sounds good. Here. I'll finish this. You go change shirts.'

CHAPTER TWELVE

Lisandra

LISANDRA WATCHED MALACHI walk away. Unless she was wrong his long stride was more rapid than usual. Yep. She hadn't been mistaken. He had wanted to kiss her and was stepping away fast from that idea.

Obviously, the thought horrified him, though she wasn't sure why. It certainly should have horrified her, but it didn't. The emotion she was feeling was more along the lines of disappointment that he hadn't followed his instincts.

What would it be like to be kissed by a man other than Richard? She'd really had too few boyfriends to have experience with this. And she certainly hadn't expected to even want the intimacy of kissing to be on her agenda only seven weeks after giving birth. Three years more likely.

But this was Malachi. It wasn't as if she hadn't noticed his wide chest, strong abs under his shirt, or watched him run powerfully along the beach paths. The man was a machine. She'd been awake in the early mornings more than a few times, sitting on the balcony, and enjoyed the sight while the boys fed.

What would it be like to be kissed by big, beautiful, kindness-personified, old-fashioned Malachi? Something stirred, deep and warm inside her, and she knew she'd been avoiding these thoughts.

Would his kiss be chaste? Perhaps not after the heat she'd seen in his eyes tonight. Would it be awkward, because sometimes she felt his awkwardness? Or would the connection she felt between them more each time he came to visit her carry them into a deeper, dangerous connection. Dangerous because she was dreaming if she thought there was a future between them.

She knew there was no future. Knew the time would come. The looming sense of loss when she had to move away and out of his life. She could just imagine his grandmother's horror that the little midwife tenant he'd invited into his home had been invited into his bed.

Crikey. Who could think of sex with all the floppy tummy and breastfeeding involved?

She gave a huff of amusement at the possibility of them actually being able to get to bed, without one or the other of the boys disturbing them. But this type of thought was a concern. Yep, she was starting to fantasise about her landlord. It was time to go. To make new plans. She'd had enough pain.

She needed to get Ginny onto finding her new for-ever home. She suspected Ginny, Malachi's secretary first before her friend, she reminded herself, had gone slow on Lisandra moving out.

She looked down at the baby between her hands and saw that he'd been fully dressed on autopilot. 'Sorry, Bennett. I wasn't paying attention to you. Bad Mummy.' And that was another reason she needed to not think silly, girly thoughts about a prince of a man who was only being kind. Full focus needed to be on her sons, her fatherless sons who needed their mother's undivided attention.

She carried Bennett across to the lounge and wedged him behind the pillow while she scooped Bastian from the pram. Then the juggle to position a baby each side at the breast with her boomerang pillow.

Done. She discovered that if she fed them every time they woke, surely more than they needed, the gaps between the feeds were get-

ting longer, her milk supply increased, and the
boys rarely cried. She was getting nearly six
hours' sleep in a row most nights and with that
came relief from the exhaustion of the first
weeks. Fingers crossed it continued. After six
weeks she was adept at juggling the boys' demands with living on her own—though Malachi's visits kept her sane.

That was all this warmth inside her was.
Her appreciation of the sanity he offered.
Nothing else.

Twenty minutes later she had the boys resettled in their pram and was pushing it from
the lift through Malachi's open door. He was
in the kitchen dishing the pizza onto a round,
heated server, cut and ready to eat.

He looked up and smiled, though he didn't
meet her eyes. 'I'll take it outside, will I?'

'Sounds great.' She parked the boys in their
usual spot against the inside window where
the breeze didn't blow on them and followed
him out into the evening light.

The last of the sun's rays had gone but there
was still light enough to see the final kite-
riders flit across the ocean. Down below the
streetlights were flicking on and the roar of
the traffic had begun to die down.

They both sat and picked up a slice of pizza

but before Malachi could take a bite his phone rang. He put the slice down.

Lisandra stood and moved to the rail overlooking the street to give him privacy. She took a bite of the crunchy crust and melted cheese and listened to Malachi say, 'I'll be there in ten minutes.' Poor Malachi.

He put his phone back in his trouser pocket and stepped across to her. 'I hope everything is all right.'

'A foetal heart trace that needs checking.'

She smiled at him. 'I'm glad they feel they can ring you any time. As a midwife myself, grumpy doctors are a difficult part of the job. I'll wrap your pizza in foil and take the boys back upstairs.'

'Or you could stay put and finish yours. It's all set up here. I might even be back.'

'I'll put yours in foil in the fridge.' She looked at the way he'd set the table with juice and glasses, pizza plates and condiments. She didn't want to waste his efforts. 'If you wish. But only because it looks so lovely here. When I've finished mine I'll go back upstairs.'

He nodded. 'Just pull the door closed when you leave if I'm not back before then.'

'Of course,' she said. But it wouldn't be the same.

So, after wrapping Malachi's pizza in foil,

and on impulse adding a quick note, she placed it in the refrigerator so he didn't get food poisoning. Lisandra sat in solitary splendour and munched her way through three slices of pizza. Seriously, her appetite was off the charts since those boys were born. She'd just risen to tidy her plates when there was a knock at the door.

She remembered that Malachi had said nobody had a key to come up in the lift so perhaps it was a service person. Now the dilemma of whether she should open the door.

Bastian, as if sensing her waver, cried, loudly, and the decision was taken from her. Whoever was out there knew she was here now.

She picked up her son first because she wouldn't be able to concentrate with him distressed in the background. When she opened the door Millicent stood there, dressed in floral silk top and pale trousers.

'Hello, Millicent. I was just leaving. Malachi's been called away.' She hadn't seen his grandmother for a couple of weeks as she'd been away on a cruise.

'Don't leave on my account.'

She felt herself swept by an intense scrutiny. Lisandra kept her smile in place. 'Not on your account.'

'May I come in?'

Lisandra realised she was blocking the door and pushed it wider, hoping she hadn't been rude.

She gestured with her hand to the interior of the apartment. 'You have more right than I do.'

Millicent raised pencilled brows. 'I don't believe that for a moment, my dear.'

Ouch, but before Lisandra could deny that, too, Millicent went on. 'It smells like pizza in here.'

'Yes. Malachi's is wrapped in the fridge in foil but I'm sure he'd share. He suggested I stay until I'd finished mine when he was called away.'

'Very sensible.' Millicent strode across the room to the kitchen and examined the boxes on the bench. 'Vegetarian and Margherita.' Over her shoulder she said, 'It would be easy to miss meals with twins. How is it going with the boys?'

'Fine.'

She left the kitchen and moved across to the pram where Bennett lay with his eyes open staring at a light fixture. 'I can't believe how much they've grown and how busy you must be.'

And was this where she could tell his

grandmother that Malachi was helping her bath them some nights through the week? She didn't think so.

She looked away from Millicent's face to Bastian in her arms. 'We're finding our routines, aren't we, little man?'

'And how's your hunt for a house going?'

And if that wasn't a hint, nothing was. 'Ginny and I have a discussion about possibilities tomorrow.' Fingers crossed. That was as bland and non-committal as she could make it but she had decided that tonight anyway. It wasn't really an untruth. She would make it happen. She'd send her a text and suggest they chat about it tomorrow. It was Sunday, so she wouldn't be interrupting her work. Just her family life—how did she end up being such a drain on the people who were helping her? She did need to get out on her own and stop relying on others.

She needed to leave here before she had to outright lie or say anything else that could be misconstrued. 'Well, lovely to see you. If you'll excuse me, I'm just going to take the boys upstairs. Malachi asked me to pull the door shut when I left, so I'll leave that in your capable hands.'

'Certainly. What time did he leave?'

Lisandra turned her wrist to see the time. 'Thirty minutes ago.'

'Then, I'll leave too. He won't be back for hours. I've never heard of him rushing a visit to the hospital...'

Her words trailed off as the door opened and Malachi walked in.

Lisandra couldn't help thinking how handsome he looked with his well-fitting suit jacket smoothed over his shoulders and his aristocratic features. She could see elements of his grandmother in him but there was nothing that wasn't masculine about Malachi.

His dark brows rose at the sight of Millicent. 'Gran. This is a surprise. Unannounced visits are becoming popular.' There was amusement and wry apology in the glance he sent Lisandra. She hadn't thought he would notice it might be uncomfortable for her for his grandmother to find her in his apartment alone. She'd underestimated his awareness. Again.

Millicent's eyes were sharp. 'A good surprise, I hope?'

'Delightful.'

'As was finding Lisandra here.'

He shifted his gaze from Lisandra to his grandmother. 'Would you like some pizza, Gran?'

'You know I don't eat pizza.'

Lisandra eased away from the two of them with Bastian and began to tuck him into the pram. She didn't know whether to keep moving towards the door or put Malachi's pizza in the oven before he got called out again.

'Then how can I help you, Gran?' This was a different Malachi. A cooler one. Not the awkward man who sometimes struggled with personal relationships, but the suave consultant obstetrician she'd glimpsed in the lift before the drama of the boys' births began.

'I was passing by. Thought I'd drop in on my favourite relative.'

'I'm your only relative.'

'I'm hoping you will remedy that, shortly.'

Lisandra winced. All righty then, this wasn't embarrassing, much. 'I think I'll take the boys upstairs.' Her comment eased into the middle of the awkward silence.

'As you wish,' Malachi said. 'I'll see you tomorrow.'

She nodded and escaped as he stepped back to the door and held it open. With her back to the room she might have pressed the lift button three or more times as she tried to hurry it up, feeling the eyes of the other two people boring into the back of her neck. She'd just push the pram in frontward and get away as fast as she could.

Finally, the lift arrived.

CHAPTER THIRTEEN

Malachi

As MALACHI SHUT his apartment door quietly his voice came out coolly determined. 'I won't have you making Lisandra feel uncomfortable, Grandmother.' No. He wouldn't have anyone making Lisandra feel uncomfortable. Not even himself.

Millicent raised her brows. 'I can't remember the last time you called me Grandmother.'

He inclined his head. 'It is rare I feel the need.'

She pulled a face. 'So, I've irritated you enough by finding your lodger in your unit? Waiting for you to come home from a hospital call, which would normally keep you away for hours?'

And there she went again, interfering where she normally wouldn't have before, and he wondered why she felt the need to now. 'I won't explain the set of circumstances, but I would appreciate if you enlightened me as to the nature of your visit.'

His grandmother moved to the lounge, sat down, and crossed her legs. He suppressed a sigh and thought about his dinner. It looked as if she wasn't going home any time soon.

'Do I have to have a reason to come here?'

'I do feel curious,' he said, as he decided he'd better eat in case the phone rang again, 'as to why you felt the need to drop in without allowing me the option of being prepared to welcome you?'

He took himself to the fridge and removed the foil-wrapped pizzas. There was a small note folded on top of the foil and with his back to his grandmother he opened it.

I do hope you didn't have to wait too long for these. They were scrumptious. Thank you. L.

He smiled to himself and slid the folded scrap into his top pocket and the open foil into the oven. He turned on the reheat cycle.

'Very nicely said, Malachi,' his grandmother's voice broke into his thoughts. 'Perhaps it's just as easy to say I'm not welcome here any more since the lodger arrived.'

He turned back to face her. Had he been harsh? 'That's not true and you know it. Besides, you've only just come back from a holiday.' He crossed the room to her and sat opposite. Crossing his own ankles. 'You are one of my favourite people.'

Gran huffed. 'I'm probably your only favourite person apart from the woman upstairs and her two babies.'

He let that go but the thought occurred to him to wonder if his dear grandmother was jealous. Why? Because he finally had someone else he cared about in his life? 'Not true. There're others. I'm fond of Ginny. And Simon is a good friend.' He considered the direction of their conversation. 'Do you have something against Lisandra?'

She blew out a disgruntled breath. 'It all happened so fast. One minute you escorting Grace and the next this Lisandra is upstairs with her babies or down here in your apartment.'

That made him frown. It just wasn't true. 'Today is only the second day she's been here since you were here last time.'

His grandmother looked taken aback. And not a little chagrined, if he wasn't mistaken. 'Oh. Then I may have jumped to conclusions.'

It did make her aspersions look a bit silly.

But this was taking the coward's way out, Malachi, he mocked himself. 'Of course, I've been to her apartment many times. I try to make it for the boys' bath times if I can get home before six.'

He watched her eyes widen with astonishment closely followed by righteous censure. He'd startled her. Not something he did often. He didn't know why he'd felt he needed to say that because he'd known it would put ideas into his gran's head. Maybe he wanted to hear her thoughts on that. Or he was just being contrary. 'I know you have my best interests at heart. But regardless of the time I spend with Lisandra, I do understand there is no future for us.'

She blinked. 'And why would that be?'

He shrugged, kept his face expressionless, he hoped. 'Her babies need a father. I have no skills there. The last thing I need do is inflict someone like my own father onto young boys.'

'Don't. That's not right.' His grandmother stood far too quickly for a lady of her age and swooped in next to him on the sofa. She touched his leg. Her face held distress. He regretted that. He hadn't meant to upset her.

'When the time comes you will be a wonderful father.'

His own turn to grimace. 'Apart from the fact that I'm never home and had no role model to learn from?'

'Well, you managed to get home tonight,' his grandmother said wryly. 'Surely a trip to the hospital and back in half an hour is a world record for you.'

'Perhaps.' He had to give her that. 'But tonight's patient issue was an easy problem to solve.'

'Mmm-hmm,' she said, her tone still dry. 'But normally would you immediately turn around and come home or would you wander off and check everybody else while you were in the vicinity?'

She had him there. 'Perhaps,' he said again.

'Yet you wanted to rush home and share pizza with the woman upstairs.'

'Yes, Gran. I suppose I did.'

His grandmother looked thoughtful and avoided his questioning look. 'She's discussing future housing with your secretary tomorrow. Did you know that?'

First he'd heard. His brow furrowed. 'No. How do you know?'

'Oh...' a suspiciously nonchalant study of fingernails drew his attention '...she mentioned it.'

'Out of the blue? She just mentioned it?' That didn't sound like Lisandra.

Gran pursed her lips. He knew that look. Guilt or guilty about something she'd said. 'I may have asked how her house-hunting was going.'

He compressed the words he wanted to say about interfering grandmothers. She had no right to put stupid ideas into Lisandra's head.

His displeasure must have shown because she patted his leg apologetically. 'I was just trying to make conversation. I didn't know then that you cared for her to this degree.'

'And where did that crazy idea come from?'

'From the emotions on your face when you look at her. Talk about her. Talk about her sons. And she's not immune to you either.' She added with obvious reluctance… 'As long as she's not a gold-digger.'

He stood. Stepped away from her. Looked down and didn't withhold the frown this time. 'I'll pretend you didn't say that.' Fortuitously the alarm rang from the oven as it automatically turned off. 'My pizza is ready. Are you sure you don't want any?'

His grandmother stood, picked up her clutch, and shook her head. 'No, thank you.

I'll take myself home.' She paused. 'I only want you to be happy. You know that?'

He walked over and opened the door for her. 'I know that.'

CHAPTER FOURTEEN

Lisandra

LISANDRA SLID BETWEEN her soft thousand-thread sheets and put her head on the best pillow she'd ever slept on. She'd have to discover where to buy one just like it.

It was early. Not that it was any different from any other night when she went to bed straight after dinner, but tonight, she didn't fall into an instant, dreamless sleep.

She tossed, punched her perfect pillow, turned on the soft sheets and groaned. She was using Malachi. And tomorrow she'd said she'd interrupt Ginny's weekend with her family with her need to search for a new home. She used people. She used to savour her independence, even with Richard. Richard had said he loved that about her.

But surely not wanting to leave just yet was reasonable. The first six weeks after the

babies arrived were the most hectic and she
didn't want to throw all of their routines into
disarray now she looked to be finally gaining
some structure to their day.

Not that she could really have structure
with twins, but everything was easy here.
How long had she really intended to stay here?
One day soon she would have to go. Stand on
her own two feet.

Here under Malachi's protection there were
so many aspects of daily living she didn't
have to worry about. Even heavy cleaning.
His housekeeper, Mrs Harris, sent her weekly
white tornado of cleaning through the loft on
a Monday when Lisandra took the boys for
their walk along the beachside path.

Groceries delivered, no steps, new appliances that all worked and glorious views to
relax with. And Malachi.

Dear Malachi, who underestimated how
much he really helped her when nobody else
could or would. Helped her just by being
one floor away or at the end of a phone call.
Who made the tension ease from her shoulders when he walked in with his calmness
and presence.

And tonight, with Malachi bathing the
boys, he'd been so good with them. So good
with her. She had to leave or she'd fall in love

with the man, something she wouldn't have believed possible six weeks ago. There was no doubt that misery lay that way.

Would she hurt him when she finally did leave, taking the babies he'd grown accustomed to with her?

His grandmother was right. She'd stayed a long time already and she was using people. Using the kindness of Malachi. She needed to go.

Bennett screamed. A high-pitched squeal that resonated through her like a blade of ice. A scream of fear and anguish that had Lisandra diving from the bed, tangling her feet in the covers in her haste through the open door of her bedroom and into theirs.

She rushed to Bennett's cot and as she passed she glanced into Bastian's small bed. His face shone waxen, white as the sheets, and his body too still. Too still. Oh, God.

She snatched him up and he lolled in her arms like a cloth effigy of himself. She screamed, 'Malachi!' towards the open outside windows, slapped her son's back and breathed a small breath over his mouth and nose then rushed towards the locked door. The door swung inwards and Malachi catapulted through towards her like a dark, shirtless ghost.

She gasped, 'He's not breathing.'

'Table.'

She spun, snatched the soft change mat and threw it down on the table and placed her son gently but swiftly onto his back as Malachi slid in to stand across from her. 'You do the airway. I'll do cardiac massage. Thirty to two.'

She knew that. Her brain started turning again. Thirty compressions to two breaths. He was an infant, not a newborn. Her infant. Her fingers shook as she held her baby's jaw, one hand each side, tilting the tiny face to open his airway. In a nightmare of horror she watched Malachi's strong and so capable fingers press rhythmically down on Bastian's Peter Rabbit pyjamas over his sternum with just the right amount of gentle force.

The fragile cage of ribs sank and rose and Lisandra felt the sobs bubbling at the back of her throat like a swarm of bees. Oh, God.

'Get ready for two breaths,' she heard him say and snapped away from herself to the man in charge. 'Now.'

She breathed two small puffs and watched the tiny chest rise and fall with each breath.

Malachi began the compressions. Again. Counting out loud. 'Get your phone. Ambulance.'

Oh, God. Yes. She spun away and into her room, snatched the phone off the bedside table and sprinted back to Malachi in time to give two more breaths. Punched the three numbers and garbled their address to the despatcher. Two more breaths and this time Bastian gasped. Flexed. Whimpered.

Malachi stopped his compressions. Bastian wailed. Lisandra wailed.

She reached to clutch her baby and cradle him against her breast. Malachi's big, warm arm circled them both and he pulled her into his naked chest. She turned her face into his hot skin and sobbed.

CHAPTER FIFTEEN

Malachi

MALACHI'S ARMS CIRCLED LISANDRA. He was careful not to crush the baby between them. He needed to step back. He needed to watch carefully the colour in Bastian's face. He needed his stethoscope and to make sure the emergency services could get in.

He needed to hold Lisandra.

The tragic wail of another baby, Bennett screaming, made him reluctantly ease his hold and step back.

'I'll get Bennett.' He stroked her face with one finger and lifted his hand to squeeze her shuddering shoulder under the thin straps of summer pyjamas. Her skin was like silk and he stepped away.

'Count his respirations.' She needed something to think about, to remember that they had the skills, that there were two of them who both knew what to do in shocking circumstances like this.

When he stepped into the room tiny fists waved as Bennett struggled in his cot so wildly he seemed almost able to climb out. The baby's eyes swung to his and held.

Malachi felt his heart squeeze. He knew. This baby knew. 'Your brother's okay.' He gathered the fisting child from his portable cot, lifted him until his downy cheek was against his own bare chest and covered that small pyjamaed back with his big hands. 'It's all right, baby. Your brother will be fine.'

He looked over his shoulder back to the lounge room where Lisandra had sunk onto the lounge with Bastian in her arms. Tears streamed down her face in glistening lines, her shoulders taut with tension, and he guessed her legs had almost given under her. Thank God, he had been here for her.

A siren keened in the distance, yes, coming closer. Malachi carried Bennett through to his mother, patting the nappy-covered bottom soothingly with one hand, cradling the back of his downy head with the other.

The baby's cheek felt warm and yet so achingly soft against his bare flesh and he realised he'd never held a newborn skin to skin against him. No wonder babies and parents alike loved it.

Lisandra's phone vibrated where it lay on the table and she looked up at it but didn't rise. Possibly she couldn't. Jelly legs no doubt. Not surprising.

He stopped beside it. 'Could be emergency services.'

'Oh. I should have got it.' Her voice rough with tears and ragged breath.

'I've got it,' he said. 'Okay?'

'Yes. Please.'

'This is Dr Malachi Madden on Lisandra Calhoun's phone. Who is this?'

'Emergency services, Doctor. The ambulance will arrive within two minutes. Is the infant breathing?'

'Yes. Stable at present.'

'Will someone be able to ensure the paramedics can reach the unit?'

'Yes. I'll come down now.' There'd be nobody else to let them in at this time of night. 'I'll leave this phone here with Miss Calhoun but if you need to contact us before I get there use my number.' He rattled off his own. 'I'll disconnect now to go down and meet them.'

He passed a swift assessing glance over Lisandra. The tears had stopped and she wiped them away as her gaze flicked between him and Bennett and back again.

'Will you be all right if I go?' Not that he had much choice, but it was better if she could see that things were meant to be in sequence.

'Of course.' Her voice shook. 'It was so close, Malachi. I nearly lost him.'

'I know. I wish I didn't have to leave you.' Wished he could still be holding her and sharing some of his strength because her eyes looked shattered.

'But someone has to let them in,' she said, and the ragged lift of her mouth dredged up a caricature of a smile. Toughing it out. Making him want to kiss her. God, she was brave.

'I'll grab a shirt on the way through. Be back as fast as I can.'

He tucked Bennett into the lounge beside her with a pillow to hold him. Bennett had stopped crying too, and his eyes were fixed on his brother.

She said softly, 'It was Bennett who saved him. He screamed and that's how I found him.'

Malachi's hand went out by itself and stroked Bennett's cheek with one gentle finger. 'Good boy. Good man.' He forced himself to step back and strode from them fast because the faster he was gone, the quicker he could come back.

He took the stairs two at a time into his own apartment where he grabbed a shirt, his phone and slipped his feet into his beach shoes, glancing once to the open door where he'd been sitting. If he hadn't been outside on the terrace he might not have heard her until it was too late.

Twenty minutes later, Malachi drove as they followed the flashing red lights of the ambulance. He steered Lisandra's car with Bennett strapped in the back in his car seat and Lisandra beside him.

They'd needed baby seats of course and he'd wondered if he should get them in his car, then shaken his head at the idiocy. Out loud he said, 'You'd never fit your baby seats in my convertible.'

He felt her gaze though he didn't turn his head. 'They just don't go with the car,' she said and there was something in her voice that sent a cold chill down his spine. As if she was saying his world and hers were too different.

He could get a different type of car. Stop. Now that was a crazy thought. Did he need to have it spelled out any more clearly that he was in over his head with Lisandra and her sons? And the reason there was no future for him hadn't changed. She needed a man who would be there for her and it was only the merest luck he'd been there tonight. If he was sensible he'd start pulling back. If not tonight, then soon.

As if she'd heard his thoughts, 'I could have driven,' she said, but her voice still shook.

'Could you have?' His voice dry because no way would she have been safe.

She huffed a beat of disgust at herself. 'Not as calmly or smoothly as you're doing, but I would have made it.'

'Bennett asked me to drive.' He tried for a joke, he didn't know why, he'd always been hopeless at them, but she made him want to try. Both of them trying not to think about the last twenty minutes.

The paramedics had asked him if he wanted to go in the back of the vehicle. He'd declined as he believed they could handle anything Bastian offered. Believed in his gut the infant was stable now. His bigger concern had been distraught Lisandra running into the back of a vehicle as she drove and harming herself and Bennett on the way to the hospital.

He'd seen the relief on her face when he'd declined and said, 'I'll bring the mother in.'

The lights of the public hospital drew close

and he parked her car in the doctors' car park as the ambulance went left into the emergency bay. He'd phoned his preferred paediatrician and had no doubt Simon would meet them in Emergency.

'This is the worst night of my life.' Then she shook her head. 'No. When Richard's heart stopped was worse because there was no coming back for him. What if Bastian inherited something from his father's medical history?'

'They'll check all that out,' he said soothingly and thought to himself, she was even braver than he'd realised. 'Were you there when he had his cardiac arrest? Did you attempt to resuscitate him?'

She nodded, her mouth tight, eyes haunted. 'It took that ambulance ten minutes to get there. It felt like hours. I knew by the time they arrived that he wasn't coming back.' Her voice sounded broken but she went on. 'Apparently the clot had been so huge his heart had nothing left to work with.'

Malachi lifted his hand off the steering wheel and touched her fingers. 'That didn't happen to Bastian. He came back fast. Let's go in so Bennett can see his brother's okay. I'll get him and pass him to you.'

He had the feeling she needed to hug her

baby while she walked in. When he climbed out, she stayed staring at the hospital and he understood her fear, felt for her, but they both knew there were efficient and skilled people inside.

By the time he lifted Bennett from his car safety capsule she was out, closing the door, and staring at the large emergency sign.

He walked to her. 'Here. Take Bennett. I'll lock the car.' Not that he needed to do anything except press a button, and as he did lights illuminated her for a moment and he could see the strain in her face.

He lifted her hand in his and her fingers were cold, freezing, shaking. 'You know if I'd had any concerns he'd have a relapse I would have gone with him.'

She shook herself as if frost had skittered along her nerves. 'Yes. Of course. Thank you.' But she hung tight to his hand as they walked towards the big doors.

Inside the lights were bright and he narrowed his eyes as he walked towards the reception desk. 'I'm Dr Madden. This is Sister Calhoun. Her baby has just arrived by the ambulance, Bastian Calhoun. Is Dr Purdy here?'

'Yes, Doctor. He's in Resus Two with Bastian if you'd like to go in.'

Her gaze flicked to Lisandra. 'I'm sorry. If

I could ask a few details, please, before you follow him.' It wasn't really a question and he saw the resigned way Lisandra nodded at the woman. She knew the way hospitals worked.

He said, 'I'll come back and get you in a minute.' Couldn't help notice the relief in her expression.

'Thank you,' she said as she turned reluctantly back to the woman.

Malachi pushed through the swinging plastic doors to the internal corridor and watched the numbers until he came to Resus Two. He knocked and entered.

Simon Purdy looked up from the resuscitation trolley where Bastian squirmed. Typical of Simon's skill with babies, the infant wasn't crying. In fact, Bastian had a fist curled around Simon's stethoscope as he stared into his face. The man was a positive baby whisperer.

To Malachi's relief Bastian's skin colour looked well perfused and they weren't using supplemental oxygen. His pulse oximeter read one hundred per cent and his heart rate ran at a normal speed. Malachi felt the tension ease from his shoulders and knew he needed to get Lisandra in here as quickly as he could to share the relief.

'Ahh. Malachi. I understand this young man

is staying with you?' Clear curiosity shone in Simon's usually serious eyes. Simon was one of the few people Malachi enjoyed the company of on the rare occasions he attended social events. 'Technically. Upstairs, but yes, I've known the twins and their mother since birth.'

'Theirs or yours?' He grinned.

A joke? They were all trying. 'Theirs.'

Simon nodded as if something had been confirmed. 'I thought you had the penthouse?'

'I have. Lisandra and the boys have the loft.'

'And more on that later,' Simon murmured as he looked down at the child. Then he looked up again. 'The woman in the jammed lift?'

Malachi inclined his head. 'Yes.'

Simon looked back at the child. 'He sounds good.' His voice gentle. 'Chest clear. The ambulance report said it took two to three minutes of cardiac massage and respiratory resuscitation to bring him back?'

'Yes.' He thought of Lisandra out there wondering. 'If you hold on a minute I'll retrieve his mother and she can tell you how she found him.'

'Ahh. The dreaded paperwork?'

Malachi nodded in agreement as he left. He could almost feel Lisandra wondering what was going on.

CHAPTER SIXTEEN

Lisandra

WHAT WAS KEEPING MALACHI? Lisandra couldn't sit. She paced. Even telling herself he'd only been gone barely two minutes didn't help. The receptionist had said she'd send a nurse to take her in but she could barely hold back the need to ask again. Malachi pushed open the plastic doors and held them open for her and she blew out the relief.

'He looks great,' he said, as if that was the essential greeting. It was. She felt her grip on Bennett loosen a fraction but she couldn't believe Malachi until she saw Bastian for herself.

'Has the paediatrician said anything?' She walked beside Malachi as the rush and scurry of a busy emergency department hurried by her.

'No. We're waiting for you. Just that the

paramedics mentioned our three minutes of resuscitation. I said you could explain how you found him.'

Beside Malachi it was as if she'd run into a wall. She faltered as if the memory weakened her legs, stupid legs, but Malachi must have noticed because he took her arm.

'He's fine. Bastian will be fine. Would you like me to take Bennett?'

Lisandra's arms tightened. 'No.'

'Through here.' He pushed open a door and then a curtain.

She saw her son under the bright lights of the resuscitator and her eyes flicked to the monitor and the reassuring numbers there, then she glanced at the tall man with the stethoscope around his neck.

'Dr Simon Purdy,' Malachi introduced, 'Lisandra Calhoun.' He added. 'Lisandra's a midwife.'

Dr Purdy stepped forward and took her hand in his big, warm fingers and squeezed. 'It's nice to meet you, but not in frightening circumstances.' He drew her closer to the re-suscitation trolley. 'Bastian is well. Doesn't appear to have any sequalae from his event.'

Sequalae—left-over medical problems. Event. Yes, she could call it that.

He went on. 'So far, I can't find anything wrong with him but of course we'll do further tests, which I'll talk about later. Are you able to tell me what alerted you that something was amiss?'

Lisandra dragged in a breath and consciously blew it out again slowly. She dropped her shoulders and forced herself to think back to that horrible moment when this nightmare began. 'I was in bed. Thankfully I couldn't sleep. And then Bennett...' She looked down at the baby in her arms. 'Bennett let out the most blood-curdling scream I've ever heard.' Her gaze drifted to Malachi. 'I never want to hear that sound again, anyway...'

She looked back at Dr Purdy. 'I scrambled out of bed towards Bennett and as I passed Bastian's cot I saw he didn't look right. Too pale. Unnaturally still.' Her breath caught. 'Not breathing.' Her eyes flicked back to the man beside her. 'I just screamed for Malachi.'

Malachi said quietly, 'The sound carried out of the window from above so I wasn't there much later than Lisandra.'

Her throat had closed at the shocking memories and somewhere inside she knew that a part of her reaction was left over from when she'd lost Richard.

She waved him on to take over the tale as she cupped her hands over her nose and mouth and closed her eyes.

Malachi continued the history while she breathed. 'We transferred him to the dining-room table and I began cardiac massage while Lisandra attended to the respiratory resuscitation.'

'How long do you think it was until you had a response, Lisandra?'

Lisandra took her hands away from her face and straightened her shoulders. She knew that Dr Purdy probably had this information from the paramedics and possibly even from Malachi, but wanted her opinion as well. 'It felt like for ever, but five rounds of thirty seconds would make it just over two and a half minutes.' She looked at Malachi and he nodded his head in agreement.

Dr Purdy said, 'The most likely cause is stomach content aspiration, causing a vagal response and arrhythmia, but we may never know why Bastian stopped breathing.'

She squeezed her hands together and imagined not knowing if her baby would stop breathing some other time. 'You mentioned tests?'

'Yes. Blood tests and a scan of his lungs

and a chest X-ray, if you're happy with us doing that?'

'Of course. Do whatever tests you think you'll need.' She looked at Malachi and then back at Dr Purdy. 'The twins' father died of a massive blood clot in the heart nine months ago.'

'I'm sorry for your loss.'

'Thank you. Of course I'm worried about cardiac anomaly being a cause.'

'At this stage I think that scenario is unlikely, but we'll certainly look into it as much as we can without being invasive.'

'Thank you.'

'You're welcome. We'll keep him overnight at least. Are you breastfeeding?'

'Yes. Fully.'

He gave her an admiring nod. 'Breastfeeding twins is no light undertaking. Both boys look well nourished and despite tonight's adventure they appear well. I see no reason why Bastian can't return to normal breastfeeds as soon as he's hungry. We'll arrange a room for you and his twin to stay near him and be available for feeds.'

'Bennett,' Malachi said. 'His brother's name is Bennett.'

Dr Purdy inclined his head and smiled. 'Bastian and Bennett. They're great names.'

* * *

Two hours later Lisandra sat in a room a few doors down from the paediatric intensive care, feeding Bennett, wishing for company. She'd just left Bastian in the ward where he would be strictly cardiac and respiratory monitored throughout the night.

Malachi had left after an hour to answer a call, in her car, to reach the maternity hospital, which was almost amusing, but she had no doubt he'd sort the logistics of vehicle change-overs tomorrow. Or Ginny would. And there she was using people again, but she couldn't imagine how she would have coped if she'd been on her own.

She rubbed her temples and held back a sob. This whole thing was a nightmare.

Bennett pulled away from her breast and tilted his head towards her, his brows coming together in a frown. He gurgled and cooed and she blew out a whoosh of breath and smiled at him. 'You're my little hero, you know that, don't you?'

Bennett cooed again.

Tension in her neck eased slightly as she lifted him up over her shoulder to rub his back. 'Yes, baby. Mummy needs to have a sleep soon and put an end to this horrible day.'

She looked up at the sound of a brief knock.

She knew that knock. Malachi was back and suddenly her world straightened.

The door opened and his head ducked around as if he was unsure if she was sleeping.

'I'm awake. Come in. Please.'

The rest of him appeared. Dear, dear Malachi. She shouldn't be so very glad to see him. He carried a disposable cup in his hand and the aroma of hot chocolate drifted across the room.

'I thought you might prefer this to a sleeping tablet.' His smile warmed her. There he went again doing something unobtrusively kind and wonderful for her.

'That is exactly what I would love. Thank you.'

'Can I take Bennett for you while you sip?'

In answer she lifted the baby towards him. 'I was just burping him. He's almost ready for his bed.'

'You look ready for your bed.' His concerned gaze travelled over her face.

She looked down at herself and grimaced. 'At least I'm in my pyjamas. And glad you suggested I bring a small bag.' She'd packed one while the paramedics and Malachi were ensuring Bastian was stable. 'It means I have my phone charger and something comfortable to sleep in that doesn't belong to the hospital.'

He was still watching her face with concern on his. 'Do you need anything else for the night?'

'No. I'm fine. Thank you for everything, Malachi.' Suddenly her throat stung with the prickles of tears stinging the backs of her eyes as well. She blinked them away. 'I don't know what I would have done without you.'

He came and sat on the bed beside her chair and took her hand in his free one while the other absently patted Bennett's back. 'You don't have to do without me.'

Not now. Or the next few weeks, anyway. Not until she did.

Lisandra turned her face away but he let go of her hand to touch her face and turn it with one finger. 'I don't know what my grandmother said to you today, but there's no rush for you to go anywhere, any time. I enjoy having you all upstairs.'

It was as if he'd seen through to what was most worrying for her. She searched his face. 'How will I know when I've outstayed my welcome?'

He smiled and shook his head. 'You could never outstay your welcome. The place would echo with emptiness if you all left.' He stood up. 'But that's for another day.'

He leant forward and brushed her cheek with his lips. His warm mouth smoothing her face as if in blessing. 'You did well today. Try to get some sleep between the feeds. I'll see if I can get here for Simon's ward round to-morrow morning.'

She knew he did a ward round on Sundays for his own patients at the maternity hospital. 'You don't need to.'

His face turned stern. 'I'll be here. Unless you don't want me to be?'

Of course she wanted him. 'Thank you. I would like that.' Time to be honest if he thought she didn't want him. She didn't want him to leave now, let alone not come back.

CHAPTER SEVENTEEN

Malachi

THE NEXT MORNING, he'd barely slept for worrying, Malachi found Lisandra in the paediatric intensive care, her back to the door, her attention focussed on her boys. As he stood at the sink to wash his hands he turned his head to study her for a moment, chin lowered and her lovely neck exposed as her hair fell away to the sides as she bent over Bastion.

Bennett lay in the pram beside her.

He knew now she'd become more than a friend since she'd moved in and he thought back to his grandmother's words.

He had grown very fond of Lisandra but fond wasn't the feeling that had made him toss restlessly in his bed last night. It was more than that. Way more. And complicated. He'd been gutted at the thought of anything happening to Bastian or Bennett and his heart had ached at the distress it all caused Lisandra. He cared. For all of them. Deeply.

He wanted to make her move down to his apartment and tell her she had to stay for ever. But that was ridiculous.

He was under no illusions about his worth in the husband and father stakes. Lisandra deserved a husband who would be there for her—not one like him, who would be absent or called away at any moment. The boys deserved a father who knew how to do all the things a young boy needed to do. One who would turn up for the important stuff. Unlike him.

He should step back. Because, if he wasn't careful, when she did leave and find a deserving partner this would become one of the most painful goodbyes of his life.

As if she sensed him, she looked up and smiled, and instead of stepping back he stepped towards her, crossing the distance between them in moments. 'Good morning, Lisandra. How did you sleep?'

'Surprisingly well between feeds. No further problems with Bastian overnight.'

His chest eased with her release of worry—though his own concern had been decreased by Simon's early phone call. 'Excellent.'

Her turn to study him. 'And you? Were you called out after you left here? You look tired.'

He heard a familiar deep rumble from behind him and Simon saved him from answering. He turned to see the paediatrician walking with the ward intensivist towards them. Malachi eased himself back to ensure Lisandra had front and centre but his mind whirled with wonder. She'd noticed he looked tired?

When Bennett started to fidget and complain at lack of attention, without thought, Malachi reached into the pram and lifted the boy to his chest, pulling his little body into him. 'Shh... Your mother is talking. She needs to discuss today's plans with Simon.'

Simon's brows went up as he blinked. 'You're very handy to have around twins, Malachi. Good to know.'

Malachi lifted his head in pretended surprise. 'Why? Are you planning to have some?' The last thing he needed was Simon to find his fascination with Lisandra and her sons funny. Wasn't going to encourage that.

Simon laughed. 'You and I don't have time for families. Just time to ensure others stay healthy.' Two months ago Malachi would have agreed with him—he wasn't so sure now as he glanced down at the small face and blue eyes peering up at him. He felt a hollow pit of emptiness at the thought of Lisandra and the boys leaving.

Simon turned to Lisandra. 'I hear Bastian behaved well overnight for the nurses. Did you think he fed well?'

She looked tired too, Malachi thought as she answered. 'He seems just the same. No problems with feeds. More hungry, if anything.'

'Good. We'll set up all the tests this morning, even though it's Sunday. Hopefully we'll have them done before lunch and if everything's fine you can take him home this afternoon.'

'Will the tests be done in this hospital?'

'Yes.' Simon stepped in closer to lean over the baby in her arms and lifted his stethoscope to place it on Bastian's chest over his heart.

Nobody spoke as he listened and then stood back. 'Heart sounds perfect. No signs of chest infection but we'll see what the chest X-ray shows. He's had all his surface swabs attended and a throat and nasal swab. The monitoring of his respirations hasn't recorded any apnoea. No alarms or any abnormalities noted during the observations overnight.'

Simon's gaze travelled between Malachi and Lisandra. 'At this stage—' he looked down at Bastian '—I'd say heart arrhythmia caused by milk aspiration. It could have been only a regurgitation during a deep sleep cycle, which in an unusual event caused his heart to miss a beat at the wrong time, but we'll see what the tests show us. I'll be back after lunch to let you know the results. If everything is fine you'll be able to take him home after that.'

Malachi nodded. All as expected. He looked to Lisandra to see if she was satisfied and found her brows lifted at him, asking for his thoughts on the plan. So he said, 'I agree.'

She nodded as if she just needed that and smiled up at Simon. 'I understand. Thank you. I'm happy with that, too.'

'Good.' Simon smiled at them both then fixed his eyes firmly on his friend. 'We'll have to meet up for another dinner, Malachi. I want to hear your news.'

'What news?' He had nothing to share with a winking Simon this morning.

'Just to hear where you're at. Talk soon.' His friend smiled and saluted Lisandra.

'He seems a lovely man,' Lisandra said as she watched Simon walk away.

Hmm. Normally. Being a nosy blighter this morning, Malachi thought, but he said, 'Great paediatrician. We went through med school together. He's the one we want to look at Bastian or Bennett for any problems.'

He needed to get back to a woman he was worried about in labour. He tucked a sleeping Bennett back into the cot. The baby didn't complain. He was getting good at this.

He pulled her car keys from his trouser pocket. 'I moved your vehicle down into the hospital parking last night and caught a cab home, so I have my car, too.' He glanced at his watch. 'Let Ginny know if you need anything. I'm sure she'll phone as soon as she finds out you're here.'

He smiled. Ginny would make sure Lisandra was fine today. 'There are two unexpected caesareans this morning so I might not get back until after lunch. Hopefully before Simon arrives, but if I don't, he'll keep me up to date. Text me if you need me and I'll answer as soon as I can.'

For the first time ever he wished he didn't have a patient waiting for him in Theatre. He wished he could go with Lisandra and Bastian and just be there with them today. Make sure they were fine. And how would Bennett be cared for? He hadn't thought of that. He'd check with Ginny and see what she could do.

CHAPTER EIGHTEEN

Lisandra

LISANDRA WATCHED MALACHI walk away and didn't like the way she felt suddenly alone and vulnerable. That was ridiculous. She had the boys and the boys had her. Her arms tightened on Bastian but after a few words of stern talking to herself she forced them to loosen.

She stood and settled Bastion back into the hospital cot and tucked him in. One of the nurses came and turned the alarm back on— it had kept going off every time she moved him so it had been silenced.

'I'll go back to my room and shower. My breakfast is waiting.' She should pack and be ready to leave, too. Though she had to keep the room until it was positive Bastian was being discharged. 'I'll be back after that.'

The nurse nodded and smiled. 'We'll phone

you if he wakes before then.' She shook her head in admiration. 'It must be so busy.'

'I'm glad they're not triplets.' Lisandra smiled. 'We do have our moments of unusual interest.' A sharp pang squeezed her chest. Like last night. Like finding him lifeless. Like almost losing her son.

The cold washed over her arms at the memories and nausea returned. Last night before Malachi came.

'Dr Madden's very good with them,' the nurse said.

Her sudden panic subsided. She lifted her chin, not seeing the woman in front of her. Seeing Malachi like a rock beside her. 'He is. I'm always very glad of his help.' She looked at the now sleeping Bastian. Turned the pram to leave. 'See you soon.' What would she do without Malachi when the time came to leave?

By the time Lisandra returned to the paediatric ward, Ginny stood beside Bastian's cot with a deep groove creasing her forehead. Her new friend wrung her hands and kept shooting glances at the monitor.

Lisandra came up beside her and touched her shoulder. 'Ginny. What are you doing here?'

Ginny spun and hugged her, warm arms

clasping her middle and for a moment Lisandra closed her eyes and took the hug gratefully. 'Malachi phoned me. Poor baby. Poor you.'

'We're all okay now. We should know more this afternoon. Did Malachi ask you to come?' Of course he did.

It had been so long since someone had comforted her like this.

Not true, her pedantic brain said, Malachi hugged her last night against his bare chest, but she didn't want to think about that with people all around her. That was something for the quiet of her own room when she had time and brain space to sort through those emotions.

Ginny was saying as she squeezed, 'This must have been such a shock.'

'Malachi shouldn't have asked you to come on your Sunday off.'

'Of course he should. He asked if I minded coming to help you with Bennett. I was here like a shot.' She held out her hands as if the choices were a no-brainer. 'I love babysitting and you have to take Bastion for testing.'

Yes, she did, and this would make it so much easier but she felt bad. 'He didn't say anything to me about doing that.'

Ginny waved her hand. 'And that's Malachi. Trying to avoid someone saying thank you.'

Ginny stepped back and looked into Lisandra's face with sudden unease in her eyes. 'I hope you don't mind we've micromanaged you into having a babysitter.'

Lisandra had to laugh. 'I can't think of a sitter I'd rather have for Bennett than you.' And her mushy brain said, *Oh, Malachi, thank you.* 'But he shouldn't have asked.'

Then she remembered her own intentions to intrude on Ginny's weekend to help her find new accommodation—so now who was the pot calling the kettle black?

Still, moving house had been pushed away with the horrific drama of Bastian's health and the tests to come. Despite Simon's reassurance, she needed to be told Bastian's heart was fine. His father's heart hadn't been. Dark dread sat like a black brick at the back of her chest, but she tried not to think of it. The tests would show up anything surely and Ginny would sit with her as they went through the traumatic morning to come.

By eleven a.m. Bastian had roared when he'd had his blood taken, complained his way past his first ever chest X-ray to see if his lungs were clear or his heart enlarged.

Had breastfed during the set-up for his ECG, stopped feeding for the recording, and gone back to his feed as if bored with all the wires. As far as Lisandra could tell the test proved the rhythm of his heart was perfectly normal from all directions.

Then he'd slept through the ultrasound of his heart to ensure the chambers and valves were functioning correctly.

During all the examinations the technicians had smiled and nodded when Lisandra had asked if everything was okay…but she needed to hear it from Simon Purdy and she had to wait until after lunch for that.

Finally, all the tests were done.

Ginny returned with a freshly made coffee when all the tests were over and for Lisandra it made her think of Malachi. Was he worried, too? Had he heard results she hadn't? Would he get a chance to come when Simon arrived with results, between his workload?

But she'd just have to wait and see. And be grateful for the bonus friend Ginny was. 'You're a star. I'll be fine now, Ginny. You go. They're both asleep. Thank you so much for your support.'

'I'm happy to stay.'

Lisandra knew her friend had had two phone calls from home asking about her ETA already.

'It's Sunday. You've worked all week. Go home to your family. Relax. I'll phone you after I see Simon for the official results.'

'If you're sure?'

'I'm sure.' She patted the pram. 'Bennett and I will just doze in the room until Dr Purdy comes,' she reassured her. 'Or Bastian wakes—whichever comes first.'

So, Ginny left, and Lisandra pushed the stroller back to her room to wait. And wait. Lunch came. She ate and waited some more. The phone rang. Bastian had woken.

On her way back to the paediatric wing Lisandra passed a woman sitting outside the glass door seemingly immersed in a book. 'Millicent?'

Millicent looked up and then stood, twisting her hands. 'Oh, Lisandra.' She chewed her lip, which seemed so out of character for the composed woman Lisandra had met before. 'I phoned Malachi this morning and he told me what happened to your dear little baby. I'm so sorry, my dear. What a dreadful worry for you.'

Millicent was the last person she'd expected to run into but her distress was obviously genuine. 'Thank you. It's kind of you to come out to see us here.'

Millicent waved that away. 'What did they say?'

'They ran tests this morning and so far everything appears to have come back normal. I'm waiting for Dr Purdy to give us the all-clear so I can take him home.'

Home. To Malachi's. And wasn't that a clanger of a word when this woman expected her to move out of her grandson's penthouse?

As if she heard her, Millicent hurried on quietly. 'I need to apologise for yesterday.'

Lisandra furrowed her brows. 'Apologise? For what?'

Millicent sighed. 'Sticking my nose in where it wasn't wanted or needed. Or so my grandson said.' She waved her hand before Lisandra could deny. 'I see the changes in Malachi since you've known him and they're all good.'

Lisandra blinked. 'In what way?'

'He's more relaxed with you than I've ever seen him with a woman.' She lifted both hands this time as if in wonder. 'It's a long story and I will share it with you one day.' She shook her head. 'But with the babies?' She blew out a happy breath. 'It's an absolute joy to see him with your boys. I need to thank you for that.'

'I'm not the one who needs thanks. Malachi has been marvellous with us.'

Millicent shook her head. There was a glint of wetness in her eyes and Lisandra felt unexpected tears herself. Though surely her own emotions were due to the horrific last twenty-four hours.

'He had a terrible childhood,' she whispered. 'Brought up by a cold man who belittled him and left him with uncaring staff. I despaired my grandson would ever find happiness.'

Where was this going? Not where it should be heading. 'Malachi's happiness isn't dependent on me. We're just friends, Millicent.'

'I know. He said.' She held up a placating hand. 'It's a start he needed. I hope you stay friends a long, long time with him. And I'm sorry if I was interfering. I'll go now.'

Lisandra felt confused and uncertain about the whole conversation, but she was sure that Millicent was upset. Strange and uncomfortable it might be, but she could see Millicent had come with the best of intentions. 'Don't go. Come in and see Bastian, at least.'

She saw the flare of pleasure. Then she

frowned. 'If Malachi finds me here, I'll be in trouble again.'

Lisandra laughed. 'Malachi adores you, even I can see that, and I doubt you're afraid of anyone, let alone your own grandson.'

'Maybe not.' Millicent lifted her chin. 'And if you're sure you don't mind, I would like to see the little one just for a moment.'

So, they trooped in, washed their hands and made their way to Bastian, who had fallen asleep again oblivious to everybody's worry.

Millicent stared down with a softness in her eyes that surprised and, if she was honest with herself, pleased Lisandra. 'He does look well,' Millicent said quietly. 'I just needed to see him for myself.'

She didn't stay long but there was no doubting her frank relief to see that Bastion looked healthy. Also unexpectedly, she hugged Lisandra before she left. 'I think you're a wonderful mother. This must have been so hard for you. I can't imagine how terrifying it would have been.'

'Thank you, Millicent. Malachi was wonderful.'

The older woman's eyes met hers. 'I'm glad.' She pressed a folded piece of paper into her hand, leaned forward and kissed Lisandra's cheek and then she strode away.

Lisandra unwrapped the piece of paper and saw Millicent's name and mobile phone number with the words *'Ring me any time'* written below in beautiful cursive script. 'Well. That was unexpected,' Lisandra murmured as she watched the door close behind Malachi's grandmother.

'Tell me about it,' said a voice behind her and Lisandra spun to find Simon Purdy standing next to her, his head swivelled to the door. 'From what I believe, Millicent does not grant her hugs often.'

'Really?'

'Really.'

'How well do you know Malachi and his family, Dr Purdy?'

'Simon. I know them well enough for you to call me Simon.' He smiled down at her. 'Malachi and I went to med school together.'

'Yes, he told me that.'

Simon shrugged. 'We worked the same ER in our early days. Malachi was a good friend when I lost my wife. I hoped one day he'd find a good woman, with luck a wonderful one like mine.' He looked down at her. 'Finally, I have hope.'

Her brows drew together. 'Cryptic,' she murmured.

Simon smiled. 'I hear he took himself off call four weekends in a row.'

She still didn't get it. 'And random.' She quirked a brow at him but couldn't help the smile at his mischievous eyes. He was teasing her, but she couldn't pin it down. But her mind was on other things and most of them about what he had to tell her about Bastian.

He raised a brow. 'You want random? You might have to do the running, but I'm cheering for you.' He glanced up, his eyes sparkling. 'Ah, yes. Here he comes.'

CHAPTER NINETEEN

Malachi

MALACHI HAD BEEN busy with two tricky caesarean sections, plus a forceps delivery in
Birthing Unit, all before lunch.

Between each event, he'd hoped to slip back
and see how Lisandra was faring, or at least
send a text, but every time he'd tried, someone had called him away. Maybe it was time
for him to look at taking on a registrar or at
least a resident to lighten his workload.

Simon and Ginny had both suggested it.
He'd always said no. He was beginning to
wonder why.

Still, he was here now, and apparently
his timing proved impeccable as he could
see Simon through the door standing beside
Lisandra.

The two of them smiled at each other, in a
very friendly way, which was a good thing.

Wasn't it? He narrowed his eyes. Simon wasn't a man Lisandra needed—he would be as unreliably available as Malachi with his paediatric workload.

He heard Simon's voice as he pushed through the door. 'Here he comes.'

He crossed the room to Lisandra's side. She looked tired, no surprise there, and he tore his eyes away to peer down at Bastian's hospital cot. The boy looked fine.

Malachi breathed out a sigh of relief, though Lisandra would have contacted him if she'd been worried. Funny how sure he was of that.

Bennett, the little champion, lay in the pram, eyes closed with his fist in his mouth, fast asleep. Malachi lifted his brows at Simon, 'Results back?'

'Not the formal, they'll come tomorrow through the usual channels. I've cc'd you in, Malachi.'

'Excellent.' He nodded. He'd be wanting to read those detailed reports and no doubt Lisandra would too. Easier to have their own copy.

'I was just about to say to Lisandra, I've looked at everything and cardiac structure and function look perfect. Nothing seen that indicates any anomaly or concern. I go back to my original diagnosis of aspiration causing a cardiac arrhythmia and a prolonged apnoea. I don't believe there will be detrimental sequalae to this event. And I don't believe Bastian, or Bennett for that matter, have an increased risk of something like this happening again.'

They could only pray, Malachi thought.

'Just bad luck?' Lisandra asked.

He nodded. 'Afraid so. And good luck you both were so good at resuscitation. I'd be happy for Bastian to go home when you're ready.'

His friend unobtrusively winked, which made Malachi frown. 'Something in your eye, Simon?'

The man grinned but at Malachi's comment he pulled his face back under control. Simon was starting to irritate him with his odd behaviour, Malachi thought grimly. Thank goodness Lisandra seemed to have missed all that silliness as she looked down at Bastian.

Simon hmphed and continued. 'I think it's important for the next forty-eight hours that Lisandra has back-up at home. Just someone she could call out to if she was worried.'

Malachi thought about that. 'Mrs Harris will be there until five on Monday. I can get her to come on Tuesday as well and I'll make sure I get home before she leaves.'

He met Lisandra's eyes. 'If you keep the loft door open, does that work for you?'

'Of course. But what if Mrs Harris doesn't want to work Tuesday?'

He shrugged. Simple. 'Then Ginny or I will have a sickie.'

Simon made a sound that he turned into a cough and Malachi felt strangely tempted to assist him with a forceful blow to the back. Unsympathetically he said, 'You okay?'

'Yes. Sorry. Just inhaled something— maybe at the thought of Dr Madden taking a sickie.' He actually laughed but turned it into another cough. Then held up his hands and continued quickly. 'That sounds like a perfect arrangement.'

He offered his business card to Lisandra. 'If you feel the need for a paediatric consult for the boys at any time you can contact me on my mobile. I'll arrange it with my secretary.'

She took the card. 'Thank you, Simon.'

Malachi held out his hand. 'We appreciate you coming, Simon. Sunday and all.' The men shook hands and Simon clapped Malachi on the back. He wasn't the one coughing, Malachi thought dryly as he winced at the blow.

'Any time.' Simon stepped back. Still grinning. Waved and disappeared.

'He's very good.'

'He is.' Malachi frowned. 'Not usually that jolly, though. Or not for a long time.' He shrugged. 'I've finished at the hospital so I'll follow you home.' He had a burning need to see Lisandra and the boys settled back into the loft again. Last night the apartment had seemed so empty.

Thirty minutes later Lisandra sat, shoes off, on his white leather couch in his apartment, feeding Bennett and Bastian while Malachi brewed a pot of French Earl Grey and set a tray with cups and saucers.

'Would you like a biscuit?' he called across from the kitchen nook and he watched the back of her head shake in denial.

'No, thanks. I still feel a bit sick from the shock of it all.'

He thought so. 'Which is why I asked you to come here first. Just relax, debrief, because I know how hard it is to run things over and over in your mind without actually talking about them to somebody else.'

She turned her head. 'Does that happen often to you? Rehashing without talking to others?'

'Not often,' he said. Only when something doesn't turn out like we all expect, he thought. 'If a baby doesn't breathe. As you know, obstetrics can be the most joyful and the most tragic of professions. The loss of a baby, that promise of the future child being stolen, is always difficult.'

'Yes,' she said softly and he knew she understood.

'It's difficult because we search for things we could have done differently that might or might not have changed the outcome.'

He put the tray on the table between them as she shifted Bennett to her shoulder. 'Here. I'll take him and you'll have a free hand.'

'Thanks.' She repositioned Bastian up to burp him. 'And I certainly understand what you're saying—all that heartbreaking questioning, Malachi. Though it only happened twice in my time in Birthing Unit and both times it proved the baby had no chance of living outside the uterus. Nothing we did would have changed the outcome.'

'Maybe so. But that doesn't help anyone.'

She shook her head in agreement as he watched her. Of course she would understand. She would understand a lot about his work because it ran parallel to hers. 'I like that you get it,' he said. He'd never had a woman friend, except other colleagues of course, who understood the sad as well as the positive aspects of his profession.

'And I like that you get it,' she copied him and they smiled at each other.

Bennett let out a huge burp and Malachi smiled. 'I'm getting better at that.' He looked down at the infant as he carried him to the pram to tuck him in. 'Or maybe Bennett's getting better at that.'

'Probably both,' she said as Bastian also relieved himself of wind.

Malachi stepped forward. 'Stay there. I'll tuck him in too.' He reached over and took him from her hands. Realised this was the first time he'd held him since cardiac massage and his chest tightened in a visceral pull of pain. God, that had been close. He felt his fingers tighten in an emotional response. He couldn't imagine a different scenario where Bastian was lost.

'Have you thought about being a mothercraft nurse?' she teased him and he pulled back from that ghastly memory. Swallowed the horror and moistened his dry mouth. It took a few seconds before he could answer calmly.

'No. But I thought about asking if I could offer you the services of one to give you a break every now and then.' He was serious about getting in help, but she laughed.

'No, thanks. I signed up for this gig and I

have easy babies. Save the mothercraft nurses
for the people who have a tough time.'

He finished tucking Bastian in, gave him
an extra pat because he could, and thought
about her words. She was doing it tough but
he didn't argue, just checked that Bennett still
looked settled, and then sat opposite her.

He reached for the tea—she'd poured his—
and broached the subject that was on both
their minds. 'Yesterday was difficult and terrifying but we've done everything we can and
can only pray it won't happen again.'

She lifted her teacup, but her hand shook
and she put it down again. 'I wondered if I
should get a baby apnoea alarm. A breathing
pad to lay him on. Something else to keep him
safe.' He understood why she'd want one and
of course she could if she wanted to, but he
wished she wouldn't.

'Of course, that's understandable, maybe
for a week or two it could be reassuring,' he
said, and they were both silent for a pause.
'But long term they can cause more stress
than they alleviate.'

She said quietly, 'That's what we told the
mothers, too.'

'The research on apnoea monitors says no
evidence was found that they impact the pre-
vention of SIDS in healthy babies.'

'I read that too,' she said. 'But is Bastian normal or at risk?'

They both thought about that.

'Simon said he felt neither of your boys had an increased risk of this happening again.'

'I know.'

'Plus the normal breathing pauses a baby does have make the alarm goes off, and cause more stress.' He watched her, wishing he could help. 'It's hard.'

'He could have died, Malachi.'

'Yes.' And that was just about enough of him sitting opposite her while she was in pain. He stood and moved past the table between them to sit beside her. Slipped his arm around her rigid shoulders and drew her head down onto his shoulder. She sucked in a breath and there was a sob at the end.

He whispered, 'I wish I could take away your worry.'

'I know. You've done a lot. So much.'

He touched her hair. 'I believe the boys will both be fine.'

She nodded against him and he found his lips brushing the silken strands under his mouth. She smelled like herbal shampoo and baby lotion and Lisandra. The most beautiful perfume in the world to him. Quietly he added, 'I like the idea of the loft door open between the two apartments. Until you feel you want to shut it again.'

'And what if I don't want to shut it?'

His heart rate jumped. But he kept his voice low. 'I'd be a happy man.'

CHAPTER TWENTY

Lisandra

LISANDRA HAD SPOKEN the truth, though she probably shouldn't have said it out loud, but her brain was truly fried by the stress of the last twenty-four hours. And she wanted access to Malachi for reassurance.

The wonderful weight of Malachi's arm around her shoulders kept her grounded even when her brain wanted to lose the plot and let her sob. Bastian was safe, she wasn't alone, the boys were happily asleep, and Malachi had her in his arms.

Slowly the tension eased as she breathed in the scent of him, that subtle, spicy aftershave she identified as his, the slab of solid muscle of his chest under her cheek. His warmth. His caring.

His mouth on her hair as he kissed her in sympathy.

What? She froze. There it was again. A gentle caress.

It was only sympathy. Empathy maybe. But she'd take the comfort while she had it.

Besides. It felt wonderful. Against her he felt wonderful. He was wonderful.

It was true. She wanted to keep the door open. Hell. She wanted to sleep down here and if he offered his bed she'd curl up next to him with the boys in the room with them.

'Would you like to sleep down here tonight?' His unexpected words penetrated and made her blink.

'Did you just read my mind?'

He shrugged. 'Maybe you read mine. I was thinking I would lie awake tonight wondering if you were awake worrying.'

'Except neither of us would get to sleep. If we did sleep the boys would wake us up for feeds.'

'True.' She heard the smile in his voice. 'But that would be your job and you would respond.'

Before she could say something, like *gee, thanks*, he went on. 'And when my phone rings and I get called out to the hospital that would be my job and you can snuggle in.'

She laughed. 'You are a beautiful man, Malachi Madden, and I'm so pleased I met you in a lift.' That was the wonderful thing about Malachi—she could say what she thought and he would tell her what he thought right back.

He said, 'Is it time for that lunch, feed, nap part of the day?'

'You remembered that "a day in the life of Lisandra and sons" routine?'

'Every word.'

She believed him. Crazy man. 'It could be time for a nap.'

'I was thinking we could lie, a little like this, on my bed, and maybe close our eyes until the next instalment of that regime appears. Neither of us slept well last night.'

She turned her head. Which was harder than it should have been because her whole body was growing heavy with exhaustion and, because Malachi was right here next to her, she could finally allow the fatigue to overwhelm her. 'You didn't sleep?'

His other hand squeezed her shoulder. 'I worried. About you. About Bastian. Even about Bennett being upset.'

Something precious and fragile inside her opened with slowly spreading petals, unfurling, stretching, reaching for the sunlight that she was beginning to see was the man beside her.

She nodded her heavy head. 'Let's lie down

and close our eyes.' And you can hug me, which was not something she did add out loud.

Malachi lifted his arm and sat forward to slide away, while she was having trouble holding her head up. It was as if she'd been given a sedative, but she knew she'd been given a gift more precious than that. She'd been given the gift of sharing the load.

While she was still thinking about that, Malachi reached and took her hand. Pulled her gently to her feet, and before she could straighten he slid one strong arm under her knees and the other around her back and lifted her into his arms. He hugged her into his chest like some olden day knight carrying his princess to his tower.

She smiled sleepily up into his face. 'You're so strong,' she teased.

'Good to know all those hours in the gym weren't wasted,' he said seriously, and she snorted indelicately against his chest, his beautiful chest, and closed her eyes. Now this had to be a dream.

CHAPTER TWENTY-ONE

Malachi

LISANDRA IN HIS arms felt wonderful, so incredibly perfect that he couldn't help the way his fingers tightened. As he stared down into her face he saw the slight curl of her beautiful lips in a secret smile but her dark lashes hid her eyes. He could feel her relaxed and trusting as she lay against him, as she should be, because he would never hurt her.

He placed her gently on the opposite side of the bed to his and thought to himself how good she looked there. Too good.

She opened her eyes, eyes such a striking blue, those eyes like the ocean outside his window, and she smiled at him as he stepped away.

'There were two of us in this nap dream,' she said. 'Are you coming?'

'Very soon.' He stepped away from the

room to the pram and pushed it so that it stood beside the bed in full view, then opened the sliding wardrobe door behind him and pulled a thin summer blanket from the shelf. He floated half of it so that it covered her and sat on his side of the bed to remove his shoes and just his belt, so the metal wouldn't press against her.

Malachi eased down beside her and slid his arm under her shoulder, turning her gently away from him and pulling her back into his chest. 'Nap,' he said with a mock firmness, and her shoulders shook slightly in amusement. Though he couldn't see her face he knew she was smiling and he felt her relax even more against him.

Within a very short time they actually slept.

Malachi woke to a woman in his arms. Lisandra in his arms. It wasn't a dream.

On the negative she was fully dressed, and on the plus side, she lay relaxed in sleep. The scent of her hair and the skin at the back of her neck surrounded him in the most delicious way. Unconsciously his hand, the one spread under her breast, tightened to pull her closer.

In unconscious response her bottom snuggled in. There, he silently groaned, that whole positive-negative thing happening again. She was there but he couldn't have her.

So, this was what it was like? To care deeply for the person asleep in your arms. This ache to hold her like this for ever. To wake every morning with Lisandra, soft and warm, and that warmth not just physical but emotionally wonderful, all around him.

If only he were a better man.

If only he could be a better father than the man who had been so disappointed and derogatory towards him.

If only...

She stretched against him and he forced himself to let her go, watched her ease sideways and then turn on her back and roll to face him. 'I wonder if this is the first time in the last weeks that I've woken on my own without the boys pressing my alarm.'

His sense of humour, one that seemed to grow and mature when he was around Lisandra, sparked. 'Did I press you with my alarm?'

She made that delightful snort that she'd made when he'd carried her across to the bed. He could see her teeth in this smile and it made his own mouth widen.

'Malachi,' she said, 'you are one of a kind.'

'Back at you, Miss Calhoun,' he murmured as he leaned forward and kissed her.

CHAPTER TWENTY-TWO

Lisandra

WAKING IN MALACHI'S arms was like starting life all over again.

That might have been because she'd allowed herself to sleep so deeply for the first time since the twins were born that she felt renewed, just by trusting that he would hear them if she didn't. Or because Malachi's arms felt so wonderful. His whole body had felt wonderful spooned against hers. Probably, that feeling of renewal came from all of the above.

When she rolled to look at him he was watching her with his hazel eyes so dark, such smouldering bedroom dark, and if she hadn't already felt his body's reaction to her against her bottom she would have seen it in his eyes.

She stared into a wondrous world she'd thought lost for ever and knew that in the short time that she'd known Malachi Madden he had grown to mean so much to her.

Strangely, she'd never had an issue with their difference in circumstance—he was ridiculously wealthy and she was...not poor, but only adequately funded—and she'd always intended to thank him for his generosity and leave.

All that had changed now because she didn't want to leave him. She wanted to lie like this, in this bed, every night, every morning, and most certainly for naps like this during the day, with Malachi's arms around her.

His beautiful eyes grew darker and she knew the moment that he'd decided to kiss her. She felt her own lips part as she stared, suddenly breathless, into the depths of his intense gaze and watched his mouth come closer.

She'd wondered what it would be like to be kissed by Malachi...but nothing prepared her.

Then the thought was gone as he brushed her lips with his, nibbled gently at her lower lip, swept his hot and heavenly mouth backwards and forwards, backwards and forwards until she was leaning into him, hungry, desperately urging him to take her mouth.

When he sealed his lips against her the

sweep of his tongue opened her to him and she breathed him in.

Welcomed him, in fact, with all her being. The gentleness, then the unexpected authority and the sweeping reverence all combining to tumble any resistance she might have had. Not that she had much because she was lost. Swirled into a sensation of pleasure, hunger, desperation...and love.

The thought exploded into her mind like fireworks in the silent room. Malachi cared. Malachi loved her. But there was sadness and despair in this kiss because Malachi didn't believe in the future.

His passion and longing brought tears to her eyes because she tasted, inhaled, sensed profoundly the sadness at the back of this kiss and she drew him closer, deeper, wordlessly reassuring him, but the sadness remained. Why was he sad?

A baby cried and Malachi pulled away well before she would have and eased himself out of the bed.

Lisandra flopped onto her back and blew out a breath. So much for wondering if Malachi could kiss. The man was a kissing machine. A master smoocher. A maestro. And there was worry when she thought about that underlying sadness she couldn't deny she'd felt and wanted to assuage.

Malachi's sadness came from somewhere deep, she knew it wasn't something they could lightly discuss, but she'd think on it and take the insight that she'd gained today and the kindness that she knew he would still offer until they could work this out.

They had to work this out, because now she knew Malachi loved her and of a certainty, she loved him.

The thought sat comfortably. Yes, she loved the quirky, blunt, generous, kind man who kissed like an angel. A wickedly sensuous angel and she never, ever, wanted him to be sad. Or for him to be alone with that sadness.

Suddenly she remembered Simon's comment: 'You might have to do the running...' For what? Had a man who'd seen them together for less than an hour known something? Something neither she nor Malachi had seen? Had Simon guessed it would be like this?

Lisandra rose from the bed and crossed to where Malachi held Bennett to his chest, patting the small back with his big hands. She wanted to slide her own hands around his waist and comfort him from behind as he'd held her, but something told her he'd put up a wall and it wouldn't go well.

Instead, she bided her time. 'Here. I'll take him.' Took her son from his hands and crossed to the white lounge and opened her blouse to feed him.

'I'll make fresh tea,' Malachi said from behind her shoulder and she heard him walk away. The sounds of the jug switching on and then more sounds as Malachi disappeared into the bedroom where the door shut.

Why was he sad? she thought and stared down at the little face watching hers. 'Why is our Malachi sad?' she said softly and Bennett paused in his drinking and stared at her with wise eyes. 'You don't know why, either, do you, little man?' she said.

'Maybe it's all too fast for him? I'm overwhelming him?' She raised her brows at Bennett. 'Are we overwhelming him? Maybe we should all go back upstairs tonight and just leave the door open like we were supposed to. Take things more slowly?' And then she heard Bastian complain that he'd been left behind in the pram.

The bedroom door opened and she heard Malachi's voice. 'Missing out, are you, young man? I know where they went. I'll take you.'

When he came around the front of the

lounge carrying Bastian, she smiled at him. 'You're talking to babies.'

'I thought I heard you chatting away?'

He passed the boomerang pillow and she slipped Bennett onto it so she could make way for his brother on the other side. Then Malachi reached for her cold cup of tea and placed it on the tray next to the teapot. 'Earl Grey again or would you like something different?'

'You're spoiling me.'

'It's Sunday. I can.'

True. He worked a lot of the time. Except when he was with her. 'Then I'll have peppermint this time, please.'

CHAPTER TWENTY-THREE

Malachi

ON MONDAY MORNING, Malachi had to force himself to go out of his own door. He'd slipped up the stairs to the loft, something he'd done a few times since Lisandra had moved back upstairs last night, to say goodbye and ensure she needed nothing before he left.

Mrs Harris would be here in fifteen minutes, a good hour before she normally came, and Lisandra hadn't wanted him to wait and make himself late.

He hated leaving her with the boys alone after he'd promised her she wouldn't be solo for the next forty-eight hours. Yet here he was going down in the lift, and leaving them all behind.

How had his life changed so much in so short a time?

Yesterday's kiss had changed everything.

He should never have made that move but she'd been impossible to resist. The feel of Lisandra's mouth against his, her sweetness and warmth, the feeling of homecoming— such sensations and emotions he'd never had with any woman, and wanted to have with Lisandra for the rest of his life.

He'd wanted to wrap her up in his arms and never let her go, but he knew he'd been a fool to open up wants and needs he'd accepted long ago would never be his.

Not surprisingly, that kiss had sent Lisandra back upstairs to the loft and confirmed something he'd been afraid of. He wanted Lisandra Calhoun with every atom of his being but he wasn't good enough for her. Or for her boys. He never would be.

Her going back upstairs to sleep was a kindness on her part.

That was fine. If nothing changed between them now, then he had more in his life than he'd ever had and he should be grateful for that.

If she stayed living in the loft.

If he hadn't chased her away with his advances.

If he could rebuild the trust he'd smashed

down and reassure her friendship was all he wanted.

Because out of everything he wanted her and the boys to stay.

Ginny was waiting for him when he reached his office. 'How are they?' she asked before he could offer a good morning.

Dear Ginny. 'No problems. Mrs Harris is there early and I need to be out of here before five tonight so Lisandra has back-up for another twenty-four hours.'

'Got it.' Ginny agreed with a determined nod, followed by an inclination towards his inner sanctum. 'And Simon Purdy's in there waiting for you.'

'Why?' Had new results for Bastian come through that he hadn't seen yet. Had they found something that put the baby at risk? He should never have left Lisandra this morning.

'He didn't say.'

Ginny's voice broke into his sudden fear and Malachi strode towards his office. 'Hold my calls until I let you know, please.'

'Yes, I will.'

He glanced back at her. 'Except Lisandra, of course.' He patted his pocket. Thank goodness for mobile phones. In fact, since he'd met Lisandra, he held gratitude for the instrument that meant she could contact him at any time even if it was to leave a message.

Ginny murmured, lifting her hand to her face, 'Of course,' and he had a suspicion she was smiling behind her fingers. Smiling at what? There could be bad news. What was wrong with everybody at the moment?

He pushed the door wider. 'Simon. I didn't expect to see you this morning. Is something wrong with Bastian's results?'

His friend had been staring out of the office window at the ocean. 'No. Of course not. I would have phoned you. Still all good.' He waved back towards Ginny. 'I had to come over to see a baby in your NICU earlier and I thought I'd catch you before you started. You're always a hard man to track down through the day.'

Malachi's overwhelming relief made him gruff. 'What can I do for you, then?' Malachi glanced at his watch. He'd only do one ward round today instead of his usual two unless the midwives had a concern about one of his patients. That would get him home earlier.

'Offering advice.' Simon's voice seemed to come from far away as Malachi wondered if Mrs Harris had arrived yet. 'Hello. Malachi? What are you thinking about?' Simon's voice intruded into his thoughts.

'Sorry. Did you say something?' He ran his hand through his hair. Stared at his friend in exasperation. 'I'm trying to work out how I'm going to get home earlier tonight before my housekeeper leaves.'

Simon leant his big shoulder against the window frame. 'I've never seen you act this way. Ever. Not about a woman.'

He did not need to be an interesting specimen for his friend to watch. 'Well, now you've seen it, you can go.'

'Ah, man...' Simon shook his head as he pushed off the window frame. 'I just wondered if you needed a hand to work it out.'

As if anyone could help the way he was. 'What's there to work out? Lisandra's a dear friend, that's all, and one day, soon, she'll move out and find a good man to marry.'

'You are a good man. A great man. Ask her to marry you.'

Malachi pulled a face and stepped to his desk and swept up the sheet of paper waiting for him there. 'I mean one who'll be a decent father to her children.' He glared up at Simon, remembering yesterday. 'You and I will go on, just like you said, saving other people's families.'

Simon raised his hands. 'I'm sorry I said that. It's not true. You would love those boys.

I think you do already. No kid needs more than a father who loves them.' Simon added gently, 'And who loves their mother.'

'Not my forte.' Pain squeezed through him. He didn't believe that was all Lisandra's boys deserved.

More quietly, Simon said, 'I think you and Lisandra are perfect together.'

'Really?' For heaven's sake. The man was delusional. 'You deduced this from your extended observation of us both?' he said dryly as he re-scanned today's theatre list, which wasn't sinking in. 'What was it? Three lots of ten minutes?'

'It didn't take long to see. Good grief, Malachi, even your grandmother approves.'

That made his head jerk up. 'What on earth makes you say that?'

'Because Millicent came in and hugged Lisandra yesterday when she checked on Bastion. I've never seen her hug anybody.'

Malachi stared. Blinked. Replayed it. 'My grandmother was in the paediatric intensive care? Yesterday?' And why was he the last to know? Then he remembered she'd phoned him in the middle of everything just after he'd left Lisandra on Sunday morning. 'She went into the public hospital?' One she hadn't been in since his grandfather had died there.

'She did.'

Now that, Malachi thought, was too much to think about and he needed to get moving.

He narrowed his eyes and stared at his friend. 'Why are you here, again?'

Simon huffed out a laugh and headed for the door. He turned and said over his shoulder, 'Because I think you could screw it up and I don't want that to happen.'

Simon shook his head at Malachi's confusion. 'Come see me if it all starts to go pear-shaped, okay? She cares about you, too.' Then his interfering friend walked away as if he hadn't thrown Malachi into total confusion.

He pushed it all away and re-examined the day's theatre list and his part in it, folded the sheet neatly, and slid it into his trouser pocket.

He was still confused about Simon's visit as he stopped at Ginny's desk. 'Please see if you can reschedule the last appointment for today and tomorrow,' he asked.

'I've already done that. Unless we're really stuck, I'll be trying for it most days.'

'Oh. Thank you.' That was a good idea. He headed for the door but stopped before he stepped into the corridor. 'Thanks for coming in yesterday, Ginny. Lisandra said you helped a lot.'

'You're both welcome,' Ginny said. 'Ward

Three asked if you could stop in there, first on your rounds, this morning.'

He nodded and started his day.

I once asked if you could stay in the first room round this morning.

He nodded and closed the day.

CHAPTER TWENTY-FOUR

Lisandra

LISANDRA WATCHED MALACHI disappear down the stairs and a minute later she heard the door close gently in his apartment.

Earlier, with the loft door open between their previously separate living spaces, it had been strange to hear all the daily minutiae of Malachi's life in his apartment downstairs.

Strange and reassuring. It was also funny how she could imagine what he was doing a lot of the time.

Then again, since she'd moved back here last night, he had reappeared in her unit so many times to check she didn't need him that she might as well have stayed down there.

She knew what she needed to take her stress away. Malachi's arms around her. In fact, she was having the devil of a time to stop thinking about his mouth on hers and how much more she wanted him holding her in his embrace.

She was in love with Malachi Madden.

She blew out a breath. That had come out of the blue. And with more force and substance than she could believe possible.

Guilt slammed into her and she winced.

What about Richard?

It was not even a year since he'd been taken from her and she'd found another man? Loved another man? Already?

They were so different, the two men she'd loved, but what she felt for Malachi didn't lessen the past she still held in a special corner of her heart.

Which reminded her. It was time to text another photo to Richard's mother. She didn't know whether to tell her about Bastian's scare or not—but decided it could be something that could wait if they ever had a chance to talk. The last thing she wanted to do was exacerbate their grief for their son.

She'd had several short but promising texts in the last weeks from Richard's mother. It seemed Josie was making headway with Clint because of the likeness of the boys to Richard when he was a baby.

Josie had taken a phone snap of Richard's

baby photo and shared it with Lisandra, who could see the resemblance as well. It made her feel her sons were more of a part of their father's estranged family. Maybe one day, maybe even with Malachi by her side, she would be asked to visit them again.

She would always be thankful for Richard and for the gift of his sons, boys she now hoped would truly become Malachi's sons. She would ensure her boys knew they'd been blessed with two wonderful fathers.

But today was a day to look to the future.

A day to drop the guilt, the blame, the denial of something incredibly special that had grown out of loss and grief and new life and new friendship.

Malachi was a wonderful man and she had forgiven herself for unexpectedly moving on from the past. Had decided there was no right length of time to grieve—be it one year, one decade, a lifetime, all could be right—but it also had to be right to hold gratitude for the unexpected gift of not being alone and for being so selflessly loved by Malachi.

Today she'd say goodbye to Richard and she would fight for Malachi.

She glanced at the aquamarine expanse outside the window and thought of the man she'd fallen in love with.

It wasn't a blind infatuation, like the crazy, consuming attraction that she suspected she might have had with Richard. This was a warts-and-all awareness. Malachi wasn't perfect and neither was she, and they both brought baggage. But she had been gifted the opportunity to unfurl a relationship with an amazing man. Hopefully, whatever was holding Malachi back would resolve enough for them to be able to find the solution to their barriers. She needed to find Malachi's fears and help him face them.

She suspected from what he'd said about marriage and not having children—which was ridiculous with the way he handled the boys—that his hang-ups had to do with his father. Millicent had said something along those lines as well.

Was Malachi's grandmother the answer?

Millicent. Millicent, who had visited her yesterday in the hospital and had looked unexpectedly shattered at Bastian's close shave with death.

Millicent, who had shared her private mobile number and had said she could ring her any time.

Today?

Lisandra knew Malachi's grandmother to be an early riser because she'd been immacu-

late and early on that first Saturday morning
when she'd met her. Let's hope that went for
today as well.

An hour later, once she'd showered, dressed,
and the boys were back asleep, Lisandra
pressed the number for Malachi's grandmother.

'Who is this?' Crisp and curt.

'Millicent. It's Lisandra. I hope you don't
mind that I called. I just wanted to say thank
you for visiting us at the hospital, yesterday.'

'Lisandra.' Instant change in tone. Phew.
'I'm so pleased you rang. How is dear Bastian this morning? And Bennett, of course.'
There was genuine concern, interest and, if
she wasn't mistaken, pleasure that Lisandra
had called. Some of the tension left her shoulders.

It did feel good to talk to Malachi's grandmother. This was what she'd hoped for from
Richard's mother. She suspected her own sad
little need was to search for a replacement for
the mother and grandmother she had lost.

'Lisandra? Are you there?'

'Sorry. I went vague for a moment. Both
boys have been perfect gentlemen since they
arrived home yesterday.' She couldn't help
her glance at the open door to the stairwell.

'Malachi insisted we leave the loft door open because Dr Purdy wanted me to have access to assistance for the next forty-eight hours.'

'What an excellent idea. So is Malachi there?'

She wished. 'No. He's gone to work but Mrs Harris has arrived an hour early and will stay until he comes home tonight. It's just for the next twenty-four hours.'

'Oh.' Did that sound like disappointment? 'That must be reassuring for you.'

'It is.' There was a pause, she felt her bravery ebb, and Lisandra winced and almost chickened out. She couldn't chicken out of loving Malachi. No. At the thought, she straightened her shoulders. 'I wondered if you'd be interested in having lunch with me today. If you're not busy, of course.

There was a small pause and Lisandra's heart sank but before it could make it all the way to her toenails, Millicent said, 'I'm free. I'd enjoy that. Thank you for thinking of me.' She sounded sincerely pleased, and Lisandra let out a sigh of relief. Malachi's grandmother went on, 'What would you like me to bring?'

Yourself, your knowledge of Malachi, your understanding, Lisandra thought. 'I have a full freezer and I did see a lovely gourmet quiche in there that I could easily slip into the oven. I'll make a green salad to go with it and we can drink tea.'

'Perfect. What time? And which apartment?' Amusement sounded in the question. Was Millicent teasing her?

She suspected she was and smiled. 'Twelve. And the loft. But if you end up through the wrong door I'm just up the stairs.'

Millicent laughed. 'Clever girl. I'll see you then.'

When Millicent knocked on the door of the loft she brought two non-alcoholic bottles of apple cider and a tray of pastries. Lisandra gestured her in. 'Welcome to my eyrie.'

'Thank you, I'm delighted you invited me. Where are the boys?'

'Asleep.' She pushed wider the crack of the door to the boy's bedroom and two little bodies lay quietly in their portable cots.

'Angels.'

'Most times,' Lisandra murmured, and the two women smiled at each other. 'I've set places at the small table on the balcony and there's a shade sail attached to the wall to keep us out of the sun.'

She'd already set the heated quiche and green salad out there under a muslin throw, expecting Millicent to be punctual. She had been. To the minute. No surprises. Which was nice.

Lisandra brought one of the bottles of apple cider and two glasses and gestured Millicent to the best seat with the clearest view out over the ocean. She stood over the glasses and poured the gold sparkling liquid.

Millicent sighed happily. 'It really is a glorious outlook.'

Lisandra eased into her own chair and breathed in the salt and the sunshine and the new aroma of apple cider and quiche.

Millicent glanced down at the visible edge of Malachi's pool that she could see. 'Have you been in the pool?'

'Lord, no.' She laughed. 'I haven't had time to have a long shower, let alone cavort in the water.'

'Pity.'

Lisandra waved that away. 'I told Malachi I wouldn't be swanning past him to use his pool.'

Millicent raised her perfect brows. Dryly she said, 'I think he might enjoy that.'

Lisandra wasn't sure what to say to that and she wasn't quite relaxed enough with her visitor to be where she wanted before she dived into the personal.

Instead of answering she began to serve the

quiche and passed Millicent the salad. The next few minutes were taken up with eating.

'Since the boys arrived it has been busy,' she said a few minutes later.

'And when do you think it'll all settle down?'

'Apart from yesterday's horror, it's getting better every day now. Since the boys passed the six-week mark. I'm starting to feel human and they don't wake me at night as much because I feed them so often through the day.'

'It seems to be working for you. Malachi did mention he helps with bath times when he's available. It seems so out of character.'

And this was what she wanted to know. 'Why is it out of character? He has a job that involves babies.'

Millicent put down her glass of cider very carefully. 'Don't get me wrong. I'm delighted. But he's always said he wasn't father material. I'm hoping the experience he's gaining from you and the boys will change his mind for the future.'

So was she. The near future. 'He's very good with them. And it's amusing how skilled he's become at encouraging wriggling feet into the small playsuits.'

Millicent sent her an approving smile. 'I love how he's grown being around you.'

The kind remark made Lisandra's cheeks warm and inside a little more of the cold part of her thawed. 'That's lovely of you to say. He is wonderful.'

Millicent lifted her head. Held Lisandra's gaze with hazel eyes a very similar colour to her grandson's. 'And can you see a future with you and Malachi?'

Lisandra shouldn't have been surprised that his grandmother had put it out there. After all, that was why she'd asked Millicent to come. To sound her out. Listen. And ask advice.

She sat back in her chair. 'No mincing words for you, is there, Millicent?'

Those perfect brows rose again. 'I'm eighty-four years old, my dear. No time to pussyfoot around if I want to see Malachi happy before I die.'

'And you think he'd be happy with me.'

'I believe so. It's early days, I know, but I think you're fond of him. Do you think you could love him?'

'Easily. The man is everything I'd want for myself and for my boys. He's wonderful company and I miss him when he's not here. As for love, it's too late already. But I'm wary there's a reason he's holding back and I don't want to push him, hurt him, or make him unhappy. He's been so kind.'

Millicent sat back with a big breath of relief. 'Thank the stars. And yes, Malachi has always been kind. So, you asked me here to find out why he's pulling back?'

It was truth time all right. 'To help me understand why,' she clarified. 'I'm thinking it had something to do with his father because, as you say, Malachi told me he would never marry and never have children. Yet, I see him exhibiting all the wonderful traits anybody could possibly wish for in a parent or husband.'

'History.' Millicent sighed. 'All tragic history. My daughter, Malachi's mother, was always impetuous, full of life but blind when she married an impossible man. And when she left him, as she had to for her own mental health, she was not permitted to take Malachi. He threatened her with the courts if she tried.'

'That's horrible.'

'It was. Who knows what would have happened if they'd both had time to cool down? But she drove away recklessly and an accident killed her.'

Millicent's eyes drifted to the ocean and she sighed. When she looked back sadness seemed wrapped around her like a dark cloud. 'Malachi's childhood changed in an instant, ignored and despised by a man who should have seen his son's worth, and dished a cold and lonely upbringing without the mother who loved him.'

When she lifted her chin her eyes glinted with unshed tears. 'His father changed that night into a dreadful man who ridiculed Malachi's kindness and undermined his son's confidence at every turn. The boy couldn't do anything right and when I offered to raise him myself to protect him, I was practically banished as well.'

'That's even worse than I imagined.' Lisandra had guessed it had not been an easy childhood, but this was crueller than she'd suspected. Poor Malachi. Poor Millicent. Poor Millicent's daughter.

'Thankfully, his father sent him to boarding school when he turned twelve. At least I could get to take him home for the weekends. Malachi was determined to do well and become a doctor. We grew close.'

'I can see that.' Lisandra touched the other woman's hand briefly. 'His voice softens when he speaks about you.'

Millicent searched her face as if she didn't believe it, but the truth was there to see. 'Thank you. I wonder sometimes.'

'Don't. He adores you.'

'And I believe he adores you.' Millicent sat

back, her face serious. 'So, what are we going to do about that?'

Lisandra understood, a lot more anyway. She had clarity now and a mission. 'I'm going to show him I love and believe in him. The rest is up to him.'

CHAPTER TWENTY-FIVE

Malachi

MALACHI MADE IT back up the lift with ten minutes to spare before five p.m. He let himself in through his apartment, thanked Mrs Harris, who smiled and waved her hand from the kitchen where she was stirring something that smelled delicious.

'Thank you for staying,' he said.

'I've had a lovely day. The table's set and there's a mild chicken curry and rice, with some papadums, if you'd like to share it with Lisandra. My special recipe.'

He wondered if curry would upset the twins, but she must have read his mind.

'She said it would be fine with the wee ones if it was mild.'

He smiled. She'd never made him a meal but he'd take it with pleasure. He'd been so intent on getting back in time he hadn't thought about the evening meal. 'Thank you, Mrs Harris. That sounds wonderful.' His stomach rumbled and he remembered he hadn't stopped for lunch.

Mrs Harris turned the stove off and departed, promising to be early tomorrow.

He put down his briefcase and did what he'd wanted to do all day. He climbed the stairs to the loft. The door stood open, of course, but still he knocked.

Lisandra sat relaxed on the lounge, a place he'd seen her so many times, with a sleepy baby over each shoulder and a big, beautiful smile that came his way like a sunbeam that warmed his whole world.

His Lisandra, his Mother Earth and lovely 'tenant', he reminded himself, that he didn't want to lose. He thought about Simon saying not to screw it up, but he had no idea where to go from here. The dreaded awkwardness crept over him like a sticky web.

'How was your day?' he asked and reached down to take Bennett from her and slide him up over his own shoulder.

'Wonderful. Mrs Harris was a doll, and we've already bathed the babies, so my day has been very smooth and social.' She leaned her cheek against the little body near her ear. 'How was yours?'

'Not quite as smooth but I did manage to make it home in time.'

She raised amused brows at his slightly stressed reply. 'Did you have time for lunch?'

He smiled at her insight. 'No. Did you?'

'Your grandmother came and we had quiche on the balcony. It was very pleasant.'

He blinked. 'Did she invite herself again?' He'd have to lay down some rules.

'No. I phoned her. She gave me her number yesterday when she came to see Bastian at the hospital.'

He'd been going to ask about that. 'Simon said he'd seen her there.'

She straightened and brought Bastian closer to her chest in a protective hug. 'Yes, she said once she'd heard the news she'd had to come. What else did Simon say? Were there any other results from the tests? Did he find something?'

'No.' He sat down next to her so that their legs touched and he hoped pushing their bodies together would give her comfort. It was instinctual and he felt her relax beside him. He held her gaze. 'Everything is fine.

'As for Simon, he came to give me a pep talk about something else.' Anxious to reassure her but, after it was out, he could have bitten the words back. He hurried on. 'All the formal test results are in and nothing was flagged. I have them on my computer and we can pore over them together when you're ready.'

Sadly, she wasn't diverted. 'What was the pep talk about?'

Not something he wanted to share like this. 'What was your talk with my grandmother about?'

She smiled at him. 'Possibly the same thing?'

He blinked. She stood up and carried Bastian to the bedroom and almost immediately she was back and took Bennett from him. 'The boys are going to bed and the adults are having a conversation.'

He sat back. An unwilling smile tugging on his lips. Lisandra didn't do awkward, and he felt the strands of unease unravel. She returned and sat beside him. Close. Incredibly close. Wonderfully close.

She even took his hand, and hers felt warm yet fragile in his, until she turned to stare into his eyes, the blue of her gaze dazzling him.

'Malachi, I've been very happy here.'

'Good.' But past tense? He wasn't sure where this was leading but he had a sinking feeling he wasn't going to like it.

She ignored his interruption. 'I've loved every minute of getting to know you, and that's for me—not just because you're a delight with the babies.' Her eyes searched his as if she needed him to hear and agree with her. 'I think you're fabulous with them. But you're also fabulous with me.'

Oh, God. She was leaving, he thought. His world came to a shuddering halt. He had to stop her. 'You don't have to go.'

She squeezed his hand. 'I don't want to go.'

He put his other over the top as if to stop her from leaving him. 'Then don't.'

Softly, he heard the words he'd dreaded, 'I can't just stay here for ever as your tenant.'

Yes, she could. Of course she could. Ridiculously, his brain screamed, he could leave if that would make it easier for her. 'Why not?'

She pulled free and sat back widening the distance between them. Raised her brow in amusement. 'When you get married your wife wouldn't be happy.'

Now that wasn't a problem. 'I'm not getting married.'

She watched his face intently. 'My turn to ask why not?'

He shrugged, the awkwardness creeping back. 'I'm not husband material.'

She widened her eyes. Gently poked him in the chest with one finger. Said very slowly, 'I think you're perfect husband material.'

He blinked. She did? 'You do?' That was unexpected. And bore thinking about. He looked towards the room where the boys lay. He certainly wasn't father material. No doubt there.

'And you are wonderful with the boys. I couldn't wish for more care.'

She leaned into him and whispered in his ear, 'And you're an amazing kisser.'

His heart began to pound and Malachi reached down and took her fingers back in his. The awkwardness had disappeared in an instant. 'I am, am I?' He shifted closer and made up that distance she'd created.

'Oh, yes. Best ever. Super.' She nodded solemnly but he could see her eyes sparkling with mischief. Blue pools daring him to fight for her.

He was being herded, he knew that, but it wasn't awkward, it was a challenge and suddenly he was very keen on getting in on the action. 'You're pretty darn hot yourself,' he said, and slid his arm around the delightful waist he adored, pulling her into his side.

'The dilemma is,' she said softly, 'I don't want to hurt you by staying if you can't see a future with us all.'

Oh, he could see it. Dream it. He just believed she deserved more. 'I can see one day you'll leave and find someone to be there for you instead of me. But until then,' he said, the words scratching and scoring his heart as they left his mouth, 'until then you could stay.'

Her face drew closer and she whispered as her mouth brushed against his, 'Why would I possibly want anyone else but you?'

And the penny dropped.

CHAPTER TWENTY-SIX

Lisandra

SHE FELT THE moment he realised she wanted him. As she had no doubt he wanted her. His shock, and delight and what felt like possessiveness in the tenseness of his body as he moved even closer. *Oh, Malachi, you adorable man,* she mentally sighed in relief as his lips pressed against hers and his hand slid firmly behind her neck to hold her there.

He took over the kiss, deeper, stronger, like steel-covered velvet and fire...my stars, this man could kiss.

She closed her eyes and sank into the swirling wonder of Malachi's mouth, felt the tension slide from her shoulders, her belly warming, and a smile growing at the corners of her mouth.

They surfaced, and with his mouth still sliding across her lips he murmured, 'So you'd like to stay here? For ever?' His mouth brushing hers and a smile in his voice.

'I'd prefer to move down to your bedroom.'

He made a noise deep and low and in assent. 'Oh, yes. Great idea. Asap. Later on, when the boys are older, they could live upstairs and we'd have more privacy than we knew what to do with.'

'Unless we filled the other rooms with children as well.'

He pulled away. 'You'd consider having more children? With me?'

'If we were blessed...then I can't wait.'

'What if I'm a terrible father?'

And there it was. His deep-seated lack of confidence that was so unfounded. 'How can you be? You're already a wonderful dad to the B twins.' She watched him blink at the word dad. It made her throat tighten and ache for all the years he'd doubted himself.

He turned his face. Looked out of the window. Hiding his eyes. 'That's just luck with babies. I don't know how to be a real father.'

'Let me help you understand.' She took both his cheeks in her hands, turned him, and stared into his face. 'The starting and ending point is love. If you can love...' She looked and could see the love in his eyes—love for her, love for the children in the next room—

how could he not see how amazing he would be? 'Anything is possible.'

'You deserve more.'

How to convince him? She hitched up her courage and dared to dream. 'Do you love me?'

'With all my heart.' No hesitation. Straight out. The words brought tears to her eyes.

She gestured to the room that held the boys. 'Do you love my sons?'

He blew out his breath softly. Nodded. Smiled. His eyes twinkled. 'I do.'

'Then you will be a wonderful father. A wise woman I know once said, "All children need is someone to love them, someone to take responsibility, and someone to provide a safe place for them to grow." Together, we can provide all of that.'

He almost looked convinced—but not quite. And she knew what it was. His big fear. 'What about the demands of my work?'

And that was his dear blindness that she loved so much. 'You will always give your best to your patients. It's not in you to do anything else. And I love you for that.'

She saw his eyes widen but there was more to say before they dwelt on her feelings. 'Who has managed to help me bath the boys more than fifty per cent of the time in the last few weeks?'

He looked thoughtful and she smiled. 'Already, you've prioritised your work hours. Managed to spend less time at the hospital without causing harm to your patients. Maybe you can even see that having enough rest actually makes you a better doctor when you are working.'

'Hmm.' Non-committal but he was listening—and, she hoped, hearing her. Because she understood his ethic.

'Because you love us, you can stay up with a sick baby when you've already done a ten-hour work day. Could stay up for me.' And there was double entendre there.

His eyes gleamed and then dulled. 'I have call. I'll always have call. What if you get fed up?'

'Yes. You have call. But not every night. You might not be able to watch them play cricket every Saturday, like some other dads, but you'll watch them when you can. You could read a story another day, and cook dinner another. Even if you're still working long hours, it's the cumulation of little things that make a good father, it's having someone who's got their back, who's there for their mother, even if not always able to be present every minute of every day—no parent can be, and it would be very unhealthy to be there all the time anyway!'

She watched the hope brighten his eyes. Saw him lift his head as he stared at her. As if she were promising him the world and not a jam-packed life full of kids and drama and scattered homelife.

He leaned his forehead against hers and she heard the breath he drew in. 'Are you sure?'

'Absolutely. If you'll have me. And my boys.'

'Please may I have you? And your boys. I can't imagine my home if you weren't here. If I lost you all I would be alone again and for the first time in a very long time I want to come home. To you. To our boys.' He shook his head. Breathed out the words, 'I'll have a family.'

She stroked his hair. 'You are my family. We are yours.'

His eyes searched hers. Serious. Intent. 'Will you marry me, Lisandra?'

Oh, Malachi, she thought. *How can I be so lucky?* 'I love you. I'd love to.'

His mouth brushed hers and he whispered against her lips. 'When?'

'Soon.'

'How soon?'

'Let's not have a total rush into this. You have to really live with us yet. Get used to the craziness that is my life.'

He considered that. She saw it in his thoughtful gaze. That he could see she wouldn't budge. Tried his own ultimatum. 'When the boys are six months old.'

'If we haven't driven you mad by then.'

He sat back. 'Do I have to wait that long for you to move downstairs?' Disappointment clear and she wanted to hug him.

'No. We can do that much earlier.'

'When?' His eyes were laughing at her, and full of love.

'Now.'

'Excellent.'

Four months later, the wedding

Malachi stood at the leafy edge of the Tweed River in golden afternoon light. In front of him stood a metal border shaped like a heart and full of flowers. The elaborate gold and cream blooms that his grandmother had organised were elegant and stylish as they twisted to shape a frame for the sharing of the vows.

Behind him the wide lawns were immaculate, the riverfront restaurant shone like a fairyland, and even Malachi had to admit the wedding centre felt a fitting place to celebrate their marriage.

Except his bride wasn't beside him, Simon was, and, as much as he enjoyed his friend's company, he really wanted Lisandra.

He'd been trying desperately to ignore the fifty people sitting on white chairs under the trees each side of the gold carpet that led to where he stood. He'd never been a person who enjoyed the limelight, but his grandmother had said this was as few guests as he could possibly have.

His bride-to-be had smiled at Millicent's insistence and laughingly agreed, and he had to admit he smiled every time he thought of the genuine warmth between the two women in his life.

As for the wedding—he just wished they'd get to the part where he could kiss the bride.

The music changed to the entrance waltz, thank the stars for that, he thought as he turned eagerly to follow the golden road to find a glimpse of the woman he loved.

Instead, Ginny floated down the carpet in some silky, very flattering gold dress, pushing the pram with the two boys in matching suits to his. His grandmother had had the tiny suits made, which he thought ridiculous for babies six months old, but Lisandra had agreed, so he had too.

Bastian was scowling, something he seemed to enjoy, and Bennett looked extremely interested in the many faces they passed.

Ginny came to a stop a little to his right, manoeuvred the pram so the page boys were sitting up to look at the congregation, and then the music swelled.

Ahh, there she was. His eyes misted for a moment, grew intensely focussed as his Lisandra, his love, his beautiful wife-to-be met his eyes and smiled with all the love he still couldn't believe she gifted him.

She stood tall, slim like a reed, her beautiful ivory gown showing glimpses of her tanned shoulders as it fell past her long legs to sweep the carpet and splay out behind her.

She floated towards him. The deep sleeves hung like bells over her hands and the bouquet of gold and bronze flowers highlighted her blonde hair as it floated free under the veil he was so desperate to lift. Malachi's heart seemed to swell in his chest as he watched her come to him. He so adored her.

* * *

Lisandra gazed down the golden length of the carpet to the man of her dreams. Malachi Madden had changed her life, had shown her kindness and generosity she'd never seen before, but most of all his selfless love had made her melt with matching joy. His eyes, his beautiful hazel eyes, cherished her, and she stepped faster as she closed the distance between them.

Unconsciously, regardless of the protocol, he stepped towards her, his hand lifted and turned to take hers as if he couldn't wait to clasp them together.

'My love,' he breathed, and she felt his long fingers close over hers. He lifted her hand to his lips and kissed her knuckles.

Together they turned and closed the distance to the celebrant, who smiled at them. Finally, the time-worn words began to flow softly like a breeze around them and two little boys cooed in their pram.

When the vows were made and Malachi had thoroughly kissed the bride, they stood together in front of the small crowd. The applause rose and her cheeks warmed. Malachi's hand was tight over hers, and she felt as if her heart would burst with happiness as they walked the length of the carpet to greet their well-wishers.

'You got the girl, Malachi,' his friend said.

'Your turn now, Simon,' Malachi replied as he shook his best man's hand.

* * * * *

Reunited With The Children's Doc
Susan Carlisle

MILLS & BOON

Susan Carlisle's love affair with books began when she made a bad grade in mathematics. Not allowed to watch TV until the grade had improved, she filled her time with books. Turning her love of reading into a love for writing romance, she pens hot medicals. She loves castles, travelling, afternoon tea, reading voraciously and hearing from her readers. Join her newsletter at susancarlisle.com.

Visit the Author Profile page at millsandboon.com.au for more titles.

Dear Reader,

Children's hospitals are by nature negative places, but so many positives can be found there—smiles, resiliency and the love of life. I hope you find all of those and more in this book. With doctors like Dylan and Marcy, a patient has every chance to live a long, happy life.

Having spent a lot of time in a children's hospital with my son, I've seen the amazing things that can happen. Through medicine, love and hope, the unthinkable can transpire, even finding the love of your life as my characters did.

I hope you enjoy this second book in the Atlanta Children's Hospital series.

I love to hear from my readers. You can reach me at www.susancarlisle.com.

Happy reading,

Susan

DEDICATION

To Josie
The granddaughter of my heart.

CHAPTER ONE

"Mornin', Dr. Nelson," said the staff tech of the cancer center as Dylan pushed through the clinic doors.

"Good morning," he called over his shoulder, not slowing down.

"You have company today," the tech returned.

He hesitated a step. "Oh, yeah, I do." As lead pediatric oncologist at Atlanta Children's Hospital, he had patients waiting, along with a full schedule. And now a researcher was here to do a new drug trial. He entered the Infusion Room and pulled up short. Aliza, one of his sweetest and sickest patients, was talking to a slim woman with her back to him. His eyes narrowed and his lips tightened. Something about the woman sitting on a rolling stool looked familiar.

Dylan's heart squeezed when Aliza laughed

and smiled. Both were rare. For the stranger to draw them from Aliza shocked him. He continued to watch as the woman worked with the port in the child's chest and carried a conversation in the calmest of manners.

Who was this winning over his most difficult patient and undertaking the care that he or one of his nurses should provide? It had taken him months to get Aliza to trust him and this woman had already achieved it. What kind of miracle worker was she?

He approached.

Aliza's mother looked at him. "Hi, Dr. Nelson."

The woman turned and Dylan's footsteps faltered. *Marcy.*

The galloping of his heart had nothing to do with racing up the stairs. Dylan had never expected to see Marcy Wingard again, yet after all these years she'd turned up in his department. He'd thought of her many times during the fifteen years since he'd last seen her. Had compared more than one woman to her.

His startled gaze locked with her wide-eyed one. Yes, the same green eyes but with a wariness in them he'd not seen before. The shock he felt matched the look on her face.

"Dylan?" Circles of pink graced her cheeks. "Uh… Dr. Nelson?"

"Yes."

She glanced at the girl and mother. "I'm Dr. Montgomery. I was told you'd be coming in. I was just telling Aliza and her mother here about how I got lost on the way to the hospital this morning."

Montgomery? Oh, yeah. She must have married. "Sounds like I need to hear that story sometime." He forced his attention back to Aliza. "How are you doing this morning?"

"I'm fine." The girl looked at her hands.

Dylan crouched on his heels beside the girl's lounge chair, getting to her eye level. "So what's going on here?" He spoke to the child, noting the thin strands of hair where once there were beautiful yellow ringlets. His words were meant for Marcy. He was protective of his patients. Dylan didn't want other doctors interfering with them unless he was present. He needed to know what Marcy was really doing there.

He couldn't help but be particular about how his patients were treated or approached. Beau, his boarding school roommate, had developed cancer while they were in school. His friend's experience had influenced Dylan's style of care. He'd heard Beau's complaints about how he was treated and taken them to heart. Dylan vowed early in his career not to be the doctor who didn't take time to get to know his patients and listen to them. Even to this day he heard Beau's voice in his head when he first met a patient. Thankful Beau had survived to talk to Dylan regularly over the phone.

"We were just getting acquainted," Marcy said.

Dylan stood then spoke to Aliza and her mother, who sat beside her daughter. "If you'll excuse us, I'd like to speak to... Dr. Montgomery for a moment."

"Sure," Aliza's mother said.

He stepped to the nurses' desk and Marcy followed. He'd not seen her since college. They'd been lab partners their senior year of undergrad and he would've liked for them to have been more. To his deep disappointment, he'd been forced to accept nothing was going to happen between them.

"Uh... Marcy it's good to see you." He cleared his throat. "What a surprise."

"For me as well." Her words sounded more formal than necessary for old friends. At one time they had been friends. Good friends.

Marcy looked the same, just a few years older. She'd aged well. She was the one that had gotten away. He'd had his fair share of women since...he'd even been engaged and deep into wedding plans when his fiancée had broken it off. It still hurt.

"Hello, Dylan. I had no idea you were working here." She touched her hair as if checking to see if it was in place. The Marcy he'd known had worn it loose, wild and free unless she had to tie it back for their work in the lab.

He remembered all too well the brush of her long chestnut-colored hair against his cheek as they leaned over a notebook, working on an experiment. Today it was shorter. It was pulled tightly back and secured at the nape of her neck. He preferred it unbound.

More often than he wished to admit, Marcy had traveled through his mind when he least expected it. He'd checked social media a few times to see if he could find her, just to see what she was doing, but hadn't found anything but professional information.

"So you're the research doctor I was told to expect."

"Yes, that's me. Sorry I didn't mention that sooner. I was just surprised to see you."

"Me too."

"Dr. Nelson, would you please come check this port?" a nurse asked from nearby.

"Marcy, if you'd excuse me. I need to see about this." He turned, almost grateful for the chance to collect himself.

"May I come with you? I need to get to know your patients. After all I'll be working with them for the next few weeks."

"Sure. I'll introduce you." At least he couldn't fault her bedside manner with Aliza. If she was that good with all his patients, he could let his guard down. He shielded them where he could. They were already under stress and fearful, and not feeling well from medicine that should be helping them. Dylan pulled a stool near his patient's lounge chair and sat. "Hi, Lucy. How're you doing today?"

The girl smiled.

Dylan always enjoyed seeing that expression because too often his patients didn't feel like giving him a smile. "Nurse Racheal says I need to have a look at your port." He glanced toward Marcy. "Do you mind if my friend Dr. Montgomery has a look too?"

"It's okay," the girl said.

Marcy moved so she stood at his shoulder. "Lucy, will you pull your T-shirt out of the

way for me? I promise this won't take long."
Dylan helped the girl adjust her shirt so he
could see the port clearly just below her left
shoulder. He searched for redness around the
site.

"I've never seen an implantable venous access port placed like that." Marcy's voice held
a tone of disapproval.

Dylan ignored her. Now wasn't time to
discuss that. Especially in front of a patient.
"Lucy, I'm going to need to touch your skin
around the port. You tell me if it hurts." He
pressed his fingertips against the girl's skin,
moving in a clockwise motion. Dylan made
it almost all the way around before the girl
winced.

"It hurts there." Lucy gave a squeak of an
answer.

"I think we should take a closer look in the
lab." He gave Lucy a reassuring smile. "Why
don't I meet you in the port lab in a few minutes? I'll take this port out and in a few weeks
we'll place another."

Mrs. Baker, Lucy's mother sagged. "You
mean we'll have to wait to get this started?"

"Yes, I know it seems like a setback but it's
only for a few weeks." Dylan continued, "Lucy's going to be fine. You wait right here, and

I'll send someone to get you when I'm ready." He patted the girl on the shoulder.

He sensed Marcy's rigid posture as she followed him across the open room toward the port lab.

When they reached the lab and were out of hearing from everyone else, Marcy asked, "Why was the port put in that way?"

Dylan faced her. "Because I didn't do it. It was done across town at another hospital. Lucy became unhappy there and her mother brought her here. She didn't want to take the port out if we didn't have to. Lucy had already been through enough trauma. I agreed but warned them this might happen."

"So what're you thinking?"

"That it might be an infection brewing." His mouth tightened.

"I saw the small area of redness." Marcy still had sharp eyes. "Could be tunnel cellulitis in the superior vena cava?"

"Maybe but I don't think so. The situation is rare and that would be more so. We'll pull it out and try antibiotics then see. If you want to be in on the procedure you need to gown up."

Fifteen minutes later Marcy stood like a statue beside him. An uneasiness he couldn't describe circled her. Lucy and her mother sat in chairs against the wall, neither of them looking happy.

His attention returned to his patient. "I hate to say it, but I think you're gonna need to have a new port," he said to the girl then looked at her mother. Tears fell from Lucy's eyes. "I don't like it any better than you do but it'd be worse if we put medicine in and it didn't go where we need it to. Trust us. We'll take care of it."

The mother nodded. "We do trust you to know what's best."

Dylan smiled. "I hope we never abuse that trust."

"Lucy," Dylan said, "why don't you get up on the table here. I'll need you to lie down." To the mother he said, "Michelle, I'm going to have you kiss Lucy then wait for her outside in the waiting room. This will only take a few minutes."

The girl scrambled up on the exam table using the footstool. Michelle kissed and hugged her. "I'll call your dad and tell him to pick up some ice cream on the way home. I think we'll both deserve it."

"Chocolate syrup too?" Lucy asked, the fear still hanging in her voice.

Her mother gave her a weak smile. "Chocolate syrup too."

"I may need to get an invite to that." Dylan came to stand beside the bed.

"You're welcome anytime," Michelle said over her shoulder as she left the room.

Lucy lay on the table in the port lab with tears in her eyes. Marcy seemed to be having much the same reaction but was covering it better.

Two nurses entered wearing the same sterile cover-ups.

Dylan smiled down at Lucy. "Dr. Montgomery will be here with me today, okay?"

The girl nodded. "It's okay."

Marcy stepped to the table. "Would you like me to hold your hand? I know that always helps me." She offered her hand, and Lucy took it.

Marcy gave the child a reassuring smile. "If it hurts just squeeze my hand."

Lucy nodded.

Dylan liked the care Marcy gave the child. As if Marcy had been through this before. "This shouldn't take long but I'm going to make you a little sleepy first."

"Just like last time?"

"Just like last time." Dylan prepared the

pain medicine. He checked around the port after the nurses had removed the protective covering, and then glanced at Marcy. Her complete attention remained on the girl as if willing her not to have any pain.

He was impressed. Most research doctors spend so much time in the lab they forget how to have empathy for a patient. Apparently not Marcy. She was great with them. Marcy had been easy to be around in college. Her disposition served her well in these situations.

Lucy's eyes drooped.

Clipping the sutures holding the port in place, he asked, "Marcy, would you hold this open while I pull the port out?"

She nodded, letting go of Lucy's hand. Taking the long surgical tweezers, she held it steady. He gently pulled the nickel-size port out from under Lucy's skin along with the catheter. Quickly one of the nurses applied a bandage and pressure to the opening. Marcy placed the instrument in a dish the other nurse held. Moments later a nurse applied butterfly strips and a bandage to Lucy's chest.

"How long before she can have another port put in?" Marcy asked.

"At least three weeks"

She winced. "Can't you do it sooner? The wait will be horrible and her parents will be in a panic at the delay. How could this happen?"

"Take it easy, Marcy. We must have patience here. This doesn't happen often, but I want to give the antibiotics time to work. I'll place the next port below this one." He spoke to one of the nurses, "Would you tell her mother she can come sit with Lucy until she wakes. After that she can go. I'd like to see Lucy back on Thursday."

"I'll take care of it." The nurse left the room.

A noise from the area of the Infusion Room grew into rhythmic rapping. A voice sang out while the others harmonized. Marcy asked, "What's going on?"

Dylan stripped out of his protective covering and she followed his lead. They left the room to stand in the infusion area. A young dark-skinned teenage boy led a group of other patients around the same age all singing and taking a part. Their harmonizing sounded wonderful. They finished the song with a slap of their hands against the loungers they all lay on. The smiles were contagious. The staff and parents clapped.

"They're good," Marcy said.

Dylan grinned. "Yeah, until they make up one about you. Now I have to interrupt them to check on their chemo, then I have clinic this afternoon. You're welcome to join me. It would be a good chance for you to review charts and put faces to patients."

"I'd liked that. I'll review what charts I can and start determining canadines for the trial on Monday."

"Sounds like a plan."

Marcy moved on into the room behind Dylan. She couldn't have been more surprised to learn he was the head of the cancer clinic where she was doing her trial. She would never have thought in a million years they'd both become oncology doctors. Life had a way of taking you down roads you hadn't thought possible. She knew that better than most.

Dylan walked toward the patient who'd sat to the right of Lucy. He turned to Marcy. "Do you mind waiting here a moment? Dan is a particularly sensitive patient. This is stressful for him, and I don't want him upset. I'll check with him first, then introduce you."

Marcy nodded. She understood. Her son,

Toby, hadn't always welcomed new faces especially at his young age. Dylan's dark chocolate gaze regarded her before he gave her a slight nod.

Dan sat in the first tan cushioned lounge chair next to a window. An IV pole stood beside his bed and a small individual TV hung on the wall.

Dylan rolled up a stool beside the patient. "How're you doing today, Dan?"

"I am okay."

"Just okay?" Dylan pulled his stethoscope from around his neck.

He glanced back to where Marcy stood looking at the charting pad. Dylan tilted his head toward her. "That's Dr. Montgomery. She's going to be helping us here for a few weeks. She'd like to meet you. I think you'll like her. Would it be okay if she joined us?"

The ten-year-old boy studied Marcy for a moment then nodded his agreement. Would Dylan have turned her away if the boy had said no? She felt like he would have. He acted protective of his patients. She liked that. It showed he cared. Toby's doctor had the same boundaries. It was nice to know a doctor thought of his patients first and treated them as people.

Dylan waved her over with a small motion of his fingers. "Dan, I'd like you to meet Dr. Montgomery."

"Hello Dan." Marcy smiled as her chest tightened. Toby would've been about this boy's age if he'd lived. She couldn't help Toby, but she believed she had the answer to giving this child many more years of life.

"Hey," the boy said weakly.

"How're you doing?" Marcy pulled a stool up beside Dylan.

You can do this.

She hadn't expected to have so much interaction with the patients. She'd expected to do medical procedures, not to get to know them as individuals. Dylan knew them all by their first name. How did he handle it when he lost one?

Dylan studied the chemo IV line running through an infusion machine attached to the rolling pole stationed beside the boy's chair. "Dan, don't you usually play a video game?"

The boy quirked his mouth. "They forgot to bring it to me. It's okay. I get tired pretty easy, so I have a hard time not taking a nap."

Marcy blinked. Toby had slept more than normal trying to regain his strength after chemotherapy.

"I'll see that a nurse brings it to you just in case you feel like playing. Maybe we'll try to get a game in." Dylan patted Dan's shoulder. "You only have a few more weeks before this chemo round will be finished. Then you can get back to school."

The boy gave Dylan a sad look. "I hope my friends still remember who I am."

"I'm sure they will," Marcy offered before she thought about speaking.

A warm look flickered in Dylan's eyes before his attention returned to Dan. "Everything looks good. I'll see you next week."

"I'll be here. Mom says I have no choice."

Dylan chuckled. "Moms have a way of making us do what we don't want to."

"Bye, Dan. It was nice to meet you." With a tight chest Marcy joined Dylan as he moved to the next patient. She continued to follow him around the room, seeing all the patients there for the day. Each one climbed to the top of her emotional pile and sat, but she never let on. Instead, she focused on the children and Dylan's interactions with them. To her amazement he knew all their names.

The last patient in the line of chairs was a seventeen-year-old girl. The smile on her face when she saw Dylan said it all. She had a crush on her doctor.

"Hey, Mindy. How're you doing?" Dylan's smile was bright.

The girl's cheeks pinked, and she touched a turban on her head where her hair should have been. "Pretty good."

"That's always nice to hear. We doctors like to know we aren't making our patients too sick. This is Dr. Montgomery. She'll be helping me out for a few weeks. Do you mind if she has a look at you?"

Marcy gave the girl a reassuring smile.

Mindy's smile dimmed. She'd obviously rather have Dylan doing her exam. "Yeah, that's okay."

Marcy took the lead in checking the chemo setup, making sure the infusion level was correct per the chart. "Mindy, I'll need to get your vitals."

She pulled on her faded cloth hospital gown. "Okay. Don't you just love these gowns. So attractive. I'm going to design some cute ones when I get well. So that cancer patients can have something pretty to wear."

Pulling the stethoscope from around her neck, Marcy prepared to listen to Mindy's heart. She'd never thought about hospital wear for patients. They *were* rather drab and ugly. "That sounds like a fine idea."

"I've already started making sketches. Would you like to see them?"

"Sure, I would." Marcy moved on to taking Mindy's respirations and pulse.

Marcy glanced at the teen's mom. She knew the pain in the parent's eyes too well. That hit too close to home. Still, Marcy refused to let her pain show. She had a job to do here, one she planned to do well.

Years ago, she'd been like Mindy's mother. Walking around in constant fear. If she got as personally involved as Dylan, could she continue to hold it together? The next few weeks would tell. After all this time she'd believed that wouldn't be a problem. That she could compartmentalize the patients and the work, remaining unemotionally involved. Dylan's way of dealing with patients certainly wasn't that.

He'd finished up with Mindy's charting then double-checked her chemo flow. "You look good today. I'll see you next week. You don't have many more weeks of this."

"I hope so. This doesn't make for a great senior year."

Dylan smiled and patted her arm. "No, it doesn't but it's necessary."

She curled up her lips. "I don't have to like it."

Dylan chuckled. "No, you don't. With your attitude you should be fine. Be ready for the prom."

"Who's going to want to take me to the prom. I don't even have any hair."

Dylan gave her a reassuring smile. "By then you should have some."

"I hope so." Mindy didn't look encouraged.

"You just wait and see."

Marcy leaned in close as if to share a secret. "I'd believe him. I've known him a long time."

Mindy smiled.

Finished with seeing patients, Dylan asked, "How about getting some lunch with me? We can catch up."

She shook her head. "I wish I could, but I have some calls to make and a few details to review before I start this trial."

"Okay." She sensed his disappointment as his lips tightened. "Maybe later, then. I'll meet you here in an hour."

"I'll be here." She went to the small closet she had been given to serve as an office.

It had been nice to learn that Dylan worked at Atlanta Children's. Nervous and out of her element with doing actual work with patients—and more disturbing, children with cancer—she couldn't help but be pleased to see a friendly face.

Still as good-looking as she remembered, his shoulders were broader and sturdier than they had been in his youth. He seemed taller as well. What hadn't changed was his ready smile. It might be the one thing she'd missed most about him.

It had already taken great emotional fortitude for her to come here. If she hadn't taken this chance, then the drug she'd been working on for years might not see its way to helping children. She'd devoted her days, many nights and holidays to work. This drug must be successful. With it might come a promotion which would give her updated equipment, along with a chance to focus on cancer advancements in the future.

Later, as she walked down the hall, she saw Dylan standing beside the doors of the Infusion Room. She blinked. He was certainly tall, dark and handsome. Where had that thought come from? She'd not noticed a man in years. How could she? She'd rarely left the lab.

His head tilted a moment as if questioning her reaction before his look turned serious. "The clinic is located in the building across the road." They started walking. "I've not even had a chance to ask you how you've been. I can't get over you being here."

"I've been good." She wasn't about to tell him she'd lost a child to cancer or had a failed marriage. "And just as surprised to see you."

"You were great this morning with the kids. I was wondering how much experience you have with clinic work?"

She shrugged. "Not much really. You know how we lab people are—we don't come out much." Her in particular. Work had become her life. Her life saver. "Why?"

"I know this is going to sound controlling, but I still have to say it." Dylan took a deep breath. "Most of the patients we'll be seeing in a few minutes are scared. Their parents are as well. Adding another stranger in their life, asking them to do something they're even more insecure about, might tip them over emotionally."

"I understand." She didn't need to be told

that. She remembered her fear as a parent too well.

"Also try to speak at their level. Catheter is a *tube*. Superior vena cava is an *artery in the neck*. No fancy medical talk."

"I have no intentions of upsetting your patients, but I do need to have contact with them to complete my research. It's time sensitive. At some point I'll need to ask them questions. I don't have the time to ask you for permission before every interaction I have with a patient."

He stopped, giving her his full attention. "I understand that. I just want you to hedge on the side of caution."

"Then there's no problem." She held his look.

"What I'm saying is, this needs to be all gently and calmly presented." He started walking again.

She hurried to keep pace with him. "Cancer is a nasty disease that doesn't wait on us to be nice. We must eradicate it. What I learn from your patients can save others."

"I'm interested in saving *these* patients and doing it without creating more emotional scars. Like fearing life."

Emotional scars she could understand well.

Her scar tissue was thick. "I promise to follow your lead." She would until she couldn't.
Her work was important too. The drug must
be tested so that these children could have
the chance to live when others hadn't. Others like Toby.

CHAPTER TWO

A FEW MINUTES later Marcy followed Dylan down a hallway with small exam rooms on each side. A nurse waited for them in front of the first closed door.

Dylan took the tech pad from her and she returned to the nurses' desk.

Marcy watched the woman in scrubs leave. "The dress around here is more casual than I expected."

"We do that on purpose. White coat syndrome is a real thing, you know. We never wear them."

"I'll keep that in mind. I'm glad I didn't bring mine. It's in the back of the closet at home."

"Where is home?" Dylan glanced at her.

"Cincinnati."

"I like the park down by the river." He went back to looking at the pad.

"I've heard it's nice." She'd never been. All her time was spent in the lab or at home sleeping.

He handed the tech pad to her. The patient Kristen Moore had been referred from a hospital a couple of hours away.

He moved into the exam room. The girl and her parents wore a terrified look.

Marcy had to admire Dylan for facing people almost daily who expect bad news. She'd been one of those people at one time. She couldn't do what Dylan did every day. It took a special person to show that compassion while giving bad news.

Dylan had always been that type of personality. He was supersmart and he'd made their long, difficult labs fun. She'd looked forward to going to the lab because of him. In an odd way he was one of the reasons she'd gone into research. He seemed to have retained his warm, easygoing nature but there was a hardness of maturity about him now. The only time she hadn't seen the humor back then was when he talked of his family.

Two months of labs passed before he mentioned either of his parents. She chattered about hers all the time. She was from a tight family. Even then she'd picked up on Dylan's loneliness where his family were concerned. He said he wouldn't be going home for the holidays because they lived too far away. They were missionaries in some South American country. She'd been tempted to invite him home with her but knew Josh wouldn't like that idea at all.

Marcy's lips thinned. She and Josh had been high school sweethearts, and their families were friends. When she and Josh got old enough, their mothers had planned their future: college for them both, then he would go to work while she went to med school. They would buy a house and have two children, a boy and a girl. She'd made promises to Josh even when there was a suggestion of interest in Dylan.

After all, she couldn't ruin everyone's plans just for a date. She didn't let it get out of hand with Dylan because Josh had been her future. More than once she asked herself "what if" where Dylan was concerned but she'd had Josh. She'd remained true to him.

Dylan's voice brought Marcy out of her reverie. "I'm Dr. Nelson. How're you feeling today? I see you live in Columbus. Are you a Georgia or Auburn fan?"

"Auburn of course. War Eagle!"

Dylan laughed. A deep masculine sound that warmed her, made her want to join him in his humor. "Well, I now know where you stand."

Marcy had no idea what they were talking about, but the girl's face lit up so that was all that mattered.

"Do you mind if I listen to your heart?" Dylan went through his routine of checking heart and respirations. Then with gentle fingertips he checked the glands in her neck. Marcy watched his face. She saw a slight tightening of his mouth. "This is Dr. Montgomery. May she have a look?"

The girl nodded agreement.

Marcy touched the girl's neck in the same area as Dylan. She felt what he must have. A lump behind her ear. Why couldn't she have done that with Toby?

Her gaze met Dylan's. He gave a slight nod then asked the girl, "How much ice cream can you eat?"

Marcy gave him an odd look. What did that have to do with the situation?

"A lot."

"Good. I'm glad to hear it. Tonight, here at the hospital, we're giving away all the ice cream you can eat. I need to have you stay here and help us eat it. Would that be all right?"

The girl looked at her parents. They watched Dylan with less enthusiasm. "Can I?"

Before the parents could answer Dylan said gently, "Kristen will need to come in for some tests."

A stricken look showed on their faces as their worst fear became reality. Marcy's heart went out to them.

"Someone'll come in to show you where to go." Dylan made some notes on the pad then smiled at the girl. "I'll want to know tomorrow how much of that ice cream you ate."

A few minutes later Marcy followed him out of the room. "That was well done, Dr. Nelson. You had her thinking about ice cream instead of being poked and prodded."

"I'd say thank you, but I hate the thought of the road the girl has ahead of her."

"Then why did you go into oncology?"

"Because I had a friend in boarding school who had cancer. I remember how scared he was. He told me what it was like. How he hated the way doctors treated him like an experiment all the time. That he wanted them to see him as a person. Talk to him so he could understand, not speak over his head.

And most of all tell him the truth. When I started this work, I promised myself I'd remember his words."

"How's he doing now?"

"Great. He has a wife and family. Still, having cancer changed his life."

"Cancer will do that." She knew too well.

Dylan gave her a questioning look. Had he heard in that statement more than she wanted to share? He started toward the next exam room. "Why did you decide to go into cancer research?"

"For the same reason as you. To help children." What she didn't say was that these days it was to redeem herself for the past, to keep the guilt at bay. "And for their parents. They suffer too."

"They do. Sometimes more than the patients." The pain he'd seen was evident in his voice.

They spent the rest of the afternoon seeing patients. Many had to have lab work and return in three to six months. Some were patients who recovered from cancer and were returning for checkups. Marcy couldn't deny she was wrung out afterward. She still needed to get to her tiny office and start working on which patients would qualify for the trial, which included checking her emails and a call to her lab.

"Do you have plans this weekend? I feel as if I should welcome you to Atlanta. Take you to dinner or something. After all, we're old friends," Dylan said as they were walking back to the hospital.

"I wish I could, but I have a lot of work to do. Especially after meeting patients today."

"Okay, but you know the old saying all work and no play or meals makes for a dull doctor."

Marcy couldn't help but smile. "I'm not sure that's how it goes but I get your meaning. But I still have work to do."

A few minutes later she entered and closed the office door behind her. She looked at her shaking hands. Taking in a couple of deep breaths, she brought her nerves under control. With each new patient it had become more difficult for her to keep her emotions behind a curtain. Dylan would have been confused if she'd broken down in tears. She had no idea venturing outside of the lab would be so difficult emotionally, yet as the afternoon progressed her nerves eased and her confidence increased. Here she understood the parents and patients.

If she wanted this research to be successful, she had to see it through. This was not only her chance for promotion, but she believed TM13 would help children live. She would be in town for six weeks but believed with three months of good solid numbers she could get the Food and Drug Administration's approval.

Monday morning, Dylan took the back way to his office in the cancer center. Over the weekend he'd pondered the return of Marcy to his life as he did chores, worked on his car and watched a couple of football games. She'd broken his heart years before, but she'd never known it.

He'd learned early in life to cover his emotions. Few knew how much he missed his family while he was in boarding school, or how much he suffered over Beau having cancer. By the time he met Marcy he'd mastered not letting anyone know his true feelings. Not that she would have been interested since she'd had a boyfriend. For all he knew now she had a husband and children waiting for her to come home.

None of that was his business anyway. They were colleagues, that was all. Yet he couldn't help being curious about her life since they'd last seen each other. Couldn't help finding her attractive still.

He was in his office catching up on a few emails and reviewing his patient list when a knock at his door drew his attention.

"Hey," Marcy said.

Today she wore a simple blouse, pants that hugged her slim hips and flat shoes, not her power suit of the other day. He liked this more relaxed version better. She looked approachable and fragile, but she was thin, too thin really.

She continued to stand in the doorway. "Sorry to bother you."

"No bother. You're here early. How can I help?"

"I just have a few questions about some of your patients."

He waved a hand toward the lone chair in front of his desk. "What do you want to know?"

She took a seat and swiped open her tech pad. "Tell me about Roger Harris. He seems like a good candidate."

"Yes, I believe he would be. He's just starting chemo."

She made a note on her pad. "What about Rena McCray?"

"I don't think so." Dylan clasped his hands and rested his chin on his fingertips. "This is her second round. She isn't reacting well to the treatment."

"Then she might just benefit from TM13."

He gave that thought. "I'll review her latest labs and let you know."

"Robert Neels."

"Robby." He corrected. "He's the guy who led the rap."

"Oh, I know who he is now." She looked up at Dylan. "Robby. He seems on the cusp of recovery, but his labs weren't good last time."

"No, they weren't. How many of these do you have?"

"I managed to get through twenty-three this morning." Marcy looked at her pad again.

Dylan pushed back from his desk. "Have you been here all weekend working?"

"Most of it. I wanted to get started on this trial."

His eyes narrowed in concern. "Is there some urgency that requires you to work all weekend and be here so early?"

"Just patients like that beautiful girl going through chemo. It amazes me she could still talk about designing clothes as sick as she's been. That she still has dreams while having chemo and losing all her hair. I think TM13 can help her."

"I already have a very high success rate." Dylan couldn't help but defend his program.

"I'm aware of your success. But I'm also aware of the struggle."

He nodded solemnly, conscious of something in her tone he couldn't quite identify. "That's true. You're just not used to working with the patients. It's easy to think of cancer in the abstract when you're in a lab poking around with test tubes but it gets personal when you deal with patients. Especially when they're children."

"I understand you have clinic again this afternoon."

"I do."

Her eyelids flicked up. "I'll be there. I'll be ready to start the new medicine trial as soon as we have all the agreements."

Dylan leaned back in his chair. "We can discuss it with the parents as we work through patients today."

Marcy turned off the pad. "Great. I'll review all their charts tonight."

Dylan's brows came together but he said

nothing. He believed in working hard but she was taking it to an entirely different level.

She looked at him. "Should I meet you at the clinic?"

"Why don't I come get you? We need to go to a different area today. What hole did they stick you in and called it an office?"

Marcy looked around his space. "The room off the conference room."

His eyes went wide with disbelief. "You mean the closet? Surely there's some place better than that."

"I'm making it work. It's better than nothing. It's nothing like your palatial office."

He huffed and then grinned. His office was functional at best, but it was large. "Finally, the Marcy I remember. Able to put me in my place." Oddly he liked that familiar teasing part of Marcy. Too much.

But why didn't that humor reach her eyes? The sparkle and delight she'd once had for life had dimmed. He'd viewed those emotions clearly on their graduation day. He only attended the ceremony so he could see her one last time. He had no family attending so he thought to share part of the day with her.

He'd found Marcy in the crowd of students wearing black robes and hurried in her direction. Just before he reached her, Marcy broke away from the group and ran into the arms of a man who had walked up. It had to be the boyfriend she'd told him about when he'd dared to ask her out. Dylan didn't bother to speak, and instead he melted into the crowd.

It wasn't her fault he'd hurt so much that day, but one thing was for sure, he wouldn't let her do that to him again.

Two days later, at a quick knock on her door, Marcy looked up to see Dylan. He stuck his head inside the supply closet turned office. "It's lunchtime. Want to…" The pleasant look left his face and was replaced with a comic look of horror. "This place is awful. How do you get any work done?"

"It's not so bad."

"You have a broad idea of bad."

Marcy chuckled. "What were you saying about something to eat?"

"I wanted to see if you would like to join me in the cafeteria."

She had to admit she was hungry. And curious about Dylan's life since college too. Was he married? She hadn't heard him say anything about a family. She'd always thought he was the type who would want a family.

Dylan surveyed the space with shelves on both sides. "You need more room than this."

"This was all that was available."

He huffed. "I have an idea. I don't use my office much. You're welcome to share mine. At least you wouldn't have to worry about people disturbing you to get to office supplies."

"I can't take your office." Marcy's denial was quick.

"You won't be. Anyway, you'll only be here for a little while. I insist."

Sharing an office with Dylan didn't sound like a good idea but at least she wouldn't be constantly disturbed. "I guess so. Since you insist."

Dylan shrugged. "Okay. We'll get it done first chance we get. You ready for some food?"

She gave him a weak smile. "If I remember correctly, you thought of little more than food when we were in college."

He sobered. "I thought of other things. But I do like a good meal." A grin popped out again.

She watched Dylan settle into an orange plastic utilitarian chair across the metal table from her in the cafeteria. Other staff dressed in surgical scrubs and office wear came and went around them.

"I can't believe that after all these years you show up in my hospital. And of all places my department. What have you been doing all this time?" Dylan sounded interested, instead of interrogative.

"Same as you, I'm sure. Medical school, fellowship and I got a job." She forked a piece of lettuce.

"Where did you go to medical school?" He took a bite out of his sandwich.

"Duke."

Dylan brows rose. "Impressive. They're doing great work there."

"They are." Marcy relaxed and took a forkful of her salad.

"Did you like living in North Carolina?"

It had been the perfect place for Josh to get a job with all the high-tech business in the area while she went to medical school. It was even a great place to raise a family. She never planned to return. After she finished chewing, she said, "I did. Enough about me. How about you? Where did you get your medical training?"

"NYU."

"That's impressive too." She smiled. He'd

been smart enough in college to get into any medical school he wished. "Who would have thought that two kids in a lab class in a small midwestern college would have both become doctors and work in the cancer field?"

"It's a small world." He continued to eat his sandwich. "What made you go into research?"

"I just always liked lab work. Cancer needs to be eradicated." The words were as flat and dry as a Texas dirt road in the summer. She didn't dare let the emotion she felt show, or she might fall apart.

"Always liked? I must be remembering wrong. You dreaded labs in college."

"Let's just say I learned to appreciate them." Because of him. She looked forward to going to lab because she had a chance to see Dylan. Almost engaged to Josh, she shouldn't have had those thoughts, but she had.

"I always saw you as someone who liked to be around people. I thought you would have gravitated toward patients." He watched her closely.

"I'm not as good with them as you are. You always had a way of making people feel valued even back then."

Dylan grinned. "You made lab my favorite class. We had a good time."

She smiled. It had been too long since she thought of those carefree days. The days before...

"Yes, we did."

He nodded. "After med school you joined the private lab company CanMed? Or was there a stop in between?"

Marcy pushed her salad away half-finished. "CanMed hired me straight out of medical school." She'd begged for the job. The desire to help find the cure to cancer burned in her, drove her.

He leaned back in his chair. "And that's what brings you to my door."

"Yes. Your hospital agreed to be a part of the TM13 trial."

He took a sip of his drink. "Which I understand is a new regime with fewer side effects and better outcomes."

Her gaze rose to meet his. She couldn't help the pride in her voice as she said, "Yes. My team developed it."

"Impressive." Dylan grinned.

"We've had outstanding success in the lab. I'm hoping for the same or better results in actual use."

He swallowed the bite. "I hope that's what we see also."

"I'm sure you do. I've seen how important your patients are to you." She met his eyes, noticing again the warmth in the dark chocolate depths.

"I'm sorry if I've been rough on you. I'd like to say I'll mellow some, but you'd be safer with just learning to deal with me. I'm protective and don't apologize for it."

She pursed her lips and nodded. "That's a positive attribute, but I'll admit it takes some getting used to."

He laughed. Loud enough to attract the attention of those around them. "Now, there's another part of the Marcy I remember. She didn't mind saying what she thought. Enough about work. Tell me, did you end up marrying that guy you were dating in college?"

The abrupt change in topic took her by surprise for a moment. "Yes, we were married for five years. And divorced years ago."

"I'm sorry to hear that." He sounded sincere.

Her lips thinned. "Those things happen."

His look met hers. "You were devoted to him when we were in college."

Her gaze dropped to her food tray. "Yeah, but life happens."

Dylan gave her a long studying look that made her squirm. She closed the preprepared salad plastic container and stared back at him. "How about you, Dr. Nelson. Is there a wife or someone special in your life?"

"Nope. I've had a couple of close calls but never made it down the aisle."

"I'm sorry to hear that, I'm sure they were too."

He chuckled. "I think it was more like they got away clean."

"That couldn't be true." It was hard to believe he hadn't been snatched up.

"Let's just say they wanted to be married to a doctor more for social reasons than because they cared about me. They expected me to be more into social engagements than my work."

"You never said anything about being interested in working with children when we were in college. But now I think about it I'm not surprised." She crossed her arms on the table, examining him as if seeing him for the first time. His easy charm and cheeky sense of humor were clear assets in the field he'd chosen to specialize in.

"Are you saying I acted like a child?" He grinned.

Marcy shook her head. "You're not going to pull me into that discussion. How did you end up here?"

"After I finished med school, I did my fellowship here and stayed."

"So you're an important part of what makes the cancer program here so good?"

He shrugged. "I guess so. But it's really the children and their parents who are the stars."

Marcy didn't feel like a star. She felt like a failure. Maybe when TM13 showed what she believed it would, that would change. That was her single focus. "We better get back to work. I have a meeting to prepare for."

CHAPTER THREE

THE NEXT DAY Dylan entered the clinic exam room followed by Marcy. "Hi, Lucy. How're you feeling?"

The girl looked at her mother then said so low he almost couldn't hear her, "Fine."

"That's good to hear. I forgot to ask the other day, do you have a dog?"

"Yes."

"You do?" Dylan's voice rose an octave.

The girl nodded.

"Is he brown or black? I've been thinking about getting a black dog but I'm not sure that's the right color."

"Mine is brown and white. His name is Rusty."

Dylan smiled. "I like that name. Does he have a rusty color?"

Lucy nodded.

"Maybe if I get a black dog, I'll name him Blackie. What do you think about that?"

Lucy brightened. "Blackie would be a good name."

He glanced a Marcy. She wore a slight smile on her lips.

"I think so too." Dylan turned serious. "Now that you've helped me with a new dog, may I have a look at where I took out the port?"

"Okay."

"Do you mind sitting on the exam table?" Dylan placed his hand on the cushioned table.

Lucy shook her head and climbed up to sit with her legs swinging over the side.

"Now I'd like you to pull your shirt up so that I can see where the port was."

The girl did as he asked. As he stepped closer, Marcy moved beside him. "The site looks good. Healing well. The antibiotics are working." He shifted.

Marcy took the spot. "May I touch, Lucy?" She nodded.

Marcy pulled a plastic glove out of the box on the wall then pulled it on. "You tell me if I hurt you." Marcy pushed around the area.

Lucy had no reaction.

Marcy stepped back, giving him a look of satisfaction.

Dylan couldn't help but be pleased and he'd really done nothing. "Mrs. Baker, Dr. Montgomery and I would like to discuss a new drug that we'd like to try on Lucy when she starts her treatment at the end of next week."

The mother sat straighter. "I thought it would be another two weeks?"

"I believed so too, but Lucy's port area is looking well enough that I think we can do it a few days earlier," Dylan explained, gesturing to Marcy.

She sat on a chair beside Mrs. Baker. "I'm a research doctor, and I've developed a new drug. I believe that it can help Lucy. I'd like to enroll her in my trial. We've had great success in the lab and I think Lucy can benefit from the drug."

Mrs. Baker looked unconvinced. "I don't know... Lucy has already had a port in. Changed hospitals. Now the infection and port removal. If I let her into this trial, what if something goes wrong. She can't take it. Her father and I can't either."

Marcy put her hand over Mrs. Baker's. "I know how you feel. You feel like you've lost control. That you don't know enough to make an informed decision. That people who you don't know are telling you to let your child be a guinea pig. That if the medicine doesn't work, then they can walk away but you are left with..." Marcy glanced at Lucy. "You have my word that I'll be there the entire way with you. I'll even give you my private number if you need to talk. That's how strongly I feel about this medicine."

Dylan watched enthralled with Marcy's compassion. For once he saw a glimmer of the girl he'd known. The one who could give as good as she got when pushed into a corner. Dylan looked at her thoughtfully. She spoke as if she'd experienced the same feelings. Had she? He had no right to know, but he couldn't help but be intrigued.

Mrs. Baker looked at Lucy. "Let me talk to my husband."

Marcy nodded. "You should. But don't take too long deciding." She squeezed Mrs. Baker's hand then stood.

Lucy's mother turned to him. "I agree with Dr. Montgomery. I think the best move is to put Lucy in the trial," he said, helping the girl off the exam table.

Lucy went to her mother, who gathered the little girl in her arms. Mrs. Baker said tearfully, "I understand. I just want Lucy to get better."

"That's what we want as well," Marcy said.

"Please let us know in the next day or so what you and Lucy's father decide."

Dylan let Marcy exit the room ahead of him. In the hall, he said softly, "You did good in there. I think they'll make the right decision and join the trial."

"I hope so."

There was a desperation in those few words that he wasn't sure had to do with Lucy joining the trial or more to do with Lucy's parents being able to live with their decision in the months to come.

On the way out of the hospital parking lot that evening Marcy's eyes narrowed as she looked through her car windshield.

Was that Dylan?

His fists rested on his hips in a fighting stance as he glared at the tire of a well-kept antique car.

She'd not seen him since they'd finished clinic rounds. Her interaction with Lucy's mother had been difficult but refreshing. For the first time since Toby had died, she could see a positive. She could clearly understand the pain and fear the family experienced when making decisions that affected their child's life. It was empowering.

She slowly pulled to a stop and opened her window. "Hey, what's going on?"

"My tire is flat again. Second time in three weeks. Apparently the new one isn't any better than the old one."

"Do you have a service?" She studied the listing car.

"Yes, but I'm not gonna mess with this tonight. The car is safe enough here. I'll get a ride home from security and worry about this tomorrow."

"I can take you home."

"Thanks. I'd appreciate that." Dylan picked up the satchel lying on the ground and climbed into the passenger seat, folding his long legs into the small space.

Marcy couldn't help but be aware of his proximity. She shook off the strange sensation and gave the car one last look before she drove toward the parking lot exit. "I had no idea you were into old cars."

"Yeah, that GTO is my pride and joy. I promised myself as soon as I finished med school I'd get one."

"You drive it every day?"

"I do. At least when it doesn't have a flat tire." She smiled at his disgusted sigh. "You need to make a right out of the parking lot. I don't live far from here." They said nothing for a minute. "Where're you staying while you're here?"

"The company rented a furnished apartment. It isn't bad. And not far from here either. I'm learning my way around. It's no joke about Atlanta traffic."

"It's one of the reasons I bought where I did." Dylan leaned back in the seat.

Marcy could feel Dylan watching her. "What're you thinking? You're staring."

He shifted in the seat but continued to watch her. "Go left at the next light. I was wondering how you became so serious. You used to be a lot more easygoing."

"I don't think when working with cancer patients I need to be jolly."

"The next street to the left and third house on the right. Black shutters." His attention went to the road ahead. "You do have a point there."

Marcy pulled into the paved drive. She didn't know what she expected but she was surprised by Dylan's choice of homes. Located in an older neighborhood on a tree-lined street, it looked nothing like an eligible bachelor's house. The homes on his street were redbrick ranch style with large yards, which were beautifully manicured. Dylan's was no exception. He obviously spent his downtime in the yard, or he had a company maintain it. Somehow, he didn't seem like the type of person that would expect someone else to do his work. At the end of his drive and behind the house was a detached garage.

She pulled to a stop next to the back door.

"Home sweet home," Dylan announced as he unfolded himself from the car. He ducked his head back into the car as he stood with the door open. "Have you had dinner? If not, why don't you come in and we can order a pizza?"

Marcy thought a moment. Why shouldn't she? She and Dylan were old friends. It was better than going home to a place that wasn't even hers. She could admit it. She was lonely. She liked him and used to love spending time with him.

Dylan had a great personality. He worked a high-stress job, but he was easygoing. He seemed to be able to separate his personal life from his life inside the hospital. She found it refreshing to be around.

Her entire future had always been planned

out. If not by her parents, then by her. Maybe that was what had drawn her to Dylan in college. He'd seemed to take life as it came instead of manipulating it to fit a plan, as she had. She'd certainly learned the hard way that didn't work. No matter her plans, Toby hadn't survived. It was time she thought less and acted more.

Dylan said nothing, waiting for her answer.

She looked at him. His brown eyes twinkled with warmth and encouragement. "I guess I could do that."

"Great." He came around the car and helped her out before going to the back door. "Come on in." He led her up a couple of steps and opened the door.

She followed him into a large kitchen area with a small dining table sitting next to a window that looked out onto the backyard. The hardwood floors gleamed. Tan curtains hung at the windows. Modern appliances filled the work area. The space had been renovated yet still held its charm.

It was just the type of home she'd always dreamed of having but never had. She and Josh had never made it out of an apartment. She could imagine how nice it would be to have a cup of tea at the table as she watched the morning come alive. To her the room spoke of life being good.

"Come on through. I'll give you the ten-cent tour even though it's only worth about a penny."

Marcy smiled.

Dylan sat his satchel on the counter dividing the small eating area from the work section of the kitchen. "It's nice to have a date that doesn't expect a five-star restaurant."

"This isn't a date but a friendly meal. You might consider changing the type of women you ask out."

He laughed. "You're right on both accounts. Come on into the den where we'll be more comfortable."

They moved through a doorway into a spacious area. She walked around his living area, looking out the front window then running her hand across the back of the worn leather recliner, which was definitely his favorite chair. A large TV was mounted on the wall across the room. A bookcase covering one long wall was filled with books and objects. What she liked best was the back wall that consisted of floor-to-ceiling windows and a French door in the middle. It had obviously been updated with loving care and attention to detail.

Marcy slipped through the French door and stepped out onto a patio made of pavers. An early fall breeze had pushed the humidity of the day away. She took a deep breath and stretched. It felt good to be out of a building. Beneath the trees around the fenced yard was ornamental grass with occasional patches of flowers. It was lovely.

On the patio Dylan had some very masculine wicker furniture with high arms and cushions. The decor suited him as well.

"Would you like to eat out here?"

She jumped at the sound of Dylan's voice, not hearing his approach. "I'd like that. It's nice to get outside when you work in a lab closed off all day. It's a real pleasure to see the outdoors instead of sealed doors and canned air."

"I guess it is."

"I love your flowers, grass...everything." She waved a hand toward the lawn.

"I can't take credit for planting it. I'm just the caretaker of the former owner's work."

"I had no idea you'd be a yard kind of guy."

"I didn't either. I find it therapeutic after a hard day at work. It's so peaceful back here.

If I'm not in the garage tinkering with the car, I spend most of my time out here. Kick off your shoes and enjoy while I go call for the pizza. Make yourself at home."

It didn't take any more invitation than that to have her removing her shoes and pulling off her socks.

He chuckled. "There's a great local pizza place down the road that delivers. So it shouldn't take long. Nothing fancy but I can promise it'll be good. I'll bring us something to drink."

"I didn't come in for you to wait on me." She made a motion to rise.

Dylan waved her down. "I'd let you wait on me, but you don't know where everything is so why don't you let me do it this time?"

She listened to the low rumble of his deep voice as he made the pizza order. There was something soothing about it. An element she shouldn't get used to, but it eased her nerves just the same.

He returned with two large plastic glasses with sports emblems on the side. They were filled to the brim with liquid.

She took a sip and sighed. "This is excellent iced tea."

"Thanks."

Marcy looked around. "You know. I expected you to have a fancy new house and a sports car."

"Remember I am the product of missionaries. I was taught to be much more frugal than that." He settled in a chair.

"Just so you know, I know something about vintage cars. They don't give them away."

He grinned. "Point taken." In a voice meant for the drama of a stage, he continued, "Despite my one obvious, nonrunning weakness I did go into medicine to help people, not for what it would buy me."

She turned serious. "In that we share a common ground."

"I've admitted to my vice. What's yours?" He watched her, waiting.

"I don't know. Let me give that some thought." She knew the answer but telling him would make him think she was crazy. She was driven to save every child who contracted cancer. She wasn't about to tell him that. She couldn't say the words. She'd failed Toby. Had failed herself and her husband. How could she admit that to a person like Dylan?

The doorbell rang. "Then I'll expect a report one day. That must be our pizza."

Half an hour later they were still out on the patio. Marcy was feeling unusually mellow and peaceful. She was grateful that Dylan hadn't pushed her earlier. He was easy company, and easy on the eyes too.

Marcy held up a piece of half-eaten pizza. "This is good stuff."

"Told you so. Best in town."

She took another bite. "You have good taste."

Dylan chuckled. "Thanks, but it's just pizza. You know when you agree on the small things you tend to agree on the bigger ones."

Marcy wrinkled her nose. She wasn't sure about that. As time went by, she and Josh had started to disagree on everything. When it came to Toby, they couldn't seem to agree on anything. Even before Toby became sick, her and Josh's marriage had shown signs of tearing apart. "Are you sure about that?"

"You know you challenged me in college and you're still doing it." He took a long draw on his tea.

Marcy had the distinct feeling he wanted to say more but he didn't. She couldn't help but smile. She remembered those days fondly. They were days before she carried around that knot of loss in her chest. The smell of guilt around her. "We definitely had some good times. You made me laugh. I think Professor Mitchell thought about separating us."

He said in a falsetto voice, "Please stop. You're embarrassing me."

"I wish that were the case, but I think you enjoyed being different from what people expect."

He lifted a shoulder then let it fall. "I care nothing about being a stereotype. And I was different than many of the students. I was on scholarship."

"You weren't stereotypical then and from what I've seen you aren't now. I don't think you need to worry about that ever happening. What's really terrifying for us mere mortals is how well you do everything." She lifted the drink glass. "Even making iced tea."

Dylan watched Marcy with her eyes closed and her face tipped to the late afternoon sun. A golden glow shone around her. It was the most relaxed he'd seen her since she'd been in Atlanta. What was she thinking?

Her manner made him believe she was hiding something. The way she spoke to Mrs. Baker sounded too much like someone who had experienced part of that mother's pain.

When he'd asked about her marrying, she'd said nothing about having a child. If she had one, where was he now? Why was she hiding him? Maybe she just didn't want Dylan to know. Yet why? He wanted to give her friendship. She could trust him with her secrets.

"Why doesn't a nice guy like you have a wife or a girlfriend?"

He was shaken out of his thoughts. "Maybe because I'm too nice."

Marcy huffed. "There's no such thing. Over half the nursing staff has a crush on you. At least half the female population of your patients do too. Regardless of age."

"I could ask you the same thing. Did you know I had a crush on you in college?"

Her eyes opened. "You did?"

Dylan gave her a narrow-eyed "you must be kidding" look. "You don't remember me asking you to go for pizza? You turned me down."

Marcy's mouth twisted and her brows rose. "I did?"

"You did. That's when I learned you had a boyfriend. I've always wondered why you didn't mention him sooner." He crossed his ankle over his knee.

"I kind of liked you too. I guess I didn't

want to ruin the fun we were having by telling you about Josh."

"You broke my heart." The words were direct, but soft; just the truth.

Marcy sat up. Her voice held concern. "Dylan, I didn't mean to."

"I know." Dylan met her gaze. "When I found out you had a boyfriend, I made sure to hide how I felt."

She clutched her hands in her lap. "I'm sorry. I wouldn't have hurt you for anything."

"You didn't know. I shouldn't have even brought it up. That was a long time ago and we were kids."

"I just want you to know I liked you more than I knew I should. I wouldn't let myself think about that. You know I looked for you at graduation. You said you were coming but I didn't see you. Did you decide not to go?"

He hadn't planned to attend the ceremony. She'd talked him into doing so. "I was there. I saw you."

"Why didn't you come say hello?" she asked, continuing to watch him.

"Because I saw you run into some guy's arms. I didn't want to intrude."

She leaned her head back on the chair cushion and closed her eyes "Yeah. That was Josh.

The boyfriend turned ex-husband. He surprised me by showing up. He was jealous of you."

Dylan sat forward. "Jealous of me? Why would he be?"

"Because I talked about you so much." The words tumbled out while her eyes remained closed.

Dylan didn't know what to say, so he said nothing. He had no doubt he hadn't been popular with the guy. "Yeah. He recognized I liked you more than I should. In hindsight I should have paid attention to the fact I could have those feelings for someone else. I might have saved Josh and me some heartache." She continued to talk as if Dylan weren't there. As if from a far-off place. "We had our life all planned out. It was going to be perfect. But life doesn't really work that way, does it? All perfect and easy. The unexpected comes along and pushes you off the road into the grass and dirt."

Dylan didn't comment right away. "No, it doesn't. We can plan and wish for something, and it never comes your way." Like him having a family close at Christmas, or a birthday cake on his actual birthday not months later.

Or a friend that didn't have to suffer with cancer. "I'm sorry if I made life difficult for you."

She looked at him then placed her hand over his. "It wasn't anything you did. What went wrong between Josh and me was all there when I was in college. I just didn't choose to see it. Or I was too young to. We were small town high school sweethearts that everyone thought would marry. We didn't disappoint. The problem was what we had as kids didn't work in the grown-up world."

Dylan said nothing, waiting on her to share more. Instead, a few minutes later Marcy's soft snoring reached his ears. He didn't have the heart to wake her just yet. She'd been keeping long hours. Too many of them in his opinion.

Boundaries where his work was concerned had always been a priority. He wanted to enjoy his life, not just fill it with obligations as his father had. Even if it was worthwhile work. Like tonight. Her hand still rested on his, and he left it there, enjoying her touch and the company he rarely had. It felt right having Marcy at his house. He'd give her a few more minutes to nap.

When Marcy slapped at a mosquito, he

said, "Hey, sleepyhead, let's go in before you get eaten up."

"I'm sorry. I didn't mean to fall sleep on you. It's so lovely out I just drifted off."

"It's more likely from the long hours you're keeping. You work harder and longer than three people put together."

"I want to get the trial right." She stretched.

He watched, entranced. She moved with such grace.

"I'm not worried about the trial. I'm concerned about you and your health. You keep a mean pace." She picked up her shoes after stuffing her socks into them. Gathering her glass, she held the door for him.

"You killing yourself won't save others' lives." Dylan stacked the plates, picked up his glass and took them to the kitchen. He placed them in the sink.

Marcy joined him, putting her glass in beside his. "Still my work needs doing."

"Yes, it does. But not taking care of yourself might mean you make a mistake. You don't want that."

"You do know I'm a big girl and decide those things on my own?"

"Hey," he said, reaching out to touch her. "I didn't mean to overstep. I apologize. You're right it's none of my business. A balance of work and play is just a pet peeve of mine. I shouldn't put that off on you."

"I understand. I'd better get going. Thanks for the pizza. It was great catching up." She stepped toward the kitchen table where she'd left her purse.

"It's not too late. Would you like to watch a movie before you go?"

She looked unsure for a moment then said, "I don't think so. I really do have some numbers I need to look at early in the morning before some patients come in. I better call it a night."

Monday morning Dylan entered the hospital looking forward to seeing Marcy. He'd not seen her Friday because of an off campus meeting. During the weekend he'd thought of calling her several times but had stopped himself. He had the sense Marcy wanted to keep him at arm's length. Or was it everyone? She wasn't the same person he'd known in college. There was a shell around her that hadn't been there before.

Either way he had no interest in being left behind again. Marcy had done it innocently, but his ex-fiancée had done it brutally by leaving him for an old boyfriend weeks before their wedding. No, he wasn't interested in having his teeth kicked in again. Especially not by a blast from his past whom he hadn't even dated. They should just remain friends. Maybe he was remembering the past too fondly?

Dylan smiled. Marcy had acted as if she liked his home. He'd enjoyed having her there. Oddly she fit. Too well and too quickly for his comfort. She added a warmth he hadn't known was missing—until he saw her again. He didn't make a habit of inviting women to his home. It was his place to decompress.

He stopped by his office to check his messages and took a half hour seeing to them. When Marcy showed up he had already started with his first case.

She quickly joined him and pulled a stool up next to the patient. "Good morning, everyone."

The mother and daughter returned the greeting.

Dylan continued to do his examination, but he couldn't deny the pleased beat of his heart at the sight of Marcy. It was nice to see the happy look on her face. She'd become more relaxed in the clinic over the last week. That shouldn't matter, after all she'd only be there for a few weeks, but somehow it did matter.

They continued around the room, seeing all the patients. Marcy spoke to each one, listening to the parents and their sick children. Every so often she placed her hand on a parent's hand or shoulder giving reassurance, as if they were sharing a bond. One he didn't understand.

Having finished with clinic and expecting a light afternoon, it was a good time to move Marcy's office.

"Hey, since we're done here, why don't we get your office moved?"

An unsure look filled her eyes. "Doing that really isn't necessary."

"But I think it is. I'm going to insist. You've been in that rathole long enough and I have plenty of room in my office to share. With the hours you've been keeping you need somewhere comfortable to work."

She shifted her weight. Today she wore her hair down and pulled back on the sides. She didn't look as stark and sad as she had the first day he'd seen her. The lines around her eyes had eased. "I must admit it's more crowded than I imagined. The interruptions are certainly greater than I thought they would be."

"Then it's settled. I'll call down and see if I can get somebody from our maintenance staff to help with the desk. I think you and I can handle the rest."

Marcy smiled. "Then I'll go started packing up."

"Give me five minutes. I'll be right behind you." Dylan pulled his phone out of his pocket, ridiculously pleased that she'd agreed to his plan.

A young man arrived from Maintenance half an hour later. Between him and Dylan, they managed to get Marcy's desk down the hall and into place without too much difficulty. Dylan had it placed at an angle giving her as much space as possible.

The man left.

Marcy entered with her arms filled with files, books and a laptop. She looked around. "This reminds me of when we had to use that old lab after Wilson created that sulfur mess during an experiment."

Dylan chuckled. "He did make a mess. Then the class had to divide up into all those smaller rooms to work. We could hardly move around." He'd loved every minute of being that close to Marcy. "Let me have some of that before you drop it," he offered, rushing toward her.

The bulk of the material was all that stood between them. He was close enough that he could smell the spring scent of her shampoo. His gaze met hers as he slid his arms along her bare ones to support the pile. Marcy blinked then released the items into his hands.

Dylan stepped back, clearing his throat. His mind shouldn't be going to how wonderful her skin felt or how bright her eyes were or, worse, how kissable her full mouth looked. He had to put a stop to those thoughts. He wasn't a college kid with a crush anymore. Getting involved with Marcy again wasn't what he needed in his life. Dylan feared she could too easily break his heart again. He set the pile on the corner of her desk. "I'll…uh… let you get settled. I have a couple of consults to see about."

He headed out of the office without a backward look. Being nice just might get him in trouble.

Marcy looked up from the work she was doing on the laptop when Dylan entered. He dropped into his chair behind his desk. They had been sharing an office for a couple of days. During that time, she'd seen little of him. Most of their interactions happened outside the too-close working environment. He had respected her space by not disturbing her when they were in the room together but that didn't mean she wasn't aware of him nearby.

He'd only clicked a few keys when his phone rang. "Yeah. I can be there in a few minutes." He hung up. Pushing back from the desk, Dylan said, "This consult case has nothing to do with your trial but it's unusual. Would you like to go with me?"

She looked at the work on the computer screen. Closing the laptop, she stood. "I'd like a break."

"Good. We're going to the cardiology floor."

"Since when do they call Oncology for help?"

Dylan headed for the stairs. "Today apparently. The patient has an extremely low platelet count."

"I see. Handling the immune system the cancer department is the most familiar with."

Dylan grinned, the gleam in his chocolate-brown \\\\\\\eyes sending her pulse racing. "You're a smart cookie."

"Thanks. Coming from you that's nice to

hear. I guess the cardiologist wants to see if you have any ideas about what's causing the drop." She hurried to keep up with him.

"That's it." Dylan pushed through the door to the stairs' then climbed.

Marcy followed him onto the next floor, They stopped at the nurses' station, where he checked in before going to the room number he was given. Dylan knocked and they entered. A young man in his late teens lay in the bed. A woman sat in a chair nearby.

"I'm Dr. Nelson. Are you Ryan?"

"Yep." The boy continued to watch the TV.

"Dr. Connors asked me to come by to see you. This is Dr. Montgomery," Dylan said, indicating her. "Do you mind if we have a look at your chest?"

"You want to see the spots, don't you?" Ryan lifted his shirt without any hesitation, showing an old incision down the center of his chest. His nonchalant action common for children who'd been in and out of the hospital most of their lives.

She and Dylan stepped closer. This was an unusual case for an oncologist. Marcy had to admit she was intrigued.

"I understand you had a heart transplant some time ago." Dylan looked at the boy.

"Yeah." Ryan focused on the game he was playing.

"Sixteen years," the woman sitting in a nearby chair said.

"That's a long time." Dylan nodded.

"He's recently had an aorta replacement and pacemaker," the woman said.

Dylan studied the red dots on the boy's chest. "Did the petechiae show up before or after that?"

"The what?" The boy looked perplexed. Dylan had his attention now. Ryan glanced at the woman who must be his mother.

"The red spots," Dylan said without taking his attention away from the boy's chest.

"Oh. After the pacemaker." Ryan's hand went to his chest.

"May I touch a moment?" Dylan asked.

"Sure." The boy lay still.

Dylan pushed on a spot. The area around the spot turned white but the spot returned to the skin when Dylan removed his fingertip. "Have you ever had platelet issues before?"

"No," the mother replied. She rose and came to stand beside the bed.

"I'm afraid they're very low. I'm going to order another round of packed blood cells to see if that'll help. If not, we have a medicine I think we need to try."

Ryan nodded.

The mother asked, "When will you start?"

Dylan gave her a reassuring look. "As soon as I can order it."

"Thanks," she said, sounding tired.

Marcy recognized the note of worry in the woman's voice because at one time she'd been that mother.

Dylan gave Ryan's mother a reassuring smile and stepped out into the hall. Marcy followed him.

"He has thrombocytopenic purpura," Marcy said.

"He does."

"You think he's going to need IVIG."

His mouth thinned. "I do."

She knew IVIG was an anticancer treatment and would cost the patient thousands of dollars per infusion. But it looked as if it might be the only way to increase the young man's platelet count. He couldn't go about life or have another procedure with his platelet count so low. He could bleed to death. There was no choice, just as there hadn't been for the treatment Toby had received.

Her heart tightened. "What's your plan if the platelets don't work?"

"I'll have him come in for IVIG infusions once a week for three weeks and see how it goes." Dylan paused. "Ryan's platelets are dangerously low but keeping him here won't make things better. Being in the hospital just increases his chance of an infection. You know the saying, 'you get sick in the hospital.'"

Marcy nodded. "That's generally the truth."

They started down the hall. Marcy faced a mother with a baby in her arms about the age Toby had been when he'd become sick. She clenched her hands. On one level, she was getting better; she didn't want to run. But after seeing the teen and now this her nerves were strung tight. This is why she belonged in a lab, where it was safer.

"Thanks for bringing me along. I better get back to work." She hurried ahead of Dylan and through the double doors. Marcy caught Dylan's surprised glance but kept walking.

CHAPTER FOUR

FOR DYLAN THE next few days moved eternally slowly while at the same time flew by. He had adjusted to sharing his office with Marcy. Sort of. More than once he found himself stopping by for something he normally would have let wait just to see what Marcy was doing. When she wasn't with him, she spent the time seeing patients in the office, working on her laptop and talking on the phone.

They were slowly rebuilding the comradery they'd enjoyed in college. At first he wasn't sure it was possible. Sharing a joke, a memory or a laugh over something that had happened during the day had improved their relationship. Now he was sure that Marcy was hiding something but that wasn't his business. She was entitled to her privacy. He didn't want people prying into his life, so why should he do it to her. Still, he couldn't stop his curiosity.

On Friday afternoon Dylan hit the final computer key in his email response and huffed. Why did he always get this job? Yet he couldn't say no.

She looked up from her laptop screen. "Something wrong?"

"Marcy, do you think you have time to help me with something?" Maybe new eyes on the project would help.

"Like what?" She sounded hesitant.

"In a few weeks the cancer caregivers are giving the Care Ball to raise money for new equipment."

"Cancer caregivers?" Marcy raised her brows, giving her a cute inquiring expression.

He had her complete attention. "They're the volunteers who support the pediatric oncology department. Do fundraisers."

"Okay. So how can I help?" With her elbows on the desk and head resting on her hands, her gorgeous green eyes searched his face.

"I've been asked to give a presentation about the department at the ball. To 'showcase it' were the words. They left it up to me to decide what I do, but it must raise money.

I hate doing this sort of stuff. Inspirational speeches aren't my thing. Please help me. I'll take any ideas."

Marcy wore a half smile. "Begging and whining will get you everywhere. Let me think about it. I have the first part of the trial settled so I have a little more time."

"I'm desperate enough to take any time you can give. Just don't think too long. They want this in four weeks." He was completely out of his depth with no idea of where to start.

"Ooh, that's a short time. That'll be about the time I leave. Do you have anything in mind?"

He shrugged. "I can always stand up there and give statistics along with how important the work we do is."

Marcy put her hand over her mouth and patted it as if stifling a yawn.

He glared at her with a grin. "Why don't you tell me how you really feel?"

She looked away from him, the expression in her eyes thoughtful. "I think you should showcase the patients."

When Dylan started to speak, she raised a hand. "I don't mean anything to sensational-ize them or be insensitive. I know how you like to protect them."

"So what do you have in mind?" He perched on the corner of her desk, slowly swinging a leg as he listened.

"I don't know yet. Maybe pictures around the room? Or videos of the patients? But that's all been done. You want something that will grab them. You know them all so well. Outside of cancer, do they have anything in common?"

"Not really. They're different ages. Live in different parts of the city. Some outside the city. I don't know."

She pursed her mouth. "There has to be something."

"They like to sing, rap. You heard them the other day. The one they made up about me was pretty funny."

Marcy's eyes brightened as she pointed her finger at him. "That's it. If we can get some of the patients to come to the ball and be among the people, and then do a song. Like one of those crowds..."

"You mean a flash mob?"

"Yeah. Make it look impromptu. They can rap something about being in the hospital or taking chemo like they did the other day. Those attending will love it. It would showcase how well the patients are doing. That despite what they're going through, they're still full of life."

Dylan looked at her for a moment. "That sounds great. The committee will love it." Before he knew what he was doing, he'd pulled her into his arms and kissed her. Realizing what he'd done, he let her go and put the desk between them. "I'm sorry. I got excited. I shouldn't have done that. You're wonderful."

She watched him with wide eyes. "I'm glad you like the idea. Now you just have to get the children and parents to cooperate."

"I'm better at that than being the idea guy. Thanks again, Marcy."

She gave a slight nod. "You're welcome."

"Don't think you're done. I'll still need your help to get it all organized."

"Are you asking or telling?" Marcy sounded unsure.

He gave her a pleading look. "Uh, I'm asking. I promise, I'm asking."

She grinned.

He returned it. "We're going to make a great team. The kids will be the stars of the show as they should be."

A week later on a Saturday afternoon Marcy checked off another item on the list she and

Dylan had made to prepare for the Care Ball. He'd insisted she come to his house to work on the details and plans. They'd put together schedules and decided on how they wanted the children to enter the room.

They had spent the last week talking to the patients and parents encouraging them to be involved with the Care Ball. They still had a few more to talk to on Monday but all in all they were encouraged.

Robby, the lead rapper, had been the patient they really had to get on board. He took more convincing than Marcy expected.

"Dr. Nelson, we're just having fun here. No one wants to hear us."

Dylan had scooted his rolling stool closer. "I think you'd be surprised. You and the others are great. Do you think we stop and clap around here just because we have nothing else to do?"

The teen had shrugged. "I haven't really thought about it. We're just passing time."

"I get that, but we need you to make this work. I'll tell you what, you and the kids come up with whatever song you want to do. Practice it. Just one. See what you think."

"I guess we could."

"Thanks, Robby. I knew I could count on you."

Marcy had to respect Dylan for nudging Robby because she knew he was concerned about them not overdoing it. After all they were all taking chemo treatments.

By the end of the week Robby had agreed. The other patients and their parents were eager to help after that.

Dylan went to the back of his house but soon returned. "We've been at this awhile. Let's take a break and go do something fun."

"I really should go to the hospital and check some numbers." Marcy closed her laptop.

Dylan's shoulders sagged. "Come on, Marcy. You work all the time. You can take an afternoon off if you want to. Especially on the weekend. I promise you'll like what I have in mind."

Really, her work was caught up, but after their kiss she felt more aware of Dylan than ever. It had been a quick meeting of lips, but the action had made her come alive like nothing had in a long time. Truthfully, she wanted him to do it again. What would it be like if he really meant it?

"I guess I could go for a little while."

Dylan placed a hand on her shoulder.

"Good. Then let's go." He started toward the door. "Come on. Time's wasting. We'll take my car."

A few minutes later she gave his car a dubious look. "Are you making any guarantees I won't have to walk home today?"

Dylan squared his shoulders. His voice filled with false hurt. "I don't appreciate my dates questioning my automobile."

At the word *date* her gaze quickly turned to him. Marcy smiled and met his laughing brown eyes. Her stomach gave a small flip. "Actually, I was just kidding."

What was happening to her? Was she flirting with Dylan? She hadn't had interest in a man in so long she couldn't imagine trying to flirt. "I'm looking forward to riding in it."

He grinned. "You'll appreciate the fact that it's fall instead of summer since there's no air-conditioning."

She laughed. "I'll make a note of that."

He opened and held the passenger car door. She settled into the seat with the fanfare of a woman testing its comfort. Running her hands along the leather upholstery of the door, she studied it.

The fleeting thought of what it would feel like to have Dylan's hand run over her skin made her breath catch. She shook her head. She shouldn't let those thoughts happen. Hopefully she'd made the right decision by going with him today.

As Dylan pulled into the main road, Marcy rolled the window down far enough that her hair blew around her face.

"Which would you like to do most—go to a plantation house or see a museum or take a train ride? Or we could go up the sky lift to the top of the mountain?"

She turned to gape at him. "Where're we going that you have all those choices?"

Dylan glanced at her before he changed lanes. "Stone Mountain. Ever heard of it?"

"No, but I think I'd like to go up on top of the mountain."

"Then that's what we'll do." Dylan followed the signs to the parking area for the sky lift.

"It's huge." Marcy looked up at the white-and-gray stone soaring from the ground. "What kind of mountain is this? I was expecting trees on top of it."

Dylan chuckled. "There are trees but around it. Stone Mountain is what is called a monadnock. It's when the hard rock remains as the ground around it erodes."

Less than an hour later they were in a cable car riding up the side of the huge stone. Marcy stood at the window, looking out. Dylan moved in close but not touching. She felt his warmth beside her. "This is beautiful. Amazing."

Soon they stopped at the top and stepped from the car. They walked over to the rail and looked out at the flat top of the stone, then past that to the view beyond. Dylan moved over to a sign posted on the wall. "We're up 825 feet and you can see sixty miles in any direction."

Marcy shifted to another area. "Can we see the hospital from here?"

Dylan stepped next to her. He raised an arm and pointed. "It's right down there. The sand-colored building next to the blue one."

"Where?" She moved in close enough that her back touched his chest and she followed the line of sight down his arm. His aftershave smelled spicy, and it took everything she had not to give in to the temptation to lean back into the warmth of his body. "I think I see it now."

Dylan shifted away.

She immediately missed his contact. "Atlanta really does have a beautiful skyline."

"It does. I like living here."

"I can understand why." She continued to look out at the city.

They spent the next thirty minutes wandering around looking from different view spots before taking the cable car down. By that time the sun had\ moved lower in the sky.

"Are you getting hungry?" Dylan asked.

"I'm all right for now."

They strolled toward the car.

Dylan said, "Are you're interested in staying for the laser show?"

"Now, that sounds interesting. I've never been to something like that. What do we do?"

A car backed out in front of them and he took her hand, directing her out of the way. She didn't pull away. It was calming to have her hand clasped in his larger one. As if he was protecting her like he did his patients. Even with the small amount of attention Dylan had shown her she could only imagine how comforting it would be under the umbrella of his love. Safe. What had her thinking about that?

"We don't do anything but watch. They shine large bright-colored lights on the curved side of the mountain and pair it with music."

"That sounds fun." Her pulse picked up.

She would be spending another evening with Dylan. This wasn't like her. It would be easy to get carried away with being around him, which she couldn't let happen. What would he think of her if he learned about her failure with Toby? That she'd missed her son's illness until it was too late, and he'd died because of her. Would Dylan trust her again? With his patients? In his life? No, she had to stay away from him. She slipped her hand from his as soon as the danger passed.

"I'd hoped you'd like the idea. I called ahead for a catered meal. We need to move the car to a closer parking lot and get the blanket."

She stopped walking and looked at him. "You planned all this?"

"Well, yes, but I was nowhere sure you'd come or stay. Work is all you think about, except for the Care Ball, but then it's part of work too. I wanted us to do something together that was just for us."

Marcy smiled. Warmth flowed through her. When was the last time someone had wanted to spend time with just her? She liked the idea too much. "I'd love a picnic."

A smile reached his eyes as if she'd given

him a present. "Good. Because that's just what we're having."

An hour later, with a blanket under his arm, Dylan carried a picnic basket they had picked up from a van in the parking lot. They made their way to the wide grassy mound in front of a large sculpture on the side of the mountain.

Dylan spread the blanket on the ground and they took a seat, stretching out their legs. "Are you ready to eat or would you like to wait for a little bit?"

Marcy lifted her face to the last of the late afternoon sun. "I think I'd like to wait. It's been a nice afternoon, Dylan. Thank you for insisting I come."

"Insist?" He gave her a shocked look as if she'd hurt his feelings.

She grinned. "Yes, I think that's an accurate word for it. But I'm glad you did."

"I'm glad you came too. I hope you haven't worried too much about work."

"I haven't. I needed somebody to push me out of the hole my head has been in." She'd never spoken truer words. The reality that she'd stopped living when Toby died suddenly swamped her.

"Are you okay? You have a strange look on your face."

"I'm fine." Yet she wasn't. Her entire world had just tilted but she couldn't let on to Dylan.

While they sat there, other people settled in around them with their blankets and chairs.

Dylan served their meals of fried chicken, rolls, a small green salad and a brownie for dessert. Along with that, Dylan had brought a bottle of wine. They made small talk about the day as they ate.

"Thanks, Dylan. I really needed this." A long purple light reflected brilliantly off the granite rock. Marcy asked, "Is this the light show?"

"Yes." As a yellow light was added he cleared away their dinner. He held up the wine bottle. "Would you like one last glass?"

"No thanks." Marcy sat with her arms wrapped around her knees. "I don't want to miss anything."

Dylan chuckled, corked the bottle and set it aside. He lay on his side with his ankles crossed and his head in his palm to watch the show.

Over the next hour Marcy became enthralled with the bright lights against the mountain set to music. After one song she leaned over and whispered, "I know this is silly for a grown-up, but this is a lot of fun."

Dylan grinned. "I don't think it's silly. I'm glad you're having a good time."

As dark settled around them the air cooled. Marcy rubbed her arms as she wrapped them around her waist. Dylan moved in closer, placing an arm over her shoulder, bringing her into his side. "I'm sorry I don't have anything warmer to offer."

"It's okay. I'm warm now." She was. Warmer than she'd been in years. It had been too long since she had real human contact. It felt nice to have Dylan caring for her. More than nice; her whole body seemed to sparkle along with the light show.

She watched the rest of the show snuggled against Dylan's side. They often sang along to the music. She could get used to this, too easily. And she could get too attached to Dylan. Something she mustn't let happen. It wasn't healthy for her or him.

With the show over, they gathered their belongings, then walked to the car. Dylan turned up the heat inside, but she missed the warmth of his touch. "That really was fun. Thank you for taking me. You're a good guy, Dylan Nelson."

Marcy deliberately made it sound like they were just friends. It was safer that way.

"Thanks. I'm glad you think so. You've never done anything like that before?"

"If I did, it was a long time ago. I've pretty much spent all my time working."

"You should take more downtime into your life. You're going to burn out if you aren't careful. You need to let your mind turn off."

He had no idea. "I know but it's harder to do than you think." Work kept her memories and guilt at bay. Work was her mechanism for survival. For finding a cure to cancer or at least something that prevented families from experiencing what she went through. "Am I all that bad? I don't remember asking for your opinion on my life." It came out more harshly than she intended.

"I'm sorry. You're right. Your life is none of my business. Forgive me for offering advice that wasn't asked for. I do have that habit."

Neither of them said anything more as he turned into his drive, but tension hovered between them. She climbed out of his car and headed toward her own. "Thanks for the evening, Dylan. I had a great time. I'm glad you insisted I go. I did need it."

"I'm glad you went too." He waited beside the steps to his back door as she left his drive.

If she'd had hope for a good evening kiss, that had gotten lost in their last conversation. And that was probably a good thing.

Tuesday, Dylan went into the hospital with his mind firmly on what he had to do that day. He'd spent too much time over the last few days rethinking his and Marcy's last exchange. He had no business offering advice about how she spent her time when he had his own issues.

His father had called again and left a message asking if Dylan had made a decision about coming to work with him in the medical mission. Sometime today Dylan would have to return that call. He wasn't looking forward to the discussion. He wanted to help his father, but Dylan liked his work here and living in Atlanta. He had no desire to move around. Stability, building a life in one place, appealed to him.

Yet not wanting to disappoint his father still tugged at him. In a strange way the fact he'd shared little of his father's life growing up made Dylan want to get some of that time back as an adult. He wasn't sure what a psychiatrist would say about that. He resented his parents for putting him last in their lives. Just for once he'd like to hear they wanted what he wanted. He feared that day might never come.

"Hey," Marcy said as she came in the door. "I didn't know if you knew that Lucy is here for her port."

"Yeah. I'm on my way. I checked my schedule earlier and saw her name on the list." He read his last email.

"Do you mind if I observe?" Marcy put her purse away in the desk and lay her laptop down.

The technology went everywhere with her. She was always prepared to do work. Something she did too much of. "Not at all. In fact, I would've been surprised if you didn't."

Twenty minutes later Lucy lay sedated on the table in the port lab as Dylan prepared to insert the port. Marcy stood across from him. He felt more than saw her unwavering gaze on what he was doing.

She'd come into the lab a few minutes after him, having stopped to speak to Lucy's mother when they passed her in the hall. There was something Marcy was able to offer Mrs. Baker that he couldn't. Maybe it was just because they were female. Marcy was good for his department. He could already tell the difference she made, and it had nothing to do with the new drug trial.

They finished the procedure in under half an hour and walked to the waiting room to speak to Lucy's mom. Dylan stood but Marcy sat beside the mother. "Lucy is doing great. She'll be sleepy today, and maybe a little sore, but she should be good to go tomorrow. Do all the things you did last time for the port. We'll start her chemo on Wednesday. They'll give you the appointment time up front. I know Dr. Montgomery has spoken to you about the TM13, but do you have any other questions?"

Mrs. Baker shook her head. "I don't think so. I'm just ready for all this to be over and for Lucy to be better."

Marcy touched her arm. "Just take one day at a time. You'll get through it. I promise."

Lucy's mother gave her a weak smile. "I hope so."

"Just know that Dr. Nelson is the best and he'll take good care of Lucy."

Dylan liked hearing a vote of confidence directed at him from Marcy. "Then we'll see you week after next to start chemo."

Mrs. Baker nodded as Marcy rose. "You have my card. Call if you need to talk."

He and Marcy said their goodbyes and walked toward the lab.

"You were really good with Lucy's mother. Giving her your number was nice. Have you ever thought about getting out of the lab and working with the cancer families? Using your knowledge outside the glass. There are hospitals that have those types of programs led by doctors. You would be great at it."

Marcy gave him a shocked look. "I can't imagine not doing the work I do."

"It wasn't always your dream to be a researcher?"

"No, it was just my dream to help people. How about you? How did you become a doctor?"

"It was always the plan. When we knew each other before, I wasn't sure it was going to work out. I took a couple of years off to work between college and med school. I needed money to live on. My parents didn't have that kind of money for school. My father is a doctor, and he's always wanted me to work with him on the mission field. I always felt there were other places I could serve where I could help people. Lately he's been pressuring me to join him."

She grabbed his arm, surprising him. "Are you seriously considering it?"

Dylan shook his head, trying to ignore the feel of her hand on his skin. "No. My place is here. I just have to make him understand that."

"Then why don't you tell him that?" Marcy's gaze was intense.

"Because I don't want to hurt his feelings. I guess it's just easier to dodge that conversation." What he didn't want to admit was that he'd found and created a home without them. He didn't want to live as his parents had. He liked his life. After not belonging anywhere, he'd found the place where he fit.

When she dropped his arm, he stopped and leaned against the wall. "Because there are few doctors in developing countries. Dad's getting older and with no one to take his place…"

She glowered at him in disbelief. "But you've put down roots here. You do great work here. Your patients depend on you too. They deserve to know you'll be here when you're needed."

"I know but my father has always believed I would become part of the family business. Despite them not being around while I was growing up, he expects me to join him." Dylan tried to keep the bitterness out of his voice but failed.

A look of disbelief made Marcy's eyes darker. "I think it would be a shame for you to leave what you have established here. It feels wrong!"

Dylan watched her curiously. Marcy sure was invested in his future when she would be leaving it in a few weeks.

"I think you're right square in the middle of the family business here in Atlanta." She stopped short of stomping a foot.

"Why would you say that?"

"You're a doctor with compassion like I've never seen before. You're helping people. Helping families. Helping children. How's that different from being a missionary. It's not the country that matters but the needs."

Why did her words ease the heaviness he carried? "I've never really thought of it like that. I always saw me not working in a developing nation as disappointing my parents and not using my skills to the best advantage."

"I'd be surprised if you aren't using them to their best advantage. I have a feeling anybody you care about you care deeply for."

Why was she so adamant about him staying? She'd be gone soon, and they wouldn't see each other again for a long time, if ever. The thought stung him more than he would like. "What about you? What happens after the trial is over? Will you disappear inside a lab again?"

"It's not a prison, you know. I'll start on the development of a new, better drug until there's a cure."

Dylan pursed his lips and shrugged, feigning indifference. "I just think you might be missing your calling."

The sound of rapping lured them both to the Infusion Room.

Dylan grinned. Robby was beatboxing and the others were adding phrases as the group, all hooked to IV lines, continued to keep rhythm. Marcy came to stand beside him.

The song came to an end and Robby picked up again. "Dr. Montgomery can give you a summary."

Lizzy, a girl of nine, added, "Anytime, with what is on her mind."

Dylan looked at Marcy. There was a smile on her face but her eyes glistened.

When the group had finished she clapped her hands enthusiastically. "That was wonderful. Even if it was about me. You guys will be stars at the ball. If you think you'll have any trouble getting there, please let Dr. Nelson or me know. We'll be glad to come get you."

"Remember, if you're not feeling up to it also let us know that. Your health is top priority," Dylan added.

Marcy turned to Dylan and said for his ears only. "How could you even think about leaving this behind?"

CHAPTER FIVE

THURSDAY MORNING, MARCY GROANED. She'd been at Atlanta Children's four weeks. Days that had changed her life.

During the day she'd spent too much time thinking about Dylan. He'd started to slip beyond her locked gate of emotions to make her want someone again. Not just someone—him. More than once she'd hoped he'd call. More than once she'd thought of calling him. It was thrilling and disconcerting to have these feelings again.

She had no desire to mislead Dylan. He certainly needed someone who wasn't scared to love. What could she ever offer him? She promised she'd never let herself care about anyone again. Having lost so much in her life already she couldn't afford to take a chance on losing someone else. More than that she couldn't trust herself to be what he needed. What if she failed him?

She went through the motions of the day pushing thoughts of Dylan away. It was the middle of the afternoon when she remembered Ryan, the heart transplant teen was due to come in for his first treatment for low platelets. She went to the clinic in search of Dylan and the boy. She found them in a small room off the main area.

The lights had been lowered. The boy sat in a cushioned recliner, looking at the TV hanging on the wall. The sports channel played. A nurse worked with the IV already in the boy's arm while Dylan held an electric pad in his hands.

Wearing a solemn expression, he looked at Ryan. "How're you feeling?"

"Fine." Ryan didn't take his gaze off the TV.

Dylan glanced at Ryan's mother, who nodded.

Ryan and his mom acted as if they were taking the situation in stride. Marcy questioned whether they really understood how bad Ryan's condition was. Or if they had just been through so much this setback was another issue in a long line of them. Either way Marcy wished she had their peace.

Marcy had been amazed after reading Ryan's chart at how he'd managed to grow to a teenager. Now he faced another ongoing issue. His mother had come close to losing her child several times. They both wore a smile of greeting when Marcy spoke to them. How did they manage to endure?

Dylan stepped to Ryan's side. "We're gonna give you some medicine called gamma globulin. It's to help increase your platelet count. May I see your chest?"

Ryan lifted his shirt.

Marcy moved to the other side of the lounge chair.

"These small red dots are caused by the platelet issue. It indicates bleeding under the skin. These petechiae should disappear as your platelet count increases. We must get your platelet count up to keep you healthy. You've got to be very careful not to hurt yourself or cause bleeding until we do."

Ryan nodded, but focused on the TV again.

"You'll need to come in once a week for three sessions in the hope we can increase your count. I must admit the sessions can be hours long. We can only put the medicine in as fast as your body will tolerate it."

Ryan nodded.

Marcy looked at his mother, who sat on the edge of the chair, her attention on Dylan.

He continued, "I'll be checking on other patients and then come back and see you. There'll be a nurse here with you the entire time. Are we good?"

"We're good," Ryan said to Dylan.

He looked at Ryan's mom.

"We're good," she said.

Dylan left the room and Marcy followed.

"Have you done this procedure before?" Marcy asked his retreating back.

He turned to her. "Several times but all on cancer kids. I've never done it on a heart transplant patient."

"Do you have any idea what to expect?" She watched him closely.

Dylan pursed his lips. "All are educated guesses on this type of patient. You never know with the immunosuppressed."

"You have a great bedside manner. I wish I had that talent." His manners were good in more ways than one.

He studied her a moment, then said, "I think you do. I think you just fear using it."

Dylan walked off. Somehow, she felt as if she'd been scolded.

Later, on her way to the office, she passed a small consult room. Ryan's mother sat there alone with her head down. Her hands rested in her lap. Marcy considered walking on, but something stopped her. She knocked. Ryan's mother looked up and Marcy entered.

"Is there a problem? Is Ryan having a reaction to the medicine?"

She shook her head. "No, I just needed a moment away."

"Then I'll leave you alone," Marcy said, moving to leave.

"No, please stay."

"Is there something I can do to help?" Marcy took a seat unsure where that question had come from. She never asked it before. But then she'd not been in a hospital setting dealing with patients on a regular basis since medical school.

Thankfully Ryan's mother didn't act as if she noticed Marcy's discomfort. Instead she continued talking. "Sometimes I just can't watch what's happening to Ryan."

"He and your family have been through a lot."

"Yeah, it just seems to always be one more thing, then one more thing." The woman's words came out weary.

"I can tell Ryan is a fighter. And so are you."

"I don't know. Some days I put up a good front for him. I don't know if he does or not. We just do what we can and live the best we can every day."

Marcy quit doing that when Toby died. "That's to be admired."

"I don't think I do anything special. I just do what must be done. I'm just a parent who loves her kid. You just do."

Hadn't Marcy done that and not made any difference? "Do you ever feel like you don't do enough?"

"Every day. I think even parents with children who are perfectly healthy feel like they don't do enough. I do the best I can with what knowledge I have at the time."

Had Marcy done that? She had, to the best of her ability.

"We can't do any more. After all, we're just human," Ryan's mother said, drawing a circle on the table with her fingertip.

Marcy had never thought about it that way. She had loved Toby. She had done all she could with the knowledge she had. The problem was she couldn't do enough.

"His dad and I make sure he knows every day that if something ever does happen to him, his mom and dad loved and wanted him to have the best life possible."

Hadn't she and Josh done that? She believed they had. "I'm sure Ryan does know that."

The woman gave her a wry smile. "I guess I better get back to him."

"I'll walk with you."

They entered the room to find Ryan still lying on the lounger. Dylan was there as well. He did a double take when he saw her walk in behind Ryan's mother. His brows rose.

"Ryan is ready to go for today. He did well. We were able to put the medicine in faster than we'd anticipated."

Ryan sat up. "I'll see you next week, Doc."

Dylan grinned. "I'll be here. Take care of yourself this week and be careful."

"Yes, sir."

Mother and son went out the door leaving the two doctors alone. Dylan said, "You and Ryan's mama looked pretty friendly there."

"We just ran into each other and had a little talk."

His mouth quirked up on one side. "Anything you want to share?"

"No, but she did give me some food for thought."

A nurse stuck her head in the doorway. "Dr. Nelson, you're needed out here a moment."

"I'll be right there." He glanced at Marcy. "See you later."

That evening Marcy was walking out of Dylan's office as he entered. "I was planning to ask you to dinner tonight, but I have a patient coming in through Emergency. I won't be leaving anytime soon."

"Oh." She knew he could sense the disappointment in her voice.

"Maybe we can do it tomorrow night."

"I'll look forward to it."

His lips spread into a bright smile. "I'm going to count on it."

Her heart swelled. She might be leaving soon, but she'd enjoy this feeling for as long as she could.

It was late. Dylan only intended to stop by his office long enough to pick up a file and his schedule for the next day. The light was still on. It wasn't like Marcy to leave it that way. He entered to find her with her head on her laptop, sound asleep.

For once she looked relaxed. All those serious lines around her eyes and mouth had eased. He brushed the soft curtain of hair back from her cheek with his finger. "Marcy."

Her eyes opened. She groaned and sat back, murmuring, "I only meant to rest my eyes, not fall asleep. What time is it?"

"Almost eleven. Way past time for us both to go home. Give me a sec and I'll walk you to your car."

"I have some more numbers to look at for a report." She opened her laptop.

He gently closed it. "That can wait until tomorrow."

To his surprise, she pulled out the drawer, retrieved her purse and stood. "You're right."

He picked up what he needed off his desk. "I'm glad you're finally listening."

"If I was more awake I might have something to say about that but right now I'm not up for witty sparring."

Dylan chuckled as he hustled her out of the office and turned off the light. "Good to know. I'm not sure I'm sharp enough to keep up."

Marcy giggled. *Giggled.* It made his blood run hotter. She sounded happy, free. Putting his hand lightly at her waist, he walked her to her car.

The parking lot only had a few cars in it at that time of day. Marcy opened the driver's door and dropped her purse inside before she turned to him. "I forgot to ask, how did the emergency go?"

Dylan pushed a hand through his hair. "I had to admit him. The boy's breathing is shallow. I'm afraid it'll be time to send in hospice soon. I never like to admit defeat."

Marcy touched his cheek then let her hand fall. Dylan had the idea she wanted to say something but couldn't get it out. "We shouldn't have to."

She sounded so sad he couldn't help but fold her into his arms. He'd worked for days not to touch her, afraid he'd want more than she could return or was willing to give, but right now they both needed human contact. To feel the other's beating heart.

Marcy gripped his shirt as she pressed her face into his chest. They stood there holding each other, absorbing each other's strength.

When she looked up, it felt like an invitation and Dylan couldn't help but place his lips on hers. Marcy's hands pulled him tighter as his mouth moved against hers. She moaned. He pressed her against the car as he teased the line of her lips.

The lights and sound of the security cart drew his attention. He quickly backed away.

"Everything okay here?" an older heavyset man asked from the cart.

"Yes. Just a late night. I was seeing her to the car."

The security guy gave Dylan a knowing nod. "Good. It's not safe for a woman to be out by herself at this time of night. Have a good evening." He drove off.

Marcy had already settled in the car.

As much as he wanted to touch her again, he didn't. "I'll follow you. Make sure you get home safely." When she started to speak, he stopped her. "Please don't argue. It's for my peace of mind too."

Marcy had stayed up for the rest of the night thinking about Dylan kissing her. She didn't understand this new feeling of insecurity. Her nerves hummed at a mere thought of Dylan. What had started as a comforting action turned to a meeting of emotions that went into overdrive. If the security man hadn't come around, she wasn't sure what might have happened in the parking lot. At least on her part.

She'd been on her own for so long. Even after Toby died and Josh wasn't around much, she hadn't had this need to see and talk to him. Dylan had gotten past her wall. She was still confident she couldn't trust herself not to let him down, but she badly wanted his touch.

The minute Toby had died, her marriage had as well. Josh accused her of letting it happen. That she'd been so focused on her fellowship she'd not paid enough attention to her child. He played the blame game. She listened. More than that, she'd started to believe it even before Josh accused her.

When she entered Dylan's office the next morning to finish what she started the night before she was shocked to find him sitting behind his desk, his head in his hands. "You look awful," she said.

His eyes were red rimmed. "Thanks. That's what every guy wants to hear."

"Sorry, that wasn't a very warm greeting, was it?" Marcy stepped down the hall, returning with a cup of hot black coffee. She set it in front of Dylan. Her heart went out to him, and she asked gently, "How's your patient?"

"Not very good."

"I'm sorry to hear that."

"I am too. Steve and his parents have been through the mill. He was in remission for four years and now the leukemia has returned."

"That's awful." She couldn't make herself leave his side, but she didn't dare touch him. Toby hadn't even had the remission time.

"Yeah, I've tried everything I know to do," Dylan said, sounding defeated. Something she'd not heard before.

Her chest tightened and she asked quietly, "Would you mind if I look at his chart?"

Dylan picked up his electronic pad and touched the screen entering a few numbers, then handed it to her. "I welcome any ideas."

She sat down behind her desk to read the boy's chart. "What kind of health is he in currently?"

"Good actually. He's started running a fever and throwing up recently. But otherwise, he's regained his weight and all his vitals are good except for his white blood count, of course."

"Then he sounds like a good candidate for what I have in mind."

Dylan looked over his desk. "And that is?"

She met his gaze. "I want to put him in my trial. Try TM13. But in bolus amounts. Stop what's going on before it starts."

"But he doesn't fit the criteria or the trial parameters." Dylan came to stand beside her desk.

"No, but I believe by the numbers and the responses I've been getting that it could help."

Dylan gave her an intense look. "We could get in trouble stepping out of protocol. Maybe even lose our medical licenses."

"We could save his life," she snapped. "I'm willing to take the chance and the flak. His case is tailor-made for what I've been working on."

Dylan didn't say anything for a moment then nodded. "I am too. Let's go see if he and his parents agree."

"Do you think they will?" She started out the door.

"I think the parents are desperate and will agree to anything. I know I would."

"I would." She would have.

"Will you explain how the medicine works and answer questions?" Dylan pushed the button to the elevator.

"Certainly."

Once again, she and Dylan were partners. They made a good team. She'd never felt like she was a real partner with Josh. With Dylan they were equals. For once since Toby's death, the guilt was pushed away to focus on the task. Because Dylan believed in her.

Dylan had been excited and relieved to see Marcy walk through the office door that morning.

The night before he couldn't help reliving their kiss. He'd promised himself he wouldn't overthink it or read more into it than there might have been. Yet, he yearned to pull her into his arms again.

Between being worried about his latest patient and the emotional upheaval with Marcy, the morning had been long and difficult. And his father had called again. Nope this wouldn't be a good day.

Even as exhausted as he was last night it had taken him hours to go to sleep. He couldn't stop thinking about Marcy. Especially her reaction to his kiss.

He'd installed her in his office, his professional life and his personal life, making him miserable and happy at the same time. Something had to give. She would be leaving in a couple weeks. His life would return to normal. Would his life be better for it? Or worse?

At least with his patient he and Marcy had a chance to help him. They'd found common cause. He liked working with her. She was efficient, intelligent, determined and compassionate. All qualities of a first-rate doctor.

Dylan knocked, then entered a room on the fifth floor. Inside sitting in a chair was Steve, a fourteen-year-old boy who should have been out playing basketball. Instead, he was stuck in the hospital. Sitting near him were his parents. Steve had grown over the years to the point he was almost too long for the bed. He'd been one of Dylan's first patients after he'd joined the staff of Atlanta Children's. If Dylan didn't known better, he would never say the boy was ill.

"Steve, Mr. and Mrs. Tiffon…this is Dr. Montgomery. She's a cancer research doctor. She's doing a trial here at the hospital right now." Dylan looked at Steve. "Do you know what a trial is?"

Steve shook his head.

"It means we give you an experimental medicine we have tested in the lab and now we're testing on a certain group of patients before we give it to everyone. There may be side effects for some. Dr. Montgomery believes this new medicine she has developed could help you. We'd like to try it on you. But we all need to agree."

Mr. and Mrs. Tiffon came to stand beside the bed. "Dr. Montgomery, why don't you explain to Steve and his parents about how the medicine works?"

"The drug is called TM13. It works on the T cells which are part of your immune system. I'm sure you've heard of those before."

The parents nodded and Steve looked bored.

"These T cells are part of our blood that fight off infection. Fight off cancer."

"We'll give you an intravenous dose starting now if you agree. Then another one or two, tomorrow and the next day. Then you'll have to come back once a week for a month. We'll be checking your blood work regularly."

"That doesn't sound much different than what it was when I was taking chemo," Steve muttered and took a moment to look at Dylan.

He nodded. "It's close to the same regimen but the medicine is different. It's new and we can't promise what side effects you might experience. The medicine hasn't been given to many people. Only tested in the lab. It may not work but we have high hopes that it will.

"What we do know is that what we've been doing isn't working." Dylan picked up the electric pad and made a note on it. "Dr. Montgomery and I are going to step outside and let you discuss this and think about it carefully."

He followed Marcy out into the hallway. They stood to one side.

"Do you think you'd agree with us if you were in their situation?" Dylan asked with concern filling his eyes.

"I would agree to anything for a chance to save my child's life."

CHAPTER SIX

"DID YOU THINK you would be this involved with the patients when you decided to oversee the trial?" Dylan leaned against the wall across the hall from Steve's room.

Marcy pursed her lips. "Actually, it hasn't been too bad. I've learned a lot. Ryan's mother made me think about things I hadn't before. And with Steve, I think I have a way to help him. If he and his parents agree."

"By the way, what does TM13 stand for? Or is it just a name pulled out of the air?"

"It's named for a patient, and it was the thirteenth time the medicine was reworked before we found the dosage that was right."

Dylan shifted. "I always hate waiting."

Marcy gave him a look of disbelief. "Isn't that more than half of what medicine is about?"

"Yeah. But I don't have to like it. I waited

so much when Beau was sick I never wanted to do it again, but then I went into a profession that waits all the time. Waits on blood work...waits for a few days to see what's going to happen. Waits until the test results are in. I still don't like it."

"Beau?"

"My roommate in boarding school."

"Oh, the friend who made you get into oncology. Will you tell me about him?" Marcy asked softly.

Dylan took a deep breath. For some reason he wanted her to know. To understand what had formed him. "Beau was my rock, my stability during a lonely time in my life. I was homeschooled for many years. Then my parents were reassigned to an area where I couldn't go to the local high school so it was decided that we, my older brother and I, would go to boarding school. Beau was my roommate and best friend. We were inseparable until Beau was ill one morning. He went to the infirmary and never returned. No one would tell me what happened. Finally Beau's mother called to tell me he had cancer and was in the hospital. I had no car and no way of visiting. All I could do was call and check on him. When I did talk to him, he sounded so depressed. That's when I decided to be a doctor and vowed to not do everything Beau's doctors did, except for making him well."

Steve's mother stepped into the hall and looked around until she spotted them and waved them inside. Marcy glanced at Dylan then led the way into Steve's room.

They were all standing around Steve's bed when he said, "I want to try it."

Dylan was positioned at the foot of the bed. "I believe you're doing the right thing."

Steve's mother, her face drawn with worry, said, "We have to try anything that might help him get better again."

"Then I'll start getting all the paperwork together. It'll take us a little while, but I'll get on it right away." Marcy gave them a reassuring smile. "I'll have to get permission to give it in a bolus fashion. As soon as I have that we'll move ahead."

Dylan, with Marcy shadowing him, headed toward his office. "I have to speak to the committee leader dealing with trials and write this up as a proposal. Get an emergency agreement."

"Today?"

"That's my plan."

"I need to decide how to incorporate this

into the trial. As it is, it won't be looked on favorably," Marcy said, her expression showing determination.

Dylan nodded. "That will help my chances of getting the okay. If he's under your trial guidelines than he'll fall under your proposals and not so much the hospital's."

"I'll write it up as a latecomer to the trail."

"Steve and his parents deserve this chance. Let's dot our 'i's and cross our 't's." Dylan looked at Marcy, hoping she would see that he shared her resolve.

"I hope that TM13 performs as I expect. That I haven't oversold it."

Marcy left to go to the clinic and organize the medicine.

By the time he'd finished what he needed to do she'd joined him again in the office. "I've ordered the medicine for Steve. I want to be there when the infusion is started."

Six hours later, when they entered Steve's room, a nurse was there, checking his vital signs. Another nurse joined them carrying a clear IV bag of TM13. She hooked it to the pole on wheels near Steve's bed. Marcy stayed out of the way as the nurse went about putting an IV in Steve's arm and securing it with tape.

Steve didn't even flinch as the nurse did what was necessary. He'd had so much experience with being in the hospital. He was a handsome youth with red hair and light blue eyes. He spoke with intelligence to Dylan about sports, baseball in particular.

Despite the conversation Dylan could tell he was keenly aware of what the nurse was doing. There were worry lines across his forehead.

Dylan could see that Marcy was watching carefully. He was positive that she hadn't given them all false hope, and prayed she was equally confident of that. She knew her facts and figures as one of the top researchers in her field.

Soon the precious clear liquid ran into Steve's vein, giving him a chance to kick out the invader. All that could be done now was to wait. The very word and action Dylan hated but was necessary.

Lab work would be taken regularly to try to catch any adverse effects, starting three hours after the dose had finished and continuing throughout the night They wouldn't know if they were making any real headway until after a few draws.

Dylan stepped out of the room and indicated for Marcy to come with him. They crossed the hall to a consult room. "I'm gonna stay around up here a little longer to see that everything's going well. You feel free to go back to the office. I'll call if something comes up."

"Okay. Can you see that lab results are forwarded to me? I want to review the findings. I'll be in the office if you need me."

Dylan checked his wristwatch. "The first blood draw won't be until 4 a.m. We won't know anything until then."

"This is our case. I'll be staying close," Marcy stated firmly. Dylan didn't argue with her any further. He was grateful to have her there. She knew all the ins and outs of TM13, had seen its reactions. He believed in Marcy's abilities as a doctor. Trusted her as a human being and admired her as a person.

Marcy sat behind her desk and checked her clock. It was still awhile before Steve's blood work would be drawn. Her phone rang. She picked it up and read one o'clock on the screen.

"Steve is throwing up." Dylan's voice held a desperate note.

She stood. "I'm on my way."

Headed to Steve's room, she stopped by the nurses' station to put on a mask and plastic gloves. She knocked then entered the room. Dylan along with the parents stood whispering in the corner, and Steve appeared to be asleep.

Dylan stepped to her.

"This isn't unexpected," she assured him. "We can handle it." Their roles had been reversed: she was now the one reassuring him. "I've seen this before. When the rate is slowed Steve should improve."

"I'll take care of that right away." Dylan stepped away to talk to the nurse who had just come in. From the look on Dylan's face, he was completely invested in Steve.

"His blood pressure and heart rate are up." The concern in Dylan's voice tightened her chest.

Marcy examined Steve's nailbeds. They had turned a dusky blue.

"He's also developed a rash on his abdomen."

Marcy checked the monitors. "You should also increase the rate of fluids."

Steve's eyelids opened.

"How're you feeling?" Dylan asked the boy.

"Not too good."

Marcy stepped to the bed. "Can you tell me what's bothering you?"

"My stomach. It's rolling." Steve wore a pained look on his face.

Marcy couldn't help but feel sorry for the boy.

Steve put his arms across his midsection and groaned.

"Nurse, could we please get some Phenergan in here," Dylan snapped, using a tone Marcy hadn't heard from him.

The young nurse hurried out of the room.

"I would also like to see a full blood panel," Marcy whispered to Dylan as she pulled a chair up beside Steve's bed later that evening.

Dylan brought his chair up next to hers. From their vantage point they were out of the way of the nurses but could see the monitor and Steve's face clearly.

She reviewed the numbers again on the digital pad then settled in the chair. She'd become concerned about Steve despite her confidence in her plan. With the additions of other medicines Steve's heart rate was coming down and BP was improving. The infusion of TM13 had been slowed but as much medicine as possible as soon as possible was the overall answer.

"Where are Steve's parents?"

Dylan settled in a chair. "I sent them home for some rest. I told them I would call them. I assured them I'd be here the entire time."

"They trust you, don't they?"

"I sure hope so."

"You're a special doctor and man, Dylan."

He gave her a thin-lipped smile as he watched Steve. "I like hearing you say so."

Hours later Marcy shifted in the metal chair with a thin cushion and narrow armrests. None of which made for a comfortable rest.

"You can sure tell these are institutional seating." Dylan yawned and stretched out his long legs, crossing them at the ankles.

"I think hospitals buy them to encourage visitors not to stay too long." She chuckled quietly.

"Why don't you get some rest? Put your head on my shoulder. I'll take the shift watching."

Marcy wasn't sure she wanted the nurses to think there was something going on between her and Dylan. She wasn't confident there was, yet that hot kiss in the parking lot said they both felt something more than friendship. Since she'd renewed her friendship with Dylan she'd started to live again. She could feel it. For too long she'd just existed. He'd filled the hole in her life with excitement and happiness.

She rested her head against Dylan's shoulder. Before she knew it, her eyelids drooped.

Dylan jostled her. She'd only been asleep for thirty minutes. "They're taking blood work right now. We should have the results back soon. I thought you'd want to see them."

Marcy groaned and uncurled, rolling her shoulders. "What I wouldn't give for a soft bed."

His gaze met hers. "Me too." Offering his hand to help her up. "Let's get a cup of coffee while we wait. Steve seems to be resting comfortably right now. The nurse is okay with checking in on him more often while we're gone. I suspect in a couple more hours his mom and dad will be here."

She and Dylan found fresh coffee in a little break room behind the nurses' station. They took a seat at a small table for four in the tiny space.

"It's been a long time since I've done an all-nighter," Marcy said.

Dylan sipped from his cup. "I don't do them often."

She studied Dylan a moment. "Steve is a special case."

"Yeah, he is. My first success case. He reminds me of Beau. Tough but easygoing."

"I think I'd like Beau. I'd like to meet him."

"You will. His family lives in Birmingham. He and Lisa will be coming for the ball. His company underwrites the event's expenses, which means all the funds raised go directly to help the children. They always make a huge donation each year."

"I look forward to it. I'll be leaving the day after the ball." Her chest tightened at the idea.

A nurse came to the doorway. "Dr. Nelson, the results are back. You can see them at the nurses' station."

They followed her to a computer, where she punched in a code and data filled the screen.

"His numbers have improved," Marcy said. "But just marginally. We've got to get them down further."

Dylan put an arm around her shoulders and squeezed. "It's going the right direction because of your recommendations."

Marcy glowed under his praise. "I don't think I can take all the credit."

"I think you should get a huge chunk of it."

"Now that we know Steve is headed in the right direction why don't you go on home and get some rest?" Dylan started out of the nurses' station. "I'll watch over Steve during the second dose."

"Why don't we both go when Steve's parents get here?"

Dylan shook his head. "Think I'll hang around awhile and see how he does. This is paperwork day anyway."

Marcy laughed. "You're using paperwork as an excuse to keep an eye on a patient."

"Yeah, I am. He's still not out of the woods yet. We have to hope the treatment works."

She squeezed his arm. "I truly believe it will."

He looked her in the eyes. "I appreciate you being here."

Marcy liked the idea that Dylan needed her and that she was able to help.

They reentered Steve's room to find him awake.

"Hey, buddy, how are you feeling?" Dylan stepped to the bed.

"Better."

Dylan looked at the monitors. "That's good

to hear. Your blood work came back with improvements this morning."

"You stayed all night?" Disbelief hung in the boy's question.

"Yep. Did you know you snore?" Dylan pulled his stethoscope from around his neck.

Steve's smile was weak, but it was a smile.

The door opened and in came his parents. They looked relieved to see their son sitting up in the bed. Dylan explained what had happened through the night and the plan for the next few days.

Minutes later Marcy stepped out in the hall behind Dylan with a sense of relief and success. She'd seen a positive sign in her life's work. What she had worked most of her adult life to achieve. It felt good but she wanted more. For once the guilt had eased.

"I'm going to stay here through the next dose." She glanced at the tech pad. "I want to see these numbers look better. I'm not satisfied. I have plenty of work I can do while I wait."

Dylan glanced at Marcy working at her desk. He'd thought it wouldn't be an issue to share his office with her, but it was turning into a real problem. He had welcomed her into his professional life and she was nudging her way into his personal life too. He was confused by his mixed emotions about her and the upheaval he felt at the change in him. He couldn't continue this way.

She would be leaving very soon. All he had to do was survive until then. Keep his hands and his lips to himself. Then his life would return to normal. Even now, looking exhausted, she pulled at him, making him want to take her into his arms.

Unable to continue being in the room with Marcy without going to her, he decided to leave her alone. He went to the Infusion Room to check on the patients there. A couple of them had questions about the ball but most were planning to attend.

"Have ya'll picked out the rap you're going to do?" He received several nods. "Anyone want to share with me?"

They all grinned and shook their heads.

An hour later he visited Steve's room. Inside, sitting beside Steve was Marcy. She was quietly talking to the boy's parents. After sleeping in a chair all night and working part of the day, Marcy still looked lovely.

It wasn't until Steve said, "Hey, Doc," that Dylan looked away.

"Hi. How're you feeling?"

"Pretty good. My stomach isn't hurting anymore." Steve put his hand on his middle.

"That's good to hear but that might not last for long. You're due for your next treatment."

The boy's face drew serious. "You think I'll be sick again."

Dylan turned as Marcy joined him beside the bed. "Maybe it won't be so bad this time."

"I hope so. It wasn't much fun last night." Steve fiddled with the edge of his blanket.

"I'm sure it wasn't," Marcy said, patting his arm. "We'll do our best to head it off this next time."

A nurse entered carrying the bag of liquid. She hung it on the pole before preparing the IV to hook it to Steve.

"We'll be here or close by all the time. All you have to do is ask for us," Marcy told him.

"Yeah, buddy, just let us know what you need."

Steve nodded then looked at the IV leading into his arm.

Marcy and Dylan stepped out the door.

"How do you think he's going to do?" Dylan asked looking back at the room with concern. He hated to put the boy through more but knew it was necessary.

"To be truthful I don't know. TM13 is strong with fewer side effects but given as a bolus dose I can't promise what might happen. That's why I'm going to stay close by. I not only need to see the results but the reactions. Plus I want to be here for them all."

"I understand how you feel so I won't try to get you to go home. But what I will do is show you where you can shower, find clean clothes and get some rest."

"That sounds nice, but I want to hang around here until still infusion is finished and I can check Steve's numbers."

Dylan sighed. "I can't fault your dedication. I plan to hang around for a while as well. Thank goodness it was a slow patient day in the clinic."

"But we do have the kids who are planning to sing coming in for practice and a pizza party this afternoon." Marcy yawned.

Dylan shook his head. "It always amazes me that they're on chemo, which often causes an upset stomach, and yet they'll still go for pizza. The strength of the young is outstanding." He regarded Marcy's pale face and reiterated his offer. "We're a phone call away, so why don't I show you where you can get a shower."

Marcy fixed him with a look. "Are you trying to tell me that I smell?"

Dylan smiled. "No more than I do. We've been at this for almost forty-eight hours. I think we deserve a shower."

Dylan directed Marcy into a locker room. "With any luck I can find you a set of scrubs to change into." He went to a cabinet and pulled out a plastic-covered prepackaged set of light blue scrubs. He handed it to her. "These should work. Please be sure to return them because you'll be charged for them."

"Thanks. I will," she said, taking the package from him.

He searched through the stack and pulled out another set of scrubs. "While you're changing, I'll check on Steve."

Marcy gave him a long look.

"Is something wrong? What's that look for?" He watched her.

"Because you are you." She gave him a quick kiss on the cheek.

He grinned. "I need to know what I did so I can do it again."

"You believe in me. Trust me with Steve."

Dylan did, even when she didn't seem to have that much confidence in herself. Did she have people in her life who didn't believe in her?

"Of course I do. Why wouldn't I? You're smart, educated and tops in your field." What he wanted to say but didn't was that she was also beautiful. He smiled. "What's not to believe in?"

She blushed a little and smiled. "Thank you. That's one of the nicest things someone has ever said to me."

Six hours later they studied Steve's blood work numbers on the computer screen.

"His white count has dropped but not far enough," Dylan noted, pointing to a number. He wasn't telling Marcy anything she didn't know.

"Yes, but it isn't enough to warrant not doing the third dose tomorrow. Just follow the same procedures as last time and I believe he'll be fine. At least the nausea was better this time around."

"I'm going to trust your judgment on this." Dylan started toward Steve's room.

Marcy's heart swelled. He trusted her. He still found her reliable. Her husband had never been able to do that after Toby's death, even before he'd started doubting her.

Dylan turned when she didn't follow. "Is something wrong?"

She smiled. "No everything is right." It wasn't until that moment she'd realized how much she needed someone to believe in her. Having Dylan's loyalty made her have faith in herself.

After the pizza party in a conference room with the patients singing at the ball, she and Dylan returned to their office.

"That went well. I think the kids are looking forward to performing now. At first I wasn't so sure. Wasn't even sure they'd show up." Marcy sank into her chair.

"Yeah, I believe they will be a hard act to follow. Marcy, I wish you'd go home. Get some sleep in a real bed, not a cot in a closet."

She gave him a defiant look and asked, "Are *you* going?"

He met her gaze. "Well, no."

"Then I think I should stay. The final dose can be given at 4 a.m., and I want to be here for it." Marcy squared her shoulders.

"But you have plenty of time to go home and come back." His tone was a plea.

"So do you," she countered.

"Okay. If we aren't going home, then at least we're going to get outside for a few min-

utes before the sun sets. I also think Steve and
his parents could use a few minutes when we
aren't hovering." He took her hand and tugged
her toward the door.

She looked around. "Where're we going?"

"For a walk. There's a park just a couple
of blocks from here." Dylan clicked off the
lights.

"I don't think—" She stopped.

He took her elbow and nudged her forward.
"Doctor's orders."

They headed out the staff door. Dylan directed her along the sidewalk and across the
street then entered a gated path. Dylan led
her along an easy trail to a creek. The birds
chirped and flew away while the squirrels
played in the trees. She watched in amazement when Dylan grabbed her arm, putting
his finger over his lips in the sign for silence.
He pointed to a rabbit.

"I must admit this is wonderful. I might
not have thought I needed it, but I did." She
smiled and rolled her shoulders.

"Sit. Let me massage your shoulders.
Those hospital chairs aren't made for sitting in a long time or sleeping." She sat on
a smooth rock and Dylan positioned himself
behind her.

"You can't be much better off." He gave her a look filled with concern.

"Then we'll take turns." He placed his hands on her shoulders and started working the tight muscles there.

"That feels so good." A few minutes later she pulled away. "Your turn now."

Dylan sat next to her and presented his broad shoulders.

"No argument?" she teased.

"Are you kidding? I'd never turn a shoulder rub down. I hope I don't embarrass myself by purring."

Marcy chuckled. She placed her hands on him, kneaded his muscles while enjoying touching him but reminding herself she shouldn't let it go beyond this. "I feel guilty about being out here in all this beauty and tranquility while Steve is going through what he is."

"He was feeling fine when we left. I gave strict instructions if that changed to call me. I hate it too, but the procedure had to be done. Guilt does no one any good."

Marcy knew that too well. "You really believe that, don't you?"

"I do. For years I felt guilty about my parents missing every major event in my life. I thought it was my fault."

She moved so she could look him in the eyes. "It wasn't. I'm sure they didn't realize how much it bothered you. Did you ever tell them?"

He shrugged. "No."

She couldn't hide her sympathy. "It still must have hurt."

"You're right about that. I just know that I won't treat my children that way." Dylan pulled a package of crackers out of his pocket. "Not much of a picnic but what I could come up with on short notice."

Marcy noticed the abrupt end to the conversation but didn't comment. They ate sitting on the rock in the last sun of the day. Dylan took her hand, gently rubbing a thumb across the top, creating a calm within her she wouldn't have thought possible.

"Thanks for bringing me out here. You were right. I needed this. It gets your head away from your worries."

Marcy shivered. Dylan pulled her close and wrapped an arm across her shoulders. "We'll stay only a few minutes longer."

Unable to help herself, she leaned her head against his chest. The fleeting thought that she'd like to stay there forever entered her mind. She pushed it away. That would never happen. She wouldn't let it. Instead of wishing for something she couldn't have, she concentrated on the water flowing over the stones in the creek.

When Dylan finally moved, she sat straighter. He stood, offered his hand and pulled her to him. Their gazes met, held. His head lowered a fraction as if he thought to kiss her before he said, "We better get back. We have a patient waiting."

He held her hand as they strolled back the way they came. They walked in silence until Dylan broke it. "What do you see yourself doing ten years from now?"

She stopped and leaned back so she could see his face. "Wow, that's an out-of-the-blue, deep question. Are you asking about my work or my personal life?"

"Both. I'd like to hear your answer." His tone implied he wouldn't let her get away with not answering. Yet she would try. "How about you go first."

Dylan didn't even have to think. "I see myself here in Atlanta working at the hospital doing what I am doing right now, saving all the children I can. Hopefully with a wife and family."

Marcy could see too well a swing set in his backyard with children playing. Him coming home from a long day and them running to welcome him. What she didn't want to see was the woman walking toward him with a smile on her face. A sick feeling clenched her stomach. The face wasn't hers. Nor the mini-van in the driveway.

"Now you." Dylan said when it took her so long to respond.

She bit her bottom lip. At one time she had dreamed. But not now.

Dylan ran a gentle finger across her mouth, easing her hold, sending a shiver of desire through her.

"I want to find a cure for this horrible dis-ease that ruins children's and families' lives."

He encouraged her to walk on. "That's admirable but don't you want something for yourself?"

Why did he have to keep pushing? That *would* be for herself. "That's what I've been working toward for the last ten years." Since Toby had died.

"No other dreams?"

"I think the one I have is large enough."

CHAPTER SEVEN

DYLAN CHECKED AND double-checked Steve's monitor and last lab work at 7 a.m. as he stood at the end of his patient's bed. The numbers were almost perfect. He looked at Marcy next to him. She glowed with pride.

Dylan's attention returned to his patient. "Your numbers look better. I'm cautiously optimistic that the drug therapy worked. You're going to have to stay here a few more days to make sure but I can see you going home."

A soft sob came from the direction of Steve's mother, who clung to his father's arm.

Dylan smiled. "I think we could all use some rest. The nurses will be keeping a watch over you. Dr. Montgomery and I are going to leave you to rest now. We'll see you tomorrow."

Steve nodded. His mother gave him and

Marcy a hug. The father shook their hands, stammering, "Thank you. Thank you."

Dylan noticed Marcy's eyes glistened as he closed the door to the room behind them. He couldn't help but burst into a grin. His arms came around Marcy, bringing her into a tight hug. "Apparently the fourth time is the charm."

"It worked," Marcy said in a breathy voice as she hugged him back.

Dylan let her go just as abruptly as he'd taken her, scared to reveal his true emotions, then put some space between them. "Yes, it did," he said. "Thanks to you, Steve has another chance. Now it's time we go home and get some real sleep. I'm exhausted and I know you must be too."

To Dylan's amazement Marcy offered him no argument. In the parking lot, Dylan said, "I arranged for Security to drive us home. Neither of us needs to be driving. We are exhausted."

Again, Marcy said nothing and just got in the car. She lay back in the seat and closed her eyes.

The sound of jackhammers and equipment surrounded Marcy's apartment when they pulled into the complex. A busted water main was being repaired.

Dylan's mouth tightened. "You can't stay here. You'll never get any sleep or a shower You can stay in my guest room."

"I don't think—"

"Be reasonable, Marcy." He waved a hand in the direction of the work. "This is a loud mess."

She looked around in defeat. "Okay, thank you. For tonight only, though."

A long roll of thunder and a loud boom woke Dylan just before midnight. He'd left the French door in his living area open letting in fresh air. Padding into the room that had grown thick and humid, he went to the wind-blown door. A storm was coming.

A movement grabbed his attention. Marcy.

She stood on the terracotta pavers with her head back and face up to the sky. As he stepped out the door, she continued to stand there as if she had no idea it would rain soon. Lightning flashed and somewhere farther off thunder shook the air.

"Marcy what are you doing out here?"

She wrapped her arms around her waist as

she shook. "I had a bad dream. He died on a night like this."

Dylan's chest tightened. Was she sleep-walking? "Who died?"

"Toby."

He waited. She must be overtired. Unable to help himself he asked, "Toby?"

"My son."

Dylan sucked in a breath. Did she know what she was saying? Had she lost a son?

"It was storming that night too." She didn't move, just spoke as if a long way away.

"A car accident?" He wanted to go to Marcy but feared startling her.

Marcy shook her head slowly. "No. From cancer."

Dylan gasped. Some of her actions and re-actions made sense now. "I'm sorry. I didn't know."

"Because I didn't want you to. That I couldn't save my own child while I was try-ing to save your patients. You wouldn't have trusted me."

Dylan was shocked she might think that, but it didn't matter now. He made his voice low and soothing and stepped closer. Another flash of lightning went across the sky. "Let's go inside, Marcy."

When she didn't move, Dylan stepped behind her. He just wanted her to feel his reassuring warmth. With deliberate movement he drew her to him. Her head fell back against his shoulder. He slowly rubbed her arm.

He kissed the top of her head. "I think there's more to the story. You can tell me. I'm a good listener. It won't go any further than me. But let's go inside."

He'd wondered about some of her actions, but she never let on how hard it must have been for her to see patients. The past had to have come back in waves. No wonder she could empathize with the parents. She'd been one of them. Knew what they felt.

"He would be ten now if he had lived. He didn't make it out of infancy."

Dylan stayed still, waited.

Her voice was dull with remembered pain. "I was so absorbed in my work trying to prevent cancer I didn't see that Toby had it. Ironic, isn't it? A cancer researcher having a child with cancer and not seeing it. It had been there growing and growing and I had no idea. I didn't recognize it." A soft sob bubbled out of her throat.

Dylan's arms tightened around her, holding her steady. Marcy didn't resist. He wanted her to know he was there to support her. He held her close, saying nothing. His ex-fiancée always complained he could only give support to his patients. That he didn't let anyone else get close enough for him to really care about them on a personal level. He cared about Marcy. Deeply. He wanted to take the pain from her.

"The storm woke me, and the memories swamped me. It doesn't happen all the time but tonight they got to me."

"Probably because of the emotional roller coaster you've been on the last three days."

A short while later, after she'd relaxed, Dylan asked softly, "Will you tell me about Toby?"

As a rule, she didn't talk about Toby to anyone. Ever. It was too difficult. For days afterward she'd relive the happy days, the sad days and the horrible moments. Still did. Let the guilt slowly eat her up. But she couldn't tell Dylan that; couldn't admit that to anyone.

They'd think she was crazy, not handling her grief. People had told her again and again that time would ease the pain. It didn't. She felt it as intensely as she ever had. The pain lingered like a bad smell. She could recognize it instantly. Yet for some reason she wanted Dylan to know. He had a way of making things better.

"By all standards Toby was a normal baby boy. When he started crying more than usual, we just thought it was a touch of croup."

"That's not uncommon."

"It is but that wasn't the problem. By this time, Josh had moved up in his firm and had to travel to sites more often. I got the majority of the care, but I was okay with that. We had great day care help as well, and an older lady came to the house. When Toby made a whistling sound as he breathed I took him to the pediatrician. He found a tumor in Toby's nose. He sent us to a pediatric oncologist. Toby was diagnosed with esthesioneuroblastoma."

"That's rare in a child." Dylan's voice said he was in doctor mode. She'd heard that tone before.

"It is. By the time it was diagnosed it was stage III." Her words came out low and measured. She had a difficult time saying them. "Less than a month later it had moved to a stage IV in the brain."

Dylan sucked in a shocked breath.

"I was a mess. Josh didn't handle it well

either. I felt—still feel—responsible for not recognizing the problem before I did. My ex blamed me. After all, I'm a doctor. I should've known. Seen it sooner."

"Marcy—"

She held up a hand. "I know what you're going to say. I've heard it all. But that doesn't change how I feel. Or the reality. The last few months of Toby's life were the worst. I took time off to be with him. Josh couldn't face what was happening and worked more not to think about it…then Toby was gone."

Dylan's arm tightened around her. She sank into his heat and comfort. Without saying a word he told her he was there for her.

She took a deep breath. "After Toby died, I threw myself into my work, which finished off my already rocky marriage. Here I am with something to really offer children with cancer, and I can't even tell the parents I see every day that I've been where they are."

Dylan continued to hold her. "But you've been helping them more than you know. I've seen you talking to Ryan's parents, Steve's and Lucy's. I even pointed out how you inter-act with them. The children and the parents all like you. I'm even more impressed now that I know about Toby."

She turned in his arms. "It just looks that way. Every day I have to remind myself to keep it together."

"Don't we all? I have to remind myself not to get too involved. Not to bring it all home with me."

"It just seems like the more progress we make with curing cancer the more children have it. It doesn't stop. I want it to stop." Her frustration tightened the muscles of her face.

He cupped her cheek, raising her face until she could see him clearly. "You and I are doing what we can to make that happen."

The moment warmed. His gaze held hers.

She needed the reassurance, the tenderness, the human interaction. It had been too long since someone had held her, desired her, comforted her. If she was honest with herself, she liked being with Dylan. Then why was she stopping herself from enjoying him while she could? It would be painful to leave him either way. She wanted the here and now. To grasp life for a change.

Instead of fighting her feelings she would accept them and share them with Dylan if he still wanted her. She pressed her lips to his.

Dylan's return kiss was gentle, caring and tentative. Soothing.

Her focus remained firmly on Dylan's tender, yet seductive lips. He pressed closer. It was a sweet reassuring kiss. Yet she wanted more. She needed someone to touch her, desire her. She leaned into him.

His mouth firmly found hers this time. His arms tightened around her as his lips pressed against hers. This wasn't a kiss of reassurance but of the want and need of a man. Her head spun. This was too much sensation. She hadn't been kissed since Josh left. Hadn't wanted that type of contact. She instinctively pushed against Dylan's chest.

His mouth immediately left hers. "I'm sorry. I shouldn't have done that."

She put some distance between them.

"You were upset. I just wanted you to feel better. I shouldn't have taken advantage of you." Yet he still wanted her in his arms again. Wanted to make that sadness he'd heard in her voice disappear.

"It's okay. I understand."

He'd forced himself to remain isolated from real emotional relationships, fearing that if he loved someone, they would leave him. After all, his parents had, Beau had no choice but to leave him, even Marcy had in her own fashion, then his fiancée. The lesson he'd learn long ago was he was destined to be alone.

Even with his parents the distance was not only in miles but emotions. They didn't know him, especially his father who couldn't understand that Dylan's place was in Atlanta not in some far-off country. He tried not to resent them, and he'd missed them desperately when he was a boy. That loneliness still colored his world. It was just as well Marcy wanted space. She would leave him soon too, for a second time.

"Let's get you inside. You're freezing. You need a warm shower before you start to shiver." Dylan led Marcy to the guest bath and turned the shower water to hot. "I'll get you something else to wear. Don't argue. Just get in."

She put a hand on his arm stopping him. Her wide sad eyes locked with his. "I'm afraid that my

life is passing me by. I have become nothing more than a lab rat. In a cage of my own making."

Dylan's chest constricted. Had he brought on this show of boldness by having her talk about the past? "You have more life to live. Plenty of love to give."

"Toby was so small and perfect. He didn't deserve to die that way." She sounded as if she were talking to herself instead of him.

"No, honey, he didn't. That's a part of life we can't do anything about."

"I can't seem to do anything about any of my life." She looked so sad, Dylan brought her against his chest. "I think you have more control than you believe. You've just been hiding and running away from your feelings. You haven't had the right person around to help you learn to live again."

She looked up with a luminous gaze. "Are you the right person?"

Dylan's chest tightened. What could he promise her? Nothing. He was self-reliant and had learned to appreciate his own company. Could he open up enough to let her in? Be the person she deserved. Dare he? Dylan took a moment to answer. "I'd like to think I could be."

Marcy couldn't remember the last time, if ever, she'd been so open with another person. Even Josh hadn't known all her fears and dreams. She wanted Dylan to see her as a desirable woman, not just a needy one. After the sad story she'd told he'd acted as if she were too fragile to touch. She'd pushed him away, but she needed his touch, wanted personal interaction. It had been so long since she'd dared to feel.

She'd held herself away from any intimate contact for so long she'd forgotten what it was like to have someone hold and kiss her. Or how her body trembled at a man's touch. Until she'd reconnected with Dylan any sexual emotions had been missing from her life. Right now, she felt too much. It was all jumbled together. Yet she knew she wanted Dylan.

Just the little bit of caring he'd given her by insisting she shower was more than she let herself experience in years. That had opened the door to need. She craved more as she stepped under the spray.

For too long she'd lived in fear, kept people at arm's length. If she didn't care, then she wouldn't get hurt. But with Dylan she was safe. He would never hurt her. She would leave soon. For once with good memories. She wanted to live for a change. At least for a little while.

Did Dylan want her? She had to be bold enough to ask.

"Dylan?"

"Yes?"

She opened the sliding glass door to the shower. "You must be cold too. Don't waste this hot water."

"Marcy?" Her name came out rusty and sexy. "Do you know what you're saying?"

"Uh, yes. I'm inviting you to share my shower."

"Marcy, do you know what you're doing to me?" His words had a strangled sound to them.

"I think so. I hope so. I want you. I want to feel alive again. To feel something. I want to sleep next to you."

Dylan wasted no time in stripping off his pajama pants. He was amazing in all his naked glory, and desire.

He stepped inside the shower and took her into his arms. "Are you sure about this? I don't want you to have any regrets in the morning."

She cupped his cheek. "The only thing I would regret is if I didn't kiss you."

"I can't deny I like that answer," he murmured, his lips finding hers with a tentative touch.

Marcy returned the kiss. She ran her hands

over Dylan's water-slick body, appreciating the dips and rises of his muscles. She intended to enjoy him for as long as possible.

His gentle touches turned urgent and the pressure of his fingertips encouraged her. His hands slipped over her body following her curves. Cupping her butt, he lifted her to him. She gripped his shoulders as his manhood stood strong and thick between them.

Marcy's hands wandered up his back and over his shoulders, encouraging him.

He wrapped her in his arms. His mouth left hers to travel across her cheek to her neck. He nipped at that tender spot behind her ear. Would she die from the pleasure? She moaned. Leaning her head to the side, she gave him better access. Her body trembled.

He kissed along her hairline to her temple as she stepped closer. His straining pulsing manhood stood hard against her middle. The fire of desire roared making her gasp.

The water cooled.

Dylan put some space between them. "I've wanted you too long to take you for the first time in a shower. You deserve better. You should be loved slow and easy, savored like a good wine."

She pressed her body tight against him and kissed him deeply.

Dylan leaned back where he could see her face. "Marcy, are you sure about this? There'll be no turning back if this continues."

Marcy went up on her toes and gave him a challenging kiss, opening her mouth in invitation. He accepted her offer and took over the kiss.

She ran her hands through his hair, along the back of his neck and across his shoulders. When he tugged at her bottom lip, she whimpered her gratification as if she'd never experienced anything so wonderful. She hadn't.

Marcy pulled away. Her gaze met Dylan's then roamed downward to his chest. She leaned forward to kiss him but thought better of it. Instead, she licked a rivulet of water running down the center of his torso. Dylan shuddered and Marcy smiled.

He nudged her away from him. "Marcy, we have to stop."

She straightened. Had she gone too far? Was Dylan disappointed in her? "Did I do something wrong?"

He groaned. "No, honey. The problem is you're doing everything too right."

Marcy smiled, her confidence restored.

"I want you more than I can say. Let's go to my bed. It's getting cold in here, anyway." He touched the tip of her hard nipple. "Even if I like what it does for your beautiful breasts."

She craved his touch, what it made her feel.

"I've wanted you since we were in college. I think I can wait ten minutes until I get you to bed."

Her face eased into relief. "You've wanted me that long?"

Dylan turned the water off and stepped out of the shower. "I think I've wanted you forever."

"You never said anything."

Taking her hand, he led her out of the shower before wrapping a towel around her shoulders. He rubbed her down, leaving her with the towel to use on her hair. "What was I going to say? *Give up your boyfriend for me?* I didn't even have enough money to take you out on a real date." He pulled a towel off the rack and dried himself.

Marcy vigorously rubbed her hair. She peeked out from under the towel. "I'm more interested in you than a date."

The skin tightened across Dylan's cheekbones. "You're so beautiful."

Heat that had nothing to do with the steamy

shower warmed her. "Thank you. Age and a baby have changed me some."

"I like the mature you. You're more beautiful than you were in college. Leave the towel." Dylan tugged the material and it fell to the floor. He took her hand. "Come on, I'd like to show you just how beautiful I think you are."

The storm had settled in.

Dylan led her to his bed. Pulling back the covers, he let her crawl in and he joined her. He lay on his side and took her hand. Bringing it to his mouth he kissed her palm. "I need to know you're sure about this. I can't have you regretting this tomorrow. If you aren't sure, it stops here, and we go to sleep. I value our friendship too much."

No one had ever shown Marcy the sensitivity and attention Dylan bestowed. He understood her. Even Josh hadn't been able to make her feel this desire. The few men she'd made herself go out with since the end of her marriage hadn't come close to doing so. She wanted Dylan. Wanted this. Needed him.

She cupped Dylan's cheek. "I would never regret anything between us. You have my word we'll always remain friends. I need to live a little. Feel alive and I want to do that with you."

Closing the distance between them, he kissed her deeply. She wrapped her arm across his chest as she slid her leg between his legs. It felt so good to have human contact. To have someone tell her she was beautiful, to make her feel desired. To believe she had something to offer.

Dylan's hand traveled along the curve of her hip to her waist until it lifted her breast. His fingers kneaded gently, teasing her nipple, making it stand erect. He rasped, "So responsive."

His mouth left hers. He kissed the hollow of her shoulder before his lips circled her nipple and sucked.

Marcy's center tightened. She leaned back giving him free access as she ran her fingers through his hair, holding him close. Her breaths turned short and shallow. Could she die from such pleasure?

"Like that, do you?" Dylan asked as he moved to the other breast.

Marcy couldn't answer. All her attention was focused on how Dylan made her feel. She pulled at him, wanting to have him against her, but he resisted.

He raised his head, meeting her look. "Lie back and let me worship you. You deserve it."

She rested against the pillows. Her fingers fisted in the sheet. Dylan continued to love on her breasts. Lava-hot need flowed through her. His lips found the valley between her breasts. He kissed her there before moving on to her shoulders. Leaving them, he moved down one arm, sucked each of her fingertips then went to the other limb.

"You taste like honey and smell like my flower garden in the spring," he murmured against her skin as he kissed her waistline.

Using the tip of his tongue, he tormented her until she lifted her hips and yelped. His palms drifted over her behind. It was as if he was learning her many facets and memorizing them. Dylan gave her a thorough examination. "Perfect."

Slowly, too slowly, his hand floated over her stomach and moved lower. Marcy held her breath. Dylan's every touch, brief or languorous, made her sensitized skin sizzle. When his lips followed the path of his hands she sucked in her breath. She grasped his hair with both hands. Her body was wired tight. She bit her bottom lip in anticipation. Where would he explore next?

Dylan sat back reaching for one of her feet. He kissed the arch. Marcy shivered. This man was going to kill her. He raised her leg further, placing another kiss on the back of her knee. She squirmed.

Desperation washed through her. "Dylan! Please."

He grinned as he lightly ran his index finger over her calf, tickling the bottom of her foot before he stopped.

She tugged on her foot, but he kept it in a gentle but secure hold.

Dylan kissed his way up her leg. He didn't stop at her knee but continued along the inside of her thigh. She lifted her hips. His hand traveled along her other leg until he brushed the outside of her center.

"Oh… Oh!" Marcy breathed. If he didn't touch her soon, she might explode.

Dylan studied her a moment with desire burning in his eyes before his lips found hers. Seconds later his finger slid into her. She bucked. His tongue matched his movements.

Marcy shattered into the air and floated on bliss, until she came back together to settle with a deep sigh on the bed as a pile of boneless flesh.

Dylan's chuckle was one of male satisfaction. "That good, huh?"

Marcy ran her hand up his arm. It had been. Even better. One like no other. "Come here, I'd like to say thank you."

"I like the sound of that." His mouth found hers.

Wrapping her arms around him, she pulled him to her. She kissed him deeply. Dylan encouraged her to open her mouth and their tongues danced. She kneaded the muscles of his back as he continued to kiss her.

"I can't wait any longer to have you." He turned to the bedside table and jerked the drawer open. Removing a package, Dylan opened it and rolled the plastic covering over his impressive manhood.

He looked at her. She couldn't miss the admiration in his eyes. It was a look she'd never seen before but knew she'd treasure. She opened her arms. He came down beside her. Her lips joined his as he found his place between her legs. His hard length nudged her center. With a flex of his hips, Dylan entered her.

She tensed. It had been so long. Dylan pulled back and she raised her hips in invitation. He pushed forward, filling her. He looked into her eyes as he pulled back, then plunged again, picking up speed.

Hot need grew intense in her, tightened, then snapped. She spun off into that heaven only Dylan could create. As she returned to the real world, he pumped faster and deeper. His intent gaze bore into hers.

She had no doubt who was loving her.

With a final surge, he released a groan of pure satisfaction, shuddered before he lowered himself on his stomach beside her. His arm remained draped over her waist as if he didn't want to let her go.

The problem was she didn't know how she could stay.

CHAPTER EIGHT

DYLAN WANTED MORE of Marcy but they both needed rest. "We should get up. We have to be at work."

For once he wished that wasn't the case. If he had his way, they'd stay in bed all day. He'd lie with Marcy in his arms forever. But there were patients depending on him. And Marcy also had her work.

She lay half on his chest, snuggled against him. Her arm hung over one of his shoulders while a leg rested over his leg. He wanted her again. Not fast and frantic like his body demanded. Instead, slow and sweet like his heart desired. But it would wait.

She fit next to him perfectly. Too much so. When she had to leave part of him would go with her. This time would be worse than when he'd been in college.

He wanted to know all about her. There

was more to Marcy than she'd shared. He needed to understand her. "Will you tell me about your marriage?"

"You don't want to hear about that. I thought you said we needed to get moving."

He kissed the top of her head. "We have time. I want to hear. I think you need to talk."

"There's not that much to tell. After graduation I went off to Duke medical school the next fall. Josh found a job in town. His degree is in civil engineering, so he had no difficulty joining a good company. We married a year later. I finished up my third year and learned during residency that I was pregnant. It wasn't the best timing, but I was happy.

"By that time, I was gone for days sometimes, and he worked long hours. We didn't see much of each other. Having a baby added pressure to the marriage. Josh was happy but I was thrilled with the baby. I had already decided cancer research was the direction I wanted to go. I loved the idea of creating something that could save many lives and it also would give me steady hours, which would work with having a family. I had it all planned out."

"I bet you even had a list." His tone held humor, but his face remained somber.

She gave him a wry smile. "I did. Toby was born that spring. He was perfect. The best thing I've ever done. I fell in love instantly."

He felt the tremor go through her body. Had he asked too much of her?

"Things had started to get rocky between Josh and me. When Toby got really sick it didn't help the situation. Josh struggled with Toby being sick. We didn't always agree. He blamed me. He piled on the guilt that I already felt." She hadn't recognized all that then. "He wasn't a bad guy. He just didn't know how to handle his pain." She paused then continued, "For that matter neither did I. In the end he couldn't let go of blaming me. He couldn't forgive me for not seeing the problem sooner. I couldn't disagree with him."

Dylan squeezed her shoulder.

"Within a year we were divorced." She sat still a moment appreciating the movement of Dylan's hand across the tense muscles of her back.

"I know from working with cancer kids, it puts a strain on a marriage to have an ill child. The parents must be completely devoted to each other and think outside themselves to survive and hold the marriage together. It puts stress on any relationship. There's a 60 percent divorce rate for parents with a chronically ill child."

"There were already problems in the marriage before Toby. I realize that now..." Marcy's voice trailed off. "You know, I've talked about that time more with you than I have anyone." She sounded perplexed by the idea. "I have to admit it's been cathartic."

"I'm glad you think you can talk to me. I'm honored. I'm sure the last few cases we've seen together have been emotional for you. But you've been great and held it together," Dylan said. "I wish I had been there to help. I wish that hadn't happened to you. To Toby." He hugged her. Tight.

She held on to him. This was where she belonged now. In Dylan's arms.

"I'm sorry that happened. You deserve better."

She met his gaze. "Thanks for saying so."

He took a moment before he spoke. "I'm glad you told me. It helps me better understand you."

Marcy settled beside him again. "Josh was right. I should've seen the signs."

Dylan rolled to his side so he faced her

then said, "Being a doctor doesn't make you all-knowing."

"I was focused on my work. Doing all I could to get started in my career. I failed in that area."

His look bore into hers. "I don't believe that for a minute, but if you did, I'm sure it won't ever happen again."

She studied him. "I know it won't because I'm not going to have any more children. I'm not sure I'll ever remarry."

Dylan sat straighter. "I think that would be sad. Some child will miss out on having a wonderful mother. The world would miss out on a child you helped raise."

She gave him a weak smile. "That's a very nice thing to say."

He took both her hands and kissed her palms. "It's the truth. I'm not just saying it to make you feel better." Why did it matter to him so much that she believed him?

An hour later, after making love to her again he used his arm that lay along Marcy's back and across her waist to jostle her. "Hey, sleepyhead, we need to get ready for work."

"Want to stay here."

"Me too but Ryan is coming in for his

treatment today. We have Steve to check in on. Maybe to send home. His parents have worried enough—they don't need to be concerned about the doctors not showing up. Then we have to go by your apartment and get your stuff. I want you here with me."

She looked at him.

"Hey, why the frown?" he asked. Marcy shifted but he was slow to let her go.

She looked away and slid across the bed as far as possible.

"Marcy?"

Dylan's gut tightened. He could feel her pulling away. That wall of bricks she'd climbed over and knocked down last night was going up again. Sadly, he didn't know any way to stop her from running to the other side without making things worse. He needed time to think about his next move. If she'd even give him a chance to make one.

"Please don't do this."

"What? Try to maintain our friendship after a night of passion?" By her look of anxiety, he feared he'd gone too far.

"We need to get to the hospital. I don't wanna analyze it, conjugate or multiply what happened between us. Let's just accept that it was."

"'It was,' as in that was the only time?"

"You know it has to be."

"Why?"

She snatched a shirt lying on a chair and jerked it on. "Because I'm only here for a little while longer. I have all this baggage that I refuse to unload on you. Last night I said too much. You're a good guy but you don't deserve that. You need a woman who can give you a home and family. I can't be that person."

It had been his experience that men and women didn't go backward after sharing a night together, but if she wanted to try, he'd go along. "Okay. If that's the way you want it."

"Thank you for being such a gentleman."

"You can thank my parents for that."

Dumbfounded, Dylan watched Marcy hurry out the bedroom door. This wasn't what he expected for the morning after. Getting up and having a leisurely cup of coffee, holding hands across the table, yes. But Marcy going out the door without a backward look hadn't entered his mind. What had happened between their perfect lovemaking hours earlier and now?

If he was a lesser man, he might've felt

used. But he knew last night had meant more to Marcy than she let on. There was a real connection between them. In fact, there always had been.

Left in a bed going cold, he stepped into the shower, which brought back sweet memories of the night before. What would it take to remind Marcy of all those moments as well?

Marcy took care of necessities in the guest bathroom then splashed water on her face. Looking in the mirror she pushed her hair into some semblance of order. She noticed a new toothbrush and toothpaste along with a hairbrush sitting on the counter. Marcy stared at herself in the mirror. What type of man thinks about putting those out?

One with a big heart. Or one who thought of others first. Stayed prepared. She found the idea sweet. And far too much to her liking. Or did Dylan have women over regularly enough to always have items on hand. She didn't appreciate that idea.

Either way she gladly took advantage of them. She jerked on her well-worn clothes. Finished she went in search of Dylan. A noise in the kitchen let her know he was in there.

Dylan, dressed for the day in a collared shirt and slacks, stood at the stove. The table had been set. Two plates sat on the bar close to him. Bacon and toast were already on them. He stirred a frying pan of eggs. "Did you find everything you needed?"

"I did. Thanks for the toothbrush and the other stuff."

He watched her. "I want my guests to be comfortable."

"I found it interesting you keep those things around." She liked the guy he had become more and more but she couldn't let this go any further for his sake.

"Not that big a mystery. I'm a missionary's kid, remember. I keep the toiletries for my family when they come to visit. Not that they show up that often."

At least she could count on her family. She didn't care for that sad note in Dylan's voice. She nodded. "About a few minutes ago—"

"Hey, we're all good. Please don't ruin it by trying to explain it away."

She sighed. "You're really a nice guy. There are too few people I could ever say that about." She meant that. He was too fine for her.

He shrugged. "Let's just say I understand

what the important stuff in life is." He took a mug off a rack. "How do you like your coffee?"

She didn't want to answer but he deserved the truth. "I'm not really a coffee drinker."

"I think I've got a few teabags that Mom left here the last time they visited."

"Thanks, but I'd rather get to the hospital. I want to check on Steve."

"I've already called. He's doing great the nurse said. After we've had a civil moment over our morning drinks we'll go see for ourselves."

She shifted from one foot to the other. "I'd rather go now."

"Running, Marcy?" He scooped fluffy eggs onto the plates before moving around her to the table. Had he taken special pains not to touch her?

"No. Yes. Maybe. I don't know, Dylan. I need to think."

He took a seat at the table. "I get that. I could do some of that too."

Marcy gave him a weak smile. "I didn't plan—"

"Please just take a seat and eat your food."

Marcy's mouth clapped shut. She did as he asked.

* * *

Half an hour later a taxi dropped Dylan and Marcy off at the hospital front door.

He asked, "Are you going to be with me in the clinic today?"

"No, I've got some numbers to review especially related to Steve. I'll be in the office most of the day. I'll check patient charts this afternoon."

"Okay, then I'll see you later."

She didn't look at him as they parted in the stairwell, but before the door closed between them Marcy turned. "I'm sorry if you think I'm treating you badly. That's not my intention. I'm just not very good with moments like the one this morning. I need to think about what I want. Just give me a little space."

"You can have all the space you want. All I want is for you to be happy."

"Thanks, Dylan."

He thought he might be too nice. This professionalism wasn't what he envisioned happening between them this morning. Yet in many ways, like Marcy, he was trying to figure out what he wanted as well. He'd been a loner for so long, it scared him to think about how much last night had meant to him.

He had no doubt he wanted Marcy back in his bed.

His mind had gone to forever. Wow, that thought brought him to an abrupt halt in the hall. Could he really think long term? Did they even want the same things? He wasn't sure they did. She was running scared from her past. It had hurt him to hear her say she didn't ever want to have children again or marry. He wasn't sure why that disturbed him, but it did.

He'd had a taste of heaven and desired more. Just having Marcy in his arms took away the loneliness that had become so much a part of his life. With Marcy he felt freer, less burdened. Wanted. Until this morning.

Dylan started down the hall again. He needed to get up to see Steve then to his other patients. Still, Marcy's attitude worried him. She wasn't the only one standing in the rain, emotionally confused, hoping for an umbrella. The problem was he didn't know how to help her through whatever was eating at her. She seemed to lock everything away, stew on it. In his opinion she carried guilt that didn't belong to her.

The piece of their complicated relationship that rubbed him raw was that Marcy acted as if she had no intention of returning to his bed. That had been the last thing he expected to happen. Despite his disappointment in her attitude, his heart couldn't help but hurt for her.

She really had been through it. More than any person or parent should have to endure. She had been so happy-go-lucky when he'd known her in college. He'd seen flashes of that person in the last few weeks before she hid it away behind a seriousness she wore like armor. He wanted to strip off that covering and see it burned to never be worn again. Then Marcy would truly smile all the time, so that it showed in her eyes.

What he needed was a plan.

Over the next two days he treated Marcy like a colleague only. They saw patients in the Infusion Room and the general clinic. Lucy had come in for her treatment. Dylan had watched from across the room as Marcy spoke to the mother. Both the women needed the interaction and support. Marcy just wasn't as aware of that fact as Lucy's mother might have been.

Despite all the times he wanted to touch Marcy, he restrained himself. He gave her cheerful good mornings and smiles. To the best of his ability, he acted as if the night they had shared was nothing more than a pleasant memory. Yet the sexual tension between them remained thick. Gradually Marcy greeted him first, shared a smile. A couple of times she even initiated the conversation.

Late Thursday afternoon he stopped by the office to pick up some papers. Marcy was working at her desk. She glanced at him but returned to her work.

"Sorry to bother you but I thought you might like to know I spoke to Steve a few minutes ago and he's doing great." The boy had been discharged two days earlier.

"That's nice to hear." She had really gone back into her dark hole.

He needed to pull her out before she forgot what it was like to have human interaction again. Dylan started for the door, stopped. "Uh, you know I never got to take you out on a date. I'd like to. I'd planned for us to have pizza years ago. I can do better now. Would you like to have dinner with me tonight? I know you have work to complete but we can go when you get done."

"Dylan—"

"It's just a simple date. Nothing more. I won't even hold your hand if you don't want me to."

"I don't know."

"It's just a meal, Marcy. Share it with me." He had to remind himself not to lose his patience.

"Okay. I'll be ready to go at six."

He grinned. "I'll pick you up then."

"We could just leave from here. I could fellow you."

"Nope. I pick up my dates. See you at six." Dylan went out the door with a spring in his step.

Marcy slid out of Dylan's car as he held the door in front of the restaurant. His car suited the surrounding decor of the gleaming silver building. In one of the many large windows hung a red neon sign flashing the name Atlanta Café.

"Oh, 1950s, I love it." She glanced back at his car. "It suits your car."

He grinned. "Noticed that, did you?"

She chuckled. "Hard to miss."

Suddenly all the unease between them was gone. They'd found their footing again.

Marcy looked around and declared, "I like it."

"I'm glad to hear it." A warm light in Dylan's eyes made her middle tingle.

Inside the restaurant the tables were covered in white tablecloths with wooden chairs and a hurricane lamp sitting in the center. There was a simple elegance to the place.

"Hello, Dylan." A smiling older woman with an apron wrapped around her waist walked up to them.

"Marla. It's been too long." Dylan gave the woman a hug.

"I guess the hospital keeps you busy." She smiled at him.

"Unfortunately, it does."

"Let me show you to a table and get you fed." She settled them in a corner out of the way in the busy restaurant.

"I guess you come here often," Marcy said, looking around the dining area.

Dylan studied the menu. "Not that often."

"But they know you so well."

"That's because I took care of Marla's granddaughter." Dylan laid the menu down.

Marcy hesitated to ask but for some reason she had to know. "How's she doing now?"

"She's perfect. In college and already planning her wedding."

The tightness in Marcy's chest left. "That's wonderful."

He started to say something but stopped

himself before picking up the menu. "I was thinking pizza tonight, how about you?"

"I would like to share a pizza with you."

A waiter came to the table, preventing them from carrying the conversation further. Dylan ordered an extra-large pizza. When the waiter left, she looked at Dylan. "Are you sure that'll be enough?"

His dark eyes held a twinkle. "If it's not I'll order more. I feel like celebrating. Steve went home. Lucy's treatments are going well. Ryan looks to be improving and I think this will be the most successful Care Ball of them all. Thanks a lot to you."

"I don't think I did all that much." Still, it felt good to have Dylan's praise. "I hope you made it clear to Steve and his parents, as well as Lucy's, that TM13 isn't a cure. They still have a fight ahead." More than once she'd felt positive about Toby's recovery, only to have her hopes dashed.

"I agree but we've made a step in the right direction this past weekend. That's always worth celebrating, even if you don't have cancer. I was just thinking it's nice to celebrate life. It's too short to hold back."

Marcy didn't respond. She mulled over what Dylan was saying. He was right. Why hadn't she heard that before? Because she wouldn't allow herself to do so. Hadn't been open to the idea. Until Dylan. All those years she hadn't been living by that lesson, what had she failed to appreciate? Happiness?

She missed him the last few days more than she wished to admit. As good as her professional work had been going her life had felt off-center without him. She'd found joy with Dylan. Shouldn't she hold on to it as long as she could? At least while she had him.

He put his elbows on the table and clasped his hands. "Tell me what you're thinking over there."

Her gaze met his. "You're always asking me that."

"Because I'm always interested." His look didn't waver.

"I was thinking that you're right."

Dylan's brows rose almost to his hairline. "You think so? I didn't know you could be that positive."

"Have I really been that bad?" She didn't want to be like that anymore.

Dylan shrugged. "Pretty bad."

"That comes from working in a lab by myself much of the time. I've forgotten how to be social."

He touched her hand for a moment. "You need to get out more. You certainly haven't had any trouble being social with parents."

"Hanging out with you has made me do better."

"I sort of like the newer Marcy who's more like the older Marcy."

She laughed. "You don't even make sense. But thanks, I think."

The waiter returned with their pizza, and they started eating without saying much.

Marcy looked at Dylan. He really was an amazing person. One that she also admired for his intellect. She'd had enough of hiding her feelings. Of acting like there was nothing between them. She only had one more week in Atlanta, and she wanted to make the most of it—with Dylan.

He put down his fork. "What's that look about? Do I have something on my face?" He picked up his napkin and wiped his mouth.

"I was just thinking." She pushed her half-finished slice away.

His eyes narrowed. "Doing that again, are you? Okay give. What're you thinking?"

Dylan was being charming yet there was an undertone of insecurity in his voice. She didn't like it. He sounded distant as if they were strangers instead of a couple who had explored each other's bodies in detail just days ago. But hadn't she been the one who'd made it uncomfortable between them? Was this what she wanted? Her mouth tightened.

Dylan didn't play games. If anything, he was the most straightforward person she'd ever known. She didn't enjoy seeing that unsure look in his eyes or the cautious way he treated her. To make matters worse, her body craved his touch. Why shouldn't she have it?

Dylan continued to stare at her quizzically. "Now I'm really curious. Please tell me what you have on your mind."

"I'm ready to go home."

All the color left his face. "I'm sorry you aren't having a good time."

She picked up a sugar packet and fiddled with the corner before she looked directly at him. "I'm having a great time. I want to go home with you."

Dylan's eyes widened. Desire flickered in them, wild and bright. His gaze didn't leave hers. He stood and dropped two large bills on the table then offered her his hand. She slipped hers into his larger one. Within minutes they were in the car.

Dylan asked with a hard note in his voice,

"Are you sure about this? I want no repeat of the other day."

"Yes. I've never been surer about anything in my life. For as long as I'm in town."

"Let me make this clear." Dylan cupped her face then ran a hand through her hair. "There won't be any going back this time. I mean that. No time to think about it. Marcy, you think about this on the way home. This won't be another one-night stand. I want you for as long as I can have you, as often as I can."

She savored the intensity of his look and the anticipation of what was to come, confident of her emotions for the first time in years.

Dylan couldn't be sure what had changed Marcy's mind. Yet he was pleased that something had. He would have kept his word, but it had begun to take its toll on him. Since college he'd been in love with Marcy. Still, he'd been determined not to push her. She would have to come to him. With her willpower he hadn't been sure she would do so anytime soon.

More than once he'd wanted to bring the subject up but didn't dare do so for fear she'd run like a rabbit. Right now, the last thing he needed was for her to feel uncomfortable around him. Something had changed after she spoke to Ryan's mother and even more so since they'd been working to care for Steve. It was as if she'd seen her worth, found her place once more in the world.

Dylan didn't know where this was headed or how long it would last but he would take what he could get and cherish every moment. He'd taken the crumbs she would give him during their college years, but this time he intended they be on equal footing. He'd been crazy about Marcy then and he still was. He was going to enjoy the here and now and worry about tomorrow then.

He wasn't even sure what he wanted out of the relationship. Until he was, he couldn't make demands on Marcy. For now, they would make the most of what time they had.

When they entered the house, Marcy took his hand and led him to his bedroom, then his bed. He grinned. There was the old Marcy. Bold, determined and happy.

"Sit, please."

Bemused and intrigued, he did as she asked.

She stepped between his legs. Cupping his face, she kissed him deeply.

This was what he'd missed over the last few days. His entire life. For Marcy to come to him. To be the aggressor. Tell and show him what she needed.

"Just so we're clear—" she used the same tone as he had "—I want you. For as long as I can have you."

His hands went to her thighs beneath her simple dress and slid up them to cup her bottom. He tugged her closer as his mouth devoured hers. It felt wonderful, right, to hold Marcy again. Her soft sounds of acceptance and desire heated his blood and made his manhood tighten.

Dylan tried to pull her down on the bed, but she stepped out of his arms. Her fingers touched the hem of his knit shirt. Slowly, too much so for him, she removed his clothing. Next, she pulled the silk of her dress over her head. The material floated to the floor.

He forced himself not to reach for her.

Her gaze remained on him. "Is this enough to let you know that I want you? Want us."

Dylan cleared his throat. "Not yet but you're getting close."

Marcy smiled as she took a deliberate step toward him.

"Come here," he growled, snatching her

hand and pulling until she fell on the bed beside him.

Marcy giggled and it was the most beautiful thing he'd ever heard.

Her arms came around his neck. Warm, smooth skin brushed against his as she slid over him. She kissed him as she went.

Could life really be this good? Not with anyone else. Only Marcy for him.

CHAPTER NINE

MARCY MARVELED AT how wonderful life could be. She'd been staying at Dylan's house since the night of their date.

Now Dylan lay on his stomach across the bed with her on her back beside him. His arm rested over her middle. She admired his amazing body in the morning sunlight.

How quickly she could get used to this. But should she? When had she become such a wanton? Since Dylan came back into her life.

He rolled over. The sheet lay low on his hips. His fingers teased the lower curve of her breasts, sending a tingle of desire through her.

"Are you planning to sleep the day away?" His voice held a gravelly, sexy tone.

"No. We have to be at the hospital when the kids practice. The ball will be here before we know it."

"We need to make sure they have their song

together and the committee understands what we're going to do. I hate to tell you but you're going to have to say a few words as well."

She was glad to have the ball to focus on because it helped her forget she would be leaving the next day. As if by a silent agreement she and Dylan hadn't talked about the impending day, but she had no doubt he was as aware of it as she was.

Dylan groaned. "You're a hard taskmaster. Your mind is always going."

"You asked for my help."

"Remind me not to make that mistake again." He grinned.

Marcy couldn't remember her life being better. She lived in a 1950s sitcom of contentment. She woke with Dylan next to her, enjoyed her breakfast in a sunny kitchen with handsome company. Her morning meal today didn't consist of grabbing a protein bar and a cup of tea on her way out the door. Even when she and Josh were married, they hadn't eaten together often. He preferred the TV to her company. Sharing breakfast with Dylan got the day off on a positive note. She'd missed the daily routine of living with another person.

It amazed her how comfortable she'd become in Dylan's house. She'd started to think of it as her own. For once in a long time, she felt as if she belonged. She'd become so attached to her new life it would hurt to leave.

To go home to what? An empty, sterile apartment when all she did was work. How long had it been since she'd been this happy? To her surprise the afternoon at Stone Mountain popped into her head. She'd been happy then. And she'd been so happy in Dylan's arms last night.

She would cherish these times when she returned to Cincinnati.

Being with Dylan was almost too comfortable. It was calming to know he was nearby and everything about him soothed her. She'd spent far too many years tied in knots about life. With Dylan each day felt easier.

Marcy had to remind herself the land of bliss was only temporary. She couldn't trust herself to make a commitment. What if she let Dylan down? She couldn't chance that. Or open herself up to the possibility of pain again. Remaining emotionally distant was a must. The huge problem was she was failing miserably: she was falling for Dylan.

Hadn't she believed herself in love before

and her marriage failed? What made her think she could handle another relationship any better?

On Wednesday evening Dylan leaned back in his kitchen chair while Marcy was busy cooking their meal. Dylan dream of a life he'd never believed possible. He enjoyed the scene more than he should. He was headed for disappointment and heartache, but he couldn't stop the oncoming train. There was something quiet and easy, a rightness to having Marcy in his life. The clouds of loneliness that filled his sky lifted to let sunshine in when she was around.

Marcy looked every bit the woman of the house. She'd pulled her hair back, and her face was flush from activity. She moved around the work area grabbing dishes, stopping occasionally to stir what was in a pot on the stove.

Could she possibly want the same things as he? The idea sent a shot of awareness through him. He liked the idea too much, but did he dare try? He'd been rejected before. What if she rejected him again? Maybe it was better to leave well enough alone. Yet he couldn't let her leave without asking her to stay. For Marcy he would take that chance.

She placed a bowl on the table. He caught her hand as she went by him, pulling her into his lap. Wrapping her arm around his neck, she kissed him.

"Marcy, I want us to figure out some way to stay together. To explore what we've started."

She shifted off his lap and looked down at him, shaking her head. "That's not what we agreed to." She waved a hand between them. "This was only until I leave. We knew we were only borrowing time."

"Can't you feel how things have changed? How good it is between us."

"Yeah, but I live in Cincinnati, and you live here. My job is there. Yours is here. I don't see how we can make that work. I have to focus on my work. If TM13 is successful I need to build on it. I won't have time to come back and forth here. Or spend time with you if you come to Cincinnati."

"I wish you wouldn't use your work as an excuse. You hide behind it. I think we have something real, something worth building on. You can work anywhere. We have labs here."

The heat of panic washed through Marcy. She shook her head more than once, wanting him to stop talking. Dylan's face blurred from the moisture in her eyes.

He reached out to her. "Marcy...?"

She took a step back. "I'm sorry if I've led you to believe that I can give more. You deserve better than me. I'm not a good risk."

Their looks met and held. "I believe you can give me all I need and more. You have a large capacity for love. Even your work is a sign of that. You just need to believe in yourself and me."

"I won't take the chance of hurting you. I won't live through the pain of knowing I did."

"Life doesn't hold promises. Who says we can't live happily ever after? I'm confident that if we want that, we have to at least try. It may not always be good but what I can promise you is I'll always be by your side. During the good or the bad."

She frantically shook her head. "I'm sorry if I've led you to believe that I need or want more than just the last few weeks. I didn't intend to. We've been playing house and I thought you understood that. I'm not who you need for the long haul. I would just disappoint you. There's someone out there for you, but it's not me."

Dylan said quietly, "It can't be you, or won't be you?"

She paused. Her chest tightened as her ears buzzed. "We don't want the same things in life. You want a family, and I can't give you that. All the baggage I was carrying a week ago I still have. It hasn't gone away. I don't trust myself any more than I did."

Dylan stood. "So because you're afraid you won't even take a chance on us? I've seen you change over the last few weeks. I know I have. We've made a good team with patients, the ball. In bed. I think if we work together, we could make this work too.

"Your fear is going to make you throw away what might be something wonderful. What's your plan? To go through life all by yourself. Hiding in your lab. Running from anybody who cares about you or wants to get close. Spending a few weeks in bed with the next man then moving on."

Marcy flinched. The idea of being with anyone but Dylan made her sick. He made her sound pathetic. She snapped, "You're the one that pushed that. I tried to tell you. You're no better. You were rejected by your parents, your fiancée, and you keep your true feelings closed off. How do you know you don't want me just because you no longer want to be alone? That I don't just fill a missing hole in your life? You haven't even said anything about how you feel about me? For all I know you just want me for the sex."

He took a step back as if she'd slapped him. "I said I wanted us to see where this goes."

She glared at him. "That's not the same as saying you love me."

His voice had taken on a tight note. "If I said that would it made a difference?"

She shook her head.

"Then why put my heart out there for you to stomp all over it? I've had that happen enough."

"Apparently I'm not the only one with fear issues."

"I may be closed off emotionally but I'm not using my job as a gilded cage, a reason not to rejoin the world. You're keeping your head buried in a lab, staying alone, half living. You have too much love to offer, too much vitality and the desire to live to the fullest to hide it. This past week has shown me that. I've watch you blossom since you got here. You are different. A good different. It's going to come out some way, I can promise you that."

"You don't know the pain of loving and losing it," Marcy all but spat.

"I don't? I watched you walk off with another guy in college. I know what it's like to spend my Christmases and birthdays away from my family. I know what it's like to be second in people's lives. You can bet I have an idea about love and loss."

She sucked in a breath as if something had hit her. "I'm sorry, Dylan. I won't add more hurt to your life, and I would. I don't trust myself not to."

"Not even enough to take a chance on us seeing what this could be. I'm not your ex-husband. I can't bring back Toby, but I can offer you a chance to have everything you ever dreamed of. All you have to do is reach out and take it." He offered his hand, palm up.

Marcy looked at it. A tear ran down her face as she silently shook her head. One of them must be realistic.

Dylan let his hand drop to his side, his face a mask of sadness and disapproval.

Unable to say anything to make him feel better, she went to what had become their bedroom.

* * *

Dylan dropped into the chair. That certainly hadn't gone as he had hoped. He wanted Marcy to wrap her arms around his neck, kiss him and say she would give them a try.

He thought they'd gotten past her earlier anxiety. But apparently it was so deeply embedded in her she couldn't see the iron door she'd bolted between living life and existing. Only, in the last few weeks he'd seen her open the door but tonight she'd firmly slammed it in his face.

Dylan sat there until well after dark. He went to his bedroom and wasn't surprised to find it empty. Stepping down the hall he found Marcy lying on the guest bed. She was curled on her side with her back to the door. He wondered if she was asleep or pretending. Still, she looked as unapproachable as a fortress wall.

He returned to his large, cold, lonely bed. As sleep slowly found him, he continued to rack his brain for some way to get past the wall Marcy had built around her heart.

Dylan woke to the sound of movement in the house. He stepped into the hall. Looking into the guest room, he found the bed tightly made. The irony didn't escape him: just like

Marcy's feelings. In the kitchen, he noticed the door ajar.

Marcy entered. She jerked to a startled stop when she saw him. "Uh, I didn't mean to wake you. I'm sorry."

"What are you doing? Sneaking out?" Dylan glanced out the door at her car. "I see you're all packed up."

"All except my purse and I'm getting that now." She turned away slightly.

"Marcy." She finally looked at him. "Don't you think we need to talk?"

She hung her head. "I think we said everything last night."

If she'd hit him in the chest it couldn't have hurt more. He stepped aside. "Okay, then I'll get out of your way."

Neither of them said anything as she retrieved the rest of her belongings. His heart sank. She was cutting him out of her life.

"You'd rather stay in a sad little apartment than be here with me." He couldn't hide his bitterness.

"I won't be there long. I'm leaving for Cincinnati today." She headed for the back door.

"When did you decide that? The Care Ball is next Saturday. You're going to miss it. The kids will be heartbroken if you aren't there."

He couldn't believe she would just run away like this.

"I'm sorry. You'll have to tell them I had to go home," she said in a soft, sad voice.

"What about your trial?" His chest hurt as if he'd been stabbed. Once again someone he cared for was walking out on him. Was that always going to happen to him?

"I have all the numbers I need right now. The others I can call and get from one of the nurses," she called over her shoulder.

"Marcy, it doesn't have to be this way." He wanted to go after her and beg her to stay but what good would that do.

"I think it's best for both of us." She still wasn't meeting his eyes.

"I know you're running." He couldn't let her get away with this without a fight.

"I'm not going to argue about it. Dylan, this is the way I want it." The pain in her voice made him question if it really was.

"Apparently," he snapped.

She put her hands on her hips and leaned toward him. "Don't act like I'm the only one with issues hanging over my head. You don't think I'm dealing with mine and I know for a fact you're not dealing with yours. With all your talk about running, you're doing your own version too. Why haven't you made it clear to your dad you'll never be joining him? You don't owe him anything. He certainly wasn't there for you. Instead, you're letting him believe there's a chance. You aren't being fair to him or you."

Dylan took a step back as if she'd slapped him. "Wow, I didn't see that coming. Are you lashing out at me because you don't want to see it in yourself?"

Her eyes widened as if she were surprised, he'd come back at her. "I think I'd better go."

"You do what you need to do. I wouldn't want to hold you here any longer than necessary." Dylan might regret his tone of voice later but right now he was hurting.

Marcy said a civil goodbye and drove away. Dylan stood in the driveway watching the back of her car go down the street, filled with loss and defeat.

CHAPTER TEN

DYLAN WAS MISERABLE. In every sense of the word. He'd believed that his other disappointments had hurt—events when his parents couldn't attend, Beau leaving so abruptly from school or even his fiancée dumping him at the last minute—but none of that compared to what he felt at the loss of Marcy.

What really bothered him was he believed she'd been happy with him. That she had changed her mind about their time together being short-lived.

He shook his head as he drank his coffee and looked out into the gloomy sky over his back garden. Even that reflected the situation and his mood.

Over the last few days he'd spent his time going through the motions of life. Marcy was gone. He missed her so deeply there was a never-ending ache in his chest.

She'd packed up and moved out of his office before he made it to work. He wouldn't have been surprised if she'd gone in under the cover of darkness to take care of it before returning to the house to pack. There had been a note on his desk saying somebody would be in to remove what was left of her stuff. As if he cared about her desk being taken away.

Her presence lingered regardless. He couldn't find a place that he didn't associate with Marcy. The hospital reminded him of her. His office still smelled of her. His house no long felt like home without her.

Marcy not only vacated his office, but she had vacated every area of his life. It had left him floundering. He'd sworn he would never be in this position again. Rejected. He'd let her in and now he was paying for it.

Once she'd only been a memory of the girl he couldn't have from college, but in a short time she'd become his world, and then left it with a gaping hole. He had no idea how to fill it.

Why couldn't they talk this out? Marcy never once said she didn't care about him. He'd called her but got no answer or return call. It was as if there had never been anything between them.

When he'd suggested they might have a future together he'd had no idea he would get such a volatile reaction. They'd been getting along so well. He'd never been happier or looking toward the future more. Apparently, he'd completely misread her. He couldn't understand how he had misjudged her feelings so acutely.

The phone rang. He went to the kitchen and picked it up off the table.

"Hey, buddy. I was just checking in about this weekend. Lisa and I are still planning to be there for the Care Ball."

"Good. I look forward to seeing you guys." Dylan tried to put enthusiasm into his voice that he didn't feel. "You're welcome here."

"Thanks, but we're going to a hotel. We're planning a little second honeymoon since the kids won't be with us." Beau sounded pleased.

"Sounds like fun." Dylan wasn't sure anything sounded like fun to him these days. He sank into a chair.

"I understand from the committee you have a special program planned."

Dylan wanted to groan. That would be the one he and Marcy had worked so hard to put together. Every day at least one of the patients or parents planning to attend the ball asked him about her. If he wanted her out of his life it would be impossible to achieve because he had constant reminders. But he didn't want her out, so those questions made it more difficult for him to survive her loss.

"I think you'll be impressed." If people were, it would be because of Marcy's efforts. It was her idea. Her leadership. Her natural interactions with the kids and parents made it come together. And she wouldn't even be there to see it.

"I hope it's not another one of your riveting speeches again this year." Beau's tone was teasing.

"I'll have to say a few words, but I promise to keep it short." Dylan didn't even feel like attending but he had no choice. He'd put on his happy face and go do what must be done just like he always had when someone had let him down.

"Dylan? You okay, buddy?"

"Yeah. Why?"

"You sound like something's bothering you."

Concern rang clear in Beau's voice. Dylan wasn't sure he wanted to rehash his actions and feelings regarding Marcy. Still doing so might help him think through what to do.

Beau was his most trusted friend. He always gave sound advice.

"It's about a woman."

Beau hissed. "That kind of problem. What's her name?"

"Marcy."

Beau's tone turned thoughtful. "Wasn't that the name of the girl you were so crazy about in college?"

"The one and the same."

"Really?" Beau sounded intrigued. "Start at the beginning."

Dylan left nothing out as he told Beau about his and Marcy's time together. He finished with, "I don't know what to do. To make matters worse this ball is like pouring salt on a wound."

"Lisa and I wondered when a woman would come along who would make you sit up and notice longer than two dates." Beau sighed. "I'm not particularly good at the love advice but my suggestion is you figure out how you really feel. Do you love her? If you do, then tell her. She might surprise you."

"I told her I care."

"Not the same thing. I know you've closed your feelings off to most people to protect yourself but sometime you're going to have to open up. Take a chance. You can't expect her to if you aren't willing to try."

"Have I really been that bad?"

"How long did it take you to get over that rotten fiancée of yours? I hear more pain in your voice over Marcy leaving than you ever had over a wedding being canceled."

Dylan couldn't disagree with Beau.

"I suggest pouring your heart out. Trust your feelings, respect hers, and maybe she'll come around."

"I don't know about that. She's been knocked down harder than most. She's running scared. I'm not sure she'll listen to me."

Putting pressure on her wasn't what he wanted to do but the longer they stayed apart the more difficult it would be to convince her they could make a life together. He believed that without Marcy his life would always be missing that special element. They belonged together. He just needed her to see that.

"I don't know if I have a chance."

"Sounds like you're scared. You'll never know unless you put yourself out there. Something you haven't been willing to do for years. You better decide how much you want her."

"At first I wanted to give her some time

to think. Now she won't answer my phone calls."

"I suggest you pack your bags and go after her before it's too late."

"She was adamant about not wanting to talk to me." Dylan fiddled with his coffee cup, twisting it around on the table.

"That might have been the case then, but what about now? She may have changed her mind. You know I had to convince Lisa I was the guy for her. I had to keep in front of her until she realized it. Lisa and I are always in your corner. We want to see you happy. It's time for you to stop brooding and go after her. Convince her you should have a life together."

"Okay. You've persuaded me. I'll get through the ball and then go to Cincinnati."

"Sounds like a plan. We'll see you at the ball. Talk more then."

"I appreciate the pep talk."

"Anytime, buddy. You've been there for me when I've needed you. Just returning the favor."

Marcy carefully slipped the test tub into the holder on her lab table in Cincinnati. She couldn't believe she'd done it. Had let it happen. The one thing in the world she'd tried to protect Dylan from was her hurting him. He deserved better than that. But she'd failed. Again. All she'd managed to do was make them both unhappy.

She couldn't look him in the eyes as she'd left his house, and even resisted looking in the rearview mirror. Earlier that night she'd slipped out to the hospital to take care of her office, then returned to the house to get the last of her belongs. It was almost a clean escape until Dylan showed up. She gasped for breath to ease the pain in her chest at the sight of him. The tightness reminded her of seeing the sunshine when under water and not being able to break the surface to gasp air. She struggled on but got nowhere.

The thought of returning to Cincinnati should have distracted her. She had some exciting research material to share yet it held no appeal. Atlanta felt more like home than where she lived. More than once she wanted to pick up the phone and tell Dylan she'd changed her mind, but she stopped in midmovement. She couldn't trust herself to be who Dylan needed in his life. It was best this way. At least that's what she kept telling herself. Daily.

That didn't mean her heart listened or that

it wasn't broken. Not since the loss of Toby had she been this despondent.

The trial continued to go well. She would be saving children's lives with the new medicine. That should be enough in her life. When she had all the information she needed she'd write her paper and submit it to the FDA. That's what she needed to concentrate on, her work, and forget about Dylan. She'd learn to live with the loss of Dylan and her love for him. Eventually.

She'd left Atlanta under the cover of dark rain clouds. She'd gone as she had come: on her own. She had to do so before she broke down and gave in to her need to run to Dylan, to tell him how much she cared and beg him to have her. Her time in Atlanta had changed her. Meeting Dylan again had transformed her. Tipped her world. She'd been happy there, but did she deserve that?

She'd been back in Cincinnati for less than a week, but it might as well have been years. Each day dragged by. She returned to her lab the evening she landed. She should have been excited about doing so. Instead she found her work rather dull and unfulfilling. After the exhilaration of being around Dylan, her life had no spark now. She missed him and the patients, the parents.

Each evening she went home to an empty apartment where she spent her time alone not even bothering to make dinner. Quickly she learned she didn't enjoy eating by herself, and she tried cooking, but it was no fun cooking for one.

Dylan's home had felt welcoming, comfortable, as if it were embracing her. It was still difficult to face her sterile living room in her equally sterile apartment building. Her space was like a cold locker room with little personality. She missed sitting on the patio with Dylan, watching the sunset, smelling the grass after a rain and seeing the beauty of the flowers.

She tried to get back into her daily routine, but she couldn't seem to make it happen. Going through the motions was the best she could manage. She'd even started keeping regular hours which drew her coworkers' interest and comments. The only problem with having regular hours was it left her more time to remember.

Years ago, she'd promised herself she wouldn't go to this place again where depression, disappointment and despair were her only emotions. Because of her past she held people at arm's length, but Dylan had gotten beyond her defenses, under her skin and into her heart. Now she had to deal with the ongoing pain once more. She wanted it to go away.

Nothing was the same without Dylan. Her coworkers had all offered her a welcome back. She wished she could have returned the sentiment but all she could think about was what she'd left behind in Atlanta.

One evening Marcy sat slumped on her sofa with the lights off staring at nothing when the phone rang. She reached for it, hoping it would be Dylan's voice on the other end. Sadly, he stopped calling days ago.

"Hi, honey. I was just checking on you. I knew it was about time for you to come back from Atlanta."

"Hey, Mom. I returned a while ago."

Her mother sighed. "I wish you'd called to let me know. How did things go?"

"Really well. I got excellent results."

"I expected nothing less. But you don't sound excited about that." Concern filled her mother's voice.

"I am."

"But?"

Marcy had remained close to her family,

especially her mother, after the death of Toby and the demise of her marriage. Marcy feared her mother worried about her too much. "Mom, do you remember my lab partner my last year in college?"

"The one you talked about all the time. Dale, Darnell...something like that."

"Dylan." How like her mother to remember.

"That's right. Dylan. You talked about him all the time. I often wondered if Josh got jealous. What about him?"

"He's the lead doctor in the cancer clinic at Atlanta Children's."

"He is? And how is he?" Her mother sound thoughtful.

"Just as nice as ever. Funny. Very intelligent. It was nice to renew our friendship." Marcy wasn't prepared to share with her mother how much there had been between Dylan and her.

"But there was more?" That was like her mother as well. She could read between the lines.

"Yes."

"Thank goodness. I was worried you might never have anything to do with a man again."

"Have I been that bad?" Had Dylan been right about her?

"Honey, this Dylan must be a very special man to get you to even look at him. You've done nothing but work since Toby died. It was as if you died with him. Are you going to stay in touch with Dylan?"

"No. I told him it would never work."

"Oh, honey, give yourself a chance to find happiness again. Life is too short not to grasp it. It sounds like you really care for this man. There's nothing wrong or disloyal about that. It's time for you to live again."

"Mom, I can't. What if I get hurt again? What if I fail him?"

"Aren't you being a little irrational? Hurt is part of life. Happiness should be too."

Marcy shook her head. "I can't live through that kind of pain again."

"What if you don't have to? Think of all you could have." The desperation in her mother's voice surprised her. She really wanted Marcy to step out, to move on and her mother was giving her no room to slip away.

"Do you really care about this Dylan?"

"I do. But I'm so scared that I'll fail him like I did Josh," she admitted.

"You didn't fail Josh. He failed you."

Marcy had never heard her talk like that.

"I should have told you that a long time ago. Instead of being there for you, he used you as a scapegoat for his grief. He wasn't the man I believed him to be."

"Mom, I've never heard you talk like this."

"I should have before now and you might not have wasted so much of your life hiding from it. Do you think Dylan loves you?"

Marcy's voice lowered. "I think he does."

"Then don't let fear hold you back from finding happiness." The determined note in her mother's voice made Marcy sit straighter.

"He wants children. I don't know if I can do that again."

"Oh, honey, you were a wonderful mother." Compassion circled her mother's words. "You will be one again."

"My work is here. He's in Atlanta. It's just too much to deal with."

"Not if you want to be with him and he wants to be with you. You'll figure it out. The real question is, are you happy without him?"

Marcy didn't have to think about that answer. "No. I'm so miserable I can't think straight."

"Then you can only be happier with him. The way I see it is you're being offered happiness and only you can decide if you want to take it or not."

"I don't know if I can."

"Talk to him, hon. Work it out."

"It may be too late." Marcy couldn't stand the thought of that being true. "There's a ball on Saturday. We were working together on the program. I ran out on him. He may not forgive me. I've treated him badly."

"Then I suggest you go find that perfect dress, pack it and get a flight to Atlanta. Don't think about it. Just do it. If you don't, you may regret it. I'll let you go so you can get to it, and I look forward to meeting Dylan."

"Love you, Mom." Marcy ended the call.

She pushed her hair out of her face. Her mother was right. It was time for her to take her life in hand. To stop living in the past.

Her life before and after Dylan were direct opposites. She knew what it was to have fun, to experience new things, to laugh over and enjoy simple pleasures that had been lost for too long. Dylan had brought all of that back to her life. And she'd rejected it!

No longer. She'd been half living. That had to stop. This was her crossroads and she had a choice: she could either go after happiness or she could continue to live in the past. She'd had enough of wallowing in misery. Dylan offered her a brighter future, him.

Now, if she could only push the negative thinking behind her. She must be strong enough to take hold of what Dylan offered, then she would grasp it with both hands and never let it go.

She had a few more calls to make before she went after that dress. She hoped Dylan liked surprises.

Dylan tugged at his tux jacket. He preferred his T-shirt and jeans, but understood the necessity of looking the part of doctor in charge. Surveying the large ballroom of the high-end hotel, he could see the committee had done what they could to set the stage to ask for donations. From the low lighting to the tables covered in black and silver cloths and the elegance of the glassware. It encouraged a good time, which should translate to money given.

Still, he wondered why money spent getting a hotel couldn't be better used as a donation without all the other stuff. Every year he questioned it. The committee always assured him it took money to make money. He let it go even though he believed Beau's money would be put to better use as a donation. Some things he had to accept. He just hoped he didn't have to accept living without Marcy.

He was taking Beau's advice. Tomorrow he was going after Marcy. It was time to step out, bare his heart. Take a chance because she was worth it. After a week of her being gone, he had no doubt he loved her. His bag was packed, flight made. First thing in the morning he was gone.

All he had to do was get through tonight, then he would convince Marcy that she was his future.

He looked around the room. It was filling up.

Round tables circled the dance floor. Varying numbers of people were seated at them. The band turned up and started to play. Couples were entering the dance floor. At one time he'd looked forward to holding Marcy as they danced. Another time, he hoped.

Dylan checked his watch. The children would perform in an hour. Until then he was to mix and mingle to encourage donations. Which he didn't enjoy doing, but it came with his job.

A hand waving in the air beckoned him to Beau and Lisa's table. They stood as he approached. Beau gathered him in a hug and clapped him on the back. Dylan took Lisa in his arms, giving her a warm embrace.

She grinned. "I hear the mighty has fallen. You are in love."

Dylan glared at his best friend then looked back to Lisa. "I am but the question is, is she?"

"I wasn't sure I'd ever hear those words out of your mouth, Dylan Nelson," she said.

"I wasn't sure I'd ever say them."

They all took seats at the table. "So what's your plan?" Lisa looked at him with eager eyes.

"I'm leaving for Cincinnati first thing in the morning. I hope to bring her back or at least work out a schedule to see each other."

"I look forward to meeting this woman that finally got the great Dylan Nelson to open his heart."

"Have I really been that bad?"

Beau and Lisa looked at each other and smiled.

A waiter offered them a flute of champagne, and Beau raised his glass and said, "To Dylan's success."

Dylan took a drink. He sure hoped he had that. He noticed one of his patients at a nearby table. "If you'll excuse me a minute, I'm going over to speak to a patient."

He'd met with most of them before he entered the room. They seemed happy and excited. Mindy hadn't been among them. "Hey, Mindy. I'm glad you made it. How're you feeling?"

"I'm good, Dr. Nelson." She wore a formal gown that hung from her slim shoulders. Tonight her hair, which he knew was a wig, was piled on top of her head.

"Good enough for a dance? This isn't the prom, but we can pretend."

The girl beamed.

Dylan offered his hand, she took it, and he led her to the floor. They danced the rest of the song and then the next before he returned her to her parents.

"Thank you for the dance," Dylan murmured, bowing slightly.

Mindy giggled, color coming to her cheeks.

"I must go now. I have a job to do. See you later." He circled the room telling people about the cancer program, what he'd like to see done and encouraging them to donate. This was his least favorite thing to do. He'd much rather stick with plain old medicine.

He checked his watch again an saw it was

almost time for the kids to perform. The bandleader had been notified to expect them. The band was to stop playing so the kids could be heard without microphones. Dylan made his way toward Beau and Lisa's table. Halfway there a bopping sound started behind them.

Robby.

Dylan quickly found his seat near Beau.

Another kid joined in. Soon the room was thumping and bumping.

Lisa leaned across Beau. "Did you know about this?"

Dylan grinned and nodded.

Robby started in with his first line of the rap. "Cancer and chemo are not fun. I'd rather be at the beach, getting sun."

The kids kept the beat.

Another spoke. "That may be so but I have to have a treatment. I'd like to give it up for Lent."

There were chuckles around the room. Everyone had stopped what they were doing to listen to the kids.

"The doctors and nurses at ACH are heaven-sent. But in my parents' pocketbook they have put a dent."

That got even more laughs.

Some of the guest joined in the thumping by tapping the tables. Robby finished the song. All the kids looked pleased and those watching appeared astounded. There was a large round of clapping.

This time Robby started with a stomp of his foot. Two or three of the kids joined in until they were all involved. Robby did the complete rap himself. This one was about life.

Dylan looked around. Several people had tears in their eyes.

As Robby finished and everyone clapped Dylan made his way to the microphone.

"Those are just a few of the patients that come to our clinic. Aren't they a talented group? As you just heard. They do this in the clinic to make the time go faster."

Everyone clapped once more. "I'd like to introduce you to a few of them. They are brave young men and women."

Dylan clicked a button on a handheld remote and a picture of Robby appeared. A picture his parent had provided. "This is Robby Neels. He's sixteen and likes fast cars along with rapping. That's obviously true." Dylan grinned at Robby. "Oh, and Robby is from Peachtree City."

Another picture flashes up on the screen.

"John Paul Walsh is a great student. He likes training dogs and dreams of being an astrophysicist."

An *oh* went around the room.

"He lives in Winder, Georgia," Dylan continued.

When he was finished introducing the kids, everyone clapped.

"If you want to know why you're here tonight these young men and women are the answer. It's not about me, or the oncology department, or even the hospital. It's about them and saving their lives, making their lives better.

"From me and my staff we appreciate you coming tonight. We hope you've had a good time so far. Everybody, I challenge you to give. Let's break a record." He was about to step down from the stage when a flash of cobalt blue caught his attention.

Marcy. Here. His eyes widened, and his heart raced. She was here.

She came up on the stage and walked toward him.

"What're you doing here?" he asked when she got close enough to him.

She smiled. "Didn't you ask me to the ball?"

He swallowed, then whispered, "Yeah."

"I'm supposed to be helping you with the program, aren't I?"

Dylan could do little more than nod like a bobble head doll.

"Hand me the microphone. We'll talk about it in a few minutes. Right now, I've got a few more announcements and these nice people are waiting on us."

There was a murmur around the room.

He gazed out at the crowd, his face heating. Marcy took the microphone, leaving him looking dumbfounded.

"Hello, I'm Dr. Marcy Montgomery. I'm a researcher whose been working in Dr. Nelson's department."

Dylan started to move off the stage.

"Dr. Nelson, don't go."

He stopped in his tracks.

"How many of you noticed that Dr. Nelson didn't need any notecards to introduce his patients?" Marcy raised her hand. People around the room joined her. "That's because he knows them. He goes around the clinic and gets to know each of them as a person. He takes time to play video games with them… which he isn't very good at." A couple of the kids snickered. "Remarkably he remembers everything about them. He's not your average doctor. I think he deserves a round of applause."

The room broke out in noise. The kids and parents stood.

Dylan hung his head in mortification. Heat filled his face. Thank goodness the lighting was dim.

"Now that you have completely embarrassed me," he hissed at her, "are you done?"

"Nope." Marcy gave him a smile. She turned to the room. "Please bear with me a minute more. I told you that I'm a researcher who has been here working in the oncology department."

Marcy looked glorious in the regal blue dress that skimmed her curves. Her hair was piled elegantly on top of her head, staying with the royal theme. Simple pearl earrings graced her ears. She left him breathless. He'd always thought her beautiful, but she was ravishing tonight. For the life of him, he'd swear he was dreaming.

Dylan saw her deep intake of breath.

"I'm also a mother of a child who died of cancer. His name was Toby. I'm working hard to find a cure and I promise you that every dollar you give will help to make that happen. Now, I hope you enjoy your evening."

Damn, Marcy was stunning in all her glory. She'd shared in public about Toby when she'd kept that secret for years. Why now? He was proud of her.

Knowing how difficult that had to have been for her, he stepped closer.

She looked at him with a shaky smile. "Dylan, do you have anything else you would like to say?"

He shook his head. There was a snicker or two in the crowd. The loudest he recognized as Beau's. He must look as bewildered as he sounded.

She continued, "Then I'll turn this back over to the band."

Dylan offered his hand to help her from the stage. With a bright smile, she slipped her hands into his. His heart took an extra beat at her touch.

"I'm so glad you're here," he said.

They had no more time before the kids surrounded them.

"You guys were wonderful," Marcy assured them as she gave them hugs.

Others came up to speak. All Dylan wanted

was to get Marcy to himself, but that didn't look like it was going to happen anytime soon.

The crowd had finally died away when he took her hand. "We need to find a place to talk."

She looked behind him.

Dylan turned and his hand tightened on Marcy's. He wasn't sure how many jolts to his system he could take tonight but this one might be the largest. Approaching them were his parents. "Mom. Dad."

His mother hurried ahead and wrapped her arms around him. "I'm so proud of you."

He held her in a hug.

When he let her go, his father stepped forward holding out his hand. "Son."

He slid his hand into his father's. The older man gripped it and pulled Dylan to him for a full hug.

"What're you guys doing here? You didn't tell me you were coming." Dylan still couldn't believe they were there.

"We got a special invitation to the Care Ball we couldn't turn down," his mother announced. "We were told that we should see how amazing our son is."

Dylan's forehead furrowed.

Before he could ask from whom, Marcy said softly, "Dylan, are you going to introduce me to your parents?"

He set aside his confusion long enough to make the introductions.

"It's a pleasure to meet you both," Marcy said.

His mother hugged her, then gushed to him, "Your patients were wonderful tonight. I was so impressed. I've heard nothing but praise for them, your program and your work."

"Thanks, Mom. It's the patients who are the stars. I still can't get over you being here."

"I'm proud of you, son," his father offered. "I don't think you've been bragging enough on your program and your importance here."

That wasn't something Dylan had been taught to do. He felt the same devotion to his work that his father did for his. He just needed his father to understand that. It was time to make it clear.

"Dad, I know you want me to come to work with you." He had his father's complete attention. "But this is where I belong. I have a practice in Atlanta where I'm doing great work that I love. I'm a cancer doctor, a darn good one. I belong here."

Marcy squeezed his hand. He appreciated her reassurance. She understood how difficult this conversation was for him.

"How long have you known this?" his father asked.

"A long time. I should've made that clear years ago. I should never have led you to believe I might join you. I'm sorry."

His father nodded. "Deep down I knew your heart wasn't in working with me. You put me off too many times when I've asked you about joining me."

"I didn't want to hurt you."

His father studied Dylan. "I can tell by the way you talked about your patients that this is where your heart is. I should have been paying closer attention to you. I would love to have you working with me, but I do understand your passion for the work you do. It's important too."

For once in Dylan's life he believed his father understood. Maybe there was a chance they could find some of what they'd lost. Dylan's throat tightened. "Thanks, Dad." He cleared his throat. "What I *can* do is come down a couple of times a year to fill in, help or give you time away. I believe in the work you do as well."

* * *

Marcy blinked back the moisture threatening to fall. What had just happened between Dylan and his dad filled her heart. Maybe she'd helped Dylan heal like he had her.

When she'd called them she had been taking a shot in the dark. It could have backfired. They might have said they wouldn't come, which Marcy would never have told Dylan. The outcome had been far better than she'd anticipated.

She'd certainly gotten Dylan's attention when she'd joined him on stage. For a moment she'd feared he'd gobble her up or, just as bad, drag her off the stage. The fire in his eyes made her blood run hot. It hadn't gone unnoticed by her that he'd moved in closer when she'd shared about Toby. Dylan knew the courage it had taken for her to say that out loud to people she didn't know. He could still be angry with her, but he'd stuck by her.

She had no doubt he would always be there for her. He would never blame her or run away from her in her time of need. Dylan would always be her rock in a storm. They would weather it together.

Josh wasn't a bad guy, he just hadn't been

the right guy for her. Dylan was. Always would be.

"Mom and Dad, I'm glad to see you but I need to speak to Marcy for a minute. If you'll excuse us." His parents gave him a perplexed look as he tugged on Marcy's hand, heading for the door.

She grinned as he checked a couple of doors along the hallway to find them locked. He said something ugly under his breath as they moved on. She asked, "What's the hurry?"

Dylan found one open. On a sound of relief, he brought her inside and closed it. In one swift motion, he put his back to the exit and pulled her into his arms. His lips found hers.

When he let her come up for air she teased, "What are you doing? Don't you know you need to be in the ballroom schmoozing?"

His gaze, hot with desire, held hers. "What I need is to be here kissing you."

His mouth found hers again. Marcy's arms went around his neck. She pressed into him. She'd missed this. Needed it. Him.

Between kisses he asked, "What're…you… doing here? I didn't…expect…you." He kissed along her neck.

A shiver went through her. "You invited me to the ball, didn't you?"

He murmured as his lips moved over her skin. "I always assumed you'd be my date. I've missed you."

Her hands ran over his shoulders. "I don't have so many offers for a night out at a ball that I can afford to turn one down."

He pulled back and looked at her. "You're telling me you were here just for a date?"

"No, I'm telling you I came because you need me here."

"You couldn't be more right about that. You'll be going home with me tonight, won't you?"

"Don't you think we need to talk before I agree to that?"

"We are talking." He kissed her again.

"I mean about our future." She quickly placed a kiss on his lips.

He looked at her again. "There'll be a future?"

"I hope so."

"Then we need to talk privately. My house is a good place for that. We won't be disturbed." He hesitated. "Or have you arranged for a hotel room?"

She grinned. "I was counting on you offering me the guest room."

"You may have to settle for the larger bedroom with a roommate."

"We should be getting back to the ball. You'll be missed." She stepped away and began straightening her dress.

"I do have some friends I'd like you to meet," Dylan replied. He pulled on his jacket making himself presentable.

He took her hand as they strolled back toward the ballroom.

"You're responsible for my parents being here, aren't you?"

"I might have given them a personal invitation. Maybe shared with them how special their son is. I hope you aren't mad?"

"No. More surprised."

"I just thought they should see you with your patients and how great you are at your job," she explained then watched for any anger he might have and found none.

"How did you find them?"

"I made a few phone calls. Then it was easy." She ran a hand across her hair.

"To whom, may I ask?"

"My first was to the head of the ball committee. She told me who the major donor was

whose first name is Beau and lives in Birmingham."

"I should have known."

"Beau and I haven't officially met but we
have spoken a number of times." She smiled.

"And he didn't even let on when I spoke to
him earlier."

"You have a good friend there. One who
cares about you." Dylan needed someone like
that in his life.

"I do. But I don't want to talk about Beau
right now. I'd like to dance with you." He
opened the ballroom door.

"And I'd like that very much."

"Come on. Let me introduce you to Beau
and Lisa. Then we're going to the dance floor
where I can hold you."

He led her to a table where a man with
dark hair and a wide smile sat beside a blonde
woman wearing a gold gleaming dress, who
beamed at them as if they knew a secret.

"I'd like for you to officially meet Beau and
Lisa Johnson. Beau and Lisa, this is Marcy
Montgomery."

The couple stood and gave her a hug. She'd
had more personal interaction in the last six
weeks than she'd had in ten years. Just weeks

ago, she would've run from it. Now she found it comforting, invigorating.

Dylan held out a chair for her beside Lisa. She slid into it. He took the one next to hers.

"Beau, I understand that you and Marcy had already met each other. Sort of."

Marcy said, "It's a pleasure to put a face to a voice."

"I feel the same. You told him didn't you."

"Yes. Not everything but I told him most of it."

They spent half an hour with the Johnsons. Marcy hoped she'd found new friends.

Dylan stood with his hand outstretched. "Marcy would you like to dance?"

She smiled at him as her heart beat faster, and said, "I'd love to."

He put his arm around her waist and led her around the floor. "I thought I might die if I didn't get you into my arms again." Her hand moved against his back. "What did Beau mean by not telling me everything?"

"He offered to pay for your parents airline tickets and the hotel room." She met his look. "For some reason he thought it was important that they stayed here tonight."

"I'll have to pay him back."

"I wouldn't do that. I think he felt like it was a donation to a good cause." She smiled.

Giving her a squeeze, he asked, "Do you know you're amazing?"

"I don't know about that, but I'm glad you think so." Dylan made her feel special.

"You've been full of surprises tonight, Dr. Montgomery."

"I wasn't sure how you would take them."

"You were worried I wouldn't be happy to see you?" His expression showed concerned.

"I wasn't very nice to you when I left. I was counting on your parents smoothing the way."

"I'm glad I could say what I needed to face-to-face. He took it better than I expected. And your actions? We can talk about those later."

Marcy didn't like the sound of that. "I thought it was rather nice of you to offer to work with him when you had time off. I think that'll be good for both of you."

"I do too."

Dylan leaned in close to her. "How much longer do you think we're gonna need to stay?"

She looked around the room. Half of the attendees had left.

"We've got our own business to take care of," he whispered against her ear.

"We can go."

He walked her back to Beau and Lisa and looked at them. "I love you both but it's time to go. Brunch at my house at eleven if you're interested. If not, I'll be home all day."

Beau asked with a grin, "What's your hurry?"

Dylan gave him a smirk and took Marcy's arm. "We have some business to discuss."

Dylan drove home slowly, despite his desire to hurry. Instead, he made sure to stay within the speed limit; he must be as careful about handling his discussion with Marcy. Despite her actions at the ball her courage was fledgling.

He pulled into the drive and turned off the car. "Did I tell you that you look lovely this evening?"

"I believe you did but it's always nice to hear."

Dylan took her hand. "I've missed you."

"I've missed you too."

"I'm taking you being here as meaning something." He had every intention of being straightforward with her.

"It does."

"Good. Come on, then. Let's go in and

talk." He helped her out of the car and into the house.

Marcy looked around the kitchen. "I've missed this room too."

"Would you like a cup of tea?"

"Oh, no, thank you. What I would really like is to borrow one of your sweatshirts and sweatpants and sit outside."

"That can be arranged." He started toward the back of the house.

She followed, stopping in the hallway in front of his bedroom door. "I need help with my zipper."

Dylan swallowed hard. He handed the clothing to her. Slowly he lowered the zipper, appreciating the silky skin beneath. Finished he said in a raspy voice, "Marcy, you should go to the guest bedroom, or we won't get to that talk tonight."

She grinned over her shoulder and hurried out.

He was waiting on the patio with a blanket for her when she joined him. "Are you sure you'll be warm enough?"

"I believe so." She took one of the chairs and pulled her legs beneath her.

Opening the blanket, he settled it over her

shoulders then took the chair beside her. "Do you want to go first or should I?"

"I would like to go first. I'm sorry about how I acted when I left. I was horrible to you. My only defense is that I was scared."

"It's okay. I wasn't any better." Dylan took her hand.

"Let me finish before you let me off the hook. I've been afraid for so long I hardly know any other emotion. I was afraid of how you make me feel. Of what you wanted from me, of the future and the list goes on. You were right. I had stopped living, had closed myself off in a lab.

"Being with you gave me freedom. Most of which I didn't know what to do with. You made me want things I'd long ago stopped dreaming of. That was scary. But the thing is, you helped me to start living again. For that I'll forever be grateful."

Dylan squeezed her hand.

"What I really came to say is that I love you. I think in some way I have since we were in college."

He gathered her into his lap. She came willingly. As he found her lips, she curled into him.

"I feared I'd never hear that," he confessed

then kissed her tenderly. When he pulled away, he said, "I love you, Marcy. I know I have since college. I loved the girl you were and the woman you've become. I've stayed closed off because I believed if I let anyone in, they'd hurt me, leave me. You've taught me that isn't fair.

"Like tonight, you gave me a wonderful gift. You gave my parents a picture of who I am. That means the world to me. That's not the action of someone who won't be there for me forever."

Marcy kissed his neck. "So, you're going to stay at Atlanta Children's and work with cancer patients."

"That depends."

She sat up quickly. "Depends?"

Dylan gave her a direct look. "On you. I'm not going to live anywhere without you."

A shiver went down her spine. He would give up his work in Atlanta and his home for what she wanted. "You would do that for me?"

"And much more." He took her hand in his. "Don't act so surprised, Marcy. I've already told you that I love you. I haven't changed my mind. I want us to create a life together. I'm hoping, based on what you've said, that you feel the same way. If I need to move to be with you, I will."

"You would give up everything for me?"

He brought her hand to his lips, looking into her eyes. "Sweetheart, I would do anything to have you in my life. I've been so miserable without you. When you were gone it was like the sun had gone out for me."

Moisture filled her eyes. "I'm such a mess."

He stroked her cheek. "And I love everything about you."

"Dylan…" Her mouth found his and the tender touch of her lips expressed her emotions. Warmth wrapped around his heart.

Marcy cupped his face with both hands. "It's time I stopped hiding behind the past. That I take a step forward. I feel like someone who has been released into the world. I've been thinking about what you've said a couple of times, that I need to consider helping cancer parents. I have a unique perspective as a doctor and as a parent."

"You do."

"When I was making all those phone calls to your parents and such, I talked to the children's hospital. They have a program that's really working. I want to go visit. Maybe there's a place at Atlanta Children's for one of those. If there was, I'd like to lead it. What do you think?"

He hugged her. "That sounds wonderful. I think you would be perfect for the job." He hesitated. "What about your research?"

"I could always do that. Maybe oversee it. I really enjoyed doing the trial so maybe I could coordinate those."

"For a woman who has lived in a lab for years you sure are busting out."

Marcy grinned. "It's because you showed me the key."

"What's that?"

"Love."

Dylan didn't say anything for a moment. When he did his voice sounded raspy. "Sweetheart, I hope I can live up to that."

She gave him a quick kiss. "I have no doubt that you can. You're my knight in shining armor."

"Any knight can fall off his horse."

"But you won't." She stood and tugged him toward the house. "Come on, I'm getting tired. It has been a big night. The rest of our talk can wait."

"We've covered the stuff that really matters." He lifted her into his arms with longing and desire pulling at him. "Now I want to show you how much I love you."

Dylan woke next morning to a warm and sweet-smelling Marcy snuggled against him. Did he dare believe it wasn't a dream?

Her gentle hand skimmed his chest hair. "I was wondering if you'd ever wake." She kissed a spot where her fingers had teased. "I've been thinking."

"Is that so?" He said playfully, his hand appreciating the silky feel of her hip.

She moved to lie across his chest, so his gaze met hers. "I'd like to have a baby."

Dylan tensed. His eyes widened. "Marcy, you don't have to do that for me. You and I can be happy as long as we have each other."

"I want more children. You'd be the most wonderful father. With you I can be a good mother."

For a moment Dylan could hardly breathe. He hadn't expected this. He'd accepted he couldn't live without her; the children he didn't know would just have to remain that way. "You were a good mother to Toby."

"I know that now. I'm working to let go of my guilt. I can't say I won't be hypervigilant to the point of making you crazy, but I'll try not to be."

"Sweetheart, we would be in it together. The good and the bad."

"I believe and feel that." She hugged him.

His brushed his hand over her hair. "Before I can't stand it any longer and want to get started on making that baby, maybe I should ask you a question."

"Question?"

"Yep." He reached over the edge of the bed. Picking up his slacks, he fished into a pocket and pulled out a small velvet bag.

Marcy leaned back. "What's in that?"

He grinned. "Something for you. This isn't very romantic, but I can't wait." He slipped a finger in the bag and came out with a sparkling diamond ring. "I had it ready because I was coming to Cincinnati to find you today."

"You were?"

"I was. Marcy, will you marry me?"

She leaned forward, kissing him on the lips and all over his face. "Yes, yes, yes."

He chuckled. "Do you want to maybe put this on your finger, so it doesn't get lost while I'm making love to you?"

She spread the fingers of her left hand wide. He slipped the ring on her fourth finger. "I love it. It's perfect. I'll have to tell your parents thank you."

"For what?"

"For having a nice guy like you."

Dylan's lips formed a pout. "How about thanking me instead?"

"I can do that." She wrapped her arms around his neck and kissed him.

EPILOGUE

MARCY APPRECIATED THE warmth of the Sunday morning sun streaming through the bedroom glass door. She picked up the envelope off the bed and opened it. "It's from Mindy. She's loving college and has a boyfriend. I thought she might never look at another male after she danced with you."

Dylan leaned back against the pillows resting at his back. "You saw that? You were already at the ball? You never said so."

Marcy grinned. "I was there watching from a staff door."

"You're a sneaky one," he teased.

"I know you made her evening. And that little bow at the end." She shook her head. "She almost glowed."

Dylan leaned toward her. "Would you glow if I bow to you?"

She smiled. "You make me glow all the time."

One of the two babies that lay between them whimpered.

"It's almost feeding time." Marcy rested a hand on the child, hoping to put her off for a minute.

"You know when you agreed to have babies it didn't mean that we had to have them all at once."

"Hey, you wanted children, and I provided them." She couldn't help the pride in her voice.

This time he leaned over enough to give her a quick kiss. "By the way, I got a note from Robby saying he has a small music contract. Pretty nice."

"He has talent. Even two years ago I could see that. Have you seen Steve lately?"

"That's right, I forgot to tell you. He came in for a semiannual visit. He's doing great. I can't believe it. It won't be long until he age's out of the children's hospital. I've been his doctor since he was four. Watched him grow up." He fingered a small pink cheek. "Now I have my own to watch."

Marcy's chest tightened at the love she saw on her husband's face.

Liz, their girl, whined again. She was Elizabeth Margaret. Elizabeth after Dylan's mother and Margaret after Marcy's mother.

"It has been old home week for me at the clinic. Lucy Baker came in. Remember her?"

Marcy nodded. "Sure I do."

"She's in remission. TM13 saved her life, I believe."

"I'm glad. Thank goodness it was approved and is now being used widely at other hospitals."

"All because of my amazing wife." He smiled at her with pride in his eyes.

"Who will now be working from home part-time and keeping up the parents' cancer support group." Marcy wasn't sure she wasn't already tired.

"Hey, what time are Beau and Lisa supposed to be here?" Dylan rolled out of bed before picking up his daughter. He gave her a tender kiss on the forehead.

"Ten thirty."

He rested the small bundle in the crook of his arm, giving her a slow swing. "Then I guess we should get moving."

"We'll be moving a lot in a few minutes. Let's not get in a hurry yet."

Dylan sat on the bed beside her. "What's wrong?"

"Nothing. I'm just happy I guess." She patted her son, who would soon be awake. His name was Johnson Toby Nelson. They were calling him John. He was named after Beau. Dylan had asked if she would like to honor Toby by John sharing the name. She'd cried into Dylan's shoulder. What had she done to deserve such a man? This life?

"You don't sound happy?" Concern laced his words.

"I am. I'm so filled with happiness."

Dylan's eyes twinkled. "Even with moving?"

Marcy had to admit they needed a larger house, but she'd fallen in love with this one just as she'd fallen in love with Dylan. "Well, maybe not that."

"At the new house I'll plant the garden. Then when we sell it many, many years from now the person can appreciate the flowers your husband planted for you."

"That sounds nice." Still, she would miss her garden here.

John whimpered.

"I guess quiet time is over." She brought her precious baby into her arms.

"Dylan," she said, sounding distracted as she gazed at him holding their daughter. "Thank you."

"For what?" A perplexed look came over his face.

"For saving me from me. I love you."

"Honey, you're the one that saved me." He gave her a long kiss.

* * * * *

MEDICAL

Pulse-racing passion

Available Next Month

All titles available in Larger Print

Tempted By The Rebel Surgeon JC Harroway
Breaking The Single Mum's Rules JC Harroway

....

Finding Their Forever Family Caroline Anderson
Redeeming Her Hot-Shot Vet Juliette Hyland

....

Brought Together By A Pup Sue MacKay
Winning The Neonatal Doc's Heart Amy Ruttan

Keep reading for an excerpt of a new title
from the Western Romance series,
THE COWBOY NEXT DOOR by Cheryl Harper

CHAPTER ONE

SARAH HEARST WAS certain of a few things when she slipped into a cushy leather seat in the boardroom of Winthrop, Marshall, and Fine, attorneys at law.

First, her great-aunt Sadie had staged her final scene perfectly. Hiring the premiere law firm in Los Angeles came with perks, including a richly paneled conference room, efficient assistants who distributed coffee and water unobtrusively and the hush of hallowed old money that had never once managed to subdue the Hearsts.

Second, Sadie would have appreciated the size and energy of the crowd. The whole family had answered the summons to hear the reading of her will and the atmosphere was more low-key family reunion than true mourning. She had always called the people in the room her "favorite do-gooders, no-gooders and charming rapscallions" and loved every one of her four nephews—Sarah's dad included—and seventeen great-nieces and great-nephews even when they were "messier than a bag of nails."

The boardroom's view of the city was unimpeded on the beautiful late summer day, but inside, they might as well have been gathered around the island of Sadie's comfortable kitchen. Bluegrass music provided a backdrop for the various conversations. Instead of a publicity shot of a perfectly turned-out Sadie, TV chef and personality, a candid shot of her in her element, with flour dotting her red-and-white-gingham-check apron and a big grin on her face, filled the screen at the head of the table.

Sarah also knew without a doubt that some of the Hearsts would be surprised at Sadie's decisions. Her great-aunt had been unpredictable and relished every minute of watching people scurry to catch up with her. As a girl, Sarah had admired Sadie's over-the-top style; she'd come to understand the strategy behind Sadie's zigging when others expected her to zag after she'd started working her way up in the family business, the Cookie Queen Corporation.

"If they don't hurry up and get this started, the executor may need his own executor. None of us are getting any younger," her baby sister, Brooke, muttered. She smoothed her perfectly knotted blond updo and twitched a heel. "I've got to make my flight this afternoon. Paul's campaign manager is meeting us for dinner. This came at the worst time." Brooke and her husband were making plans to move into the mayor's mansion someday. Winning this election to the New York City Council was the critical first step.

"Too busy in New York to properly pay respects to Aunt Sadie," Sarah's middle sister, Jordan, said softly. She jostled Sarah as she crossed her arms with a huff.

Brooke and Jordan had been together for a full ride from the airport without an argument, so the cease-fire was clearly winding down.

Sarah didn't roll her eyes. She counted that a victory.

The lawyer executing Sadie's will, Howard Marshall, was both impressive and elderly, and the two qualities together meant he kept no schedule other than his own. Sadie had always done things as she liked and on her own time. This gathering would be no different. Fussing wouldn't change a thing, and Jordan's fidgeting suggested she agreed more with her younger sister than she'd ever want anyone to know.

As the peacemaker of the group, Sarah bit back the urge to shush her sisters, but if Brooke reminded her one more time how important it was that she get back to New York that evening, Sarah was going to...

"Thank you for joining us," Howard Marshall said as he opened the folder in front of him. "I'll be forwarding a copy of the letters Sadie left for each of you after this reading. Today we're here to cover the bequests Sarah Abigail Hearst outlined in her will." He cleared his throat, licked his finger and turned the page slowly. Hearing the lawyer call her great-aunt Sarah illuminated how clearly the world had changed. If Sadie were here, she'd smack him wherever she could reach, head or arm or chest, and remind him she only answered to Sadie. Being named after Sadie had always made Sarah proud. Today she was proud and heartbroken all over again that Sadie was really gone.

"Sadie did her own writing, so you will excuse the..." Howard sniffed. "Ahem, casual tone and hear these words in her voice, if you please."

Jordan bumped her shoulder again. "You okay?" she whispered.

Sarah nodded and wrapped her hand around Jordan's on one side and Brooke's on the other while they listened to Howard Marshall outline the bequests connected with the Cookie Queen Corporation, including the small corporate headquarters near Los Angeles, and the fortune Sadie had amassed over a lifetime as top baker, television chef and name brand for kitchen appliances and a line of Western wear.

A Los Angeles home and New York apartment and other large assets would be sold and the proceeds divided equally between Sadie's list of heirs after the final sale.

Simple enough. There were keepsakes left to each member of the family, and Sadie hadn't made any rules on keeping, selling or trading. As always, her gifts were true gifts, no strings attached.

As the lawyer's reading slowed, Sarah felt the weight of her sisters' stares. Their names had been conspicuously absent from the list of keepsakes and special notes.

"The final items are rather...delicate. Thus, Sadie wanted to handle telling you herself." Howard Marshall lifted his chin in a sharp motion to give his assistant a signal. Behind him, Sadie's photo became a video.

"Well, now, if this isn't the sorriest bunch of rascals I ever saw gathered in one place. Not a solitary tear to be seen." Sadie tsked and shook her head. Sarah tried to guess when it had been recorded. Her aunt had never gone gray, thanks to the best salons money could reserve. Until the end, she'd preferred a red lip and dark mascara. She might have recorded this video last month or last century, honestly.

Sadie waggled her finger. "I better not see any tears when I gaze down from my comfy cloud at you all. I'm celebratin' today, and you better be, too. I'm guessing Howie's almost finished reading my will. Let's tie up business, shall we? Wilson, raise your hand."

Wilson Douglas, Sadie's chief financial officer, followed Sadie's order.

"Aw, put your hand down, Wil. Everyone at this table knows who you are." Sadie chuckled. "First. My four darling nephews will form a new board of directors, with Wilson Douglas serving as the fifth member. During my last contract negotiation with Wil, I included a clause about what should happen if I died before the end of said contract." She held her hands out as if to say, "and here's where we ended up."

"Wilson will step up to lead The Cookie Queen Corporation. His position is guaranteed for one year. At the end of that year, either Wil or the board of directors may make a change there, but he will continue to serve on the board for a period of at least five years. Nobody knows the business better than Wil. I trust him with my baby."

Sarah studied Wilson Douglas's face. He was not shocked. He and his boss must have discussed her plans for the board of directors in advance. His firm jaw indicated he was prepared to honor Sadie's wishes even if her family bucked the decision.

Sadie cupped a hand over her eyes. "Michael, you better be at this table."

Sarah watched her oldest cousin straighten in his seat. "I'm here." A flush covered his cheeks when he realized he was responding to a video. Michael was the first of all the great-nephews and as such, took his position as eldest seriously. Michael took everything seriously; he marched through the Cookie Queen headquarters as if he were the official hall monitor. His "management by walking around" had earned him his own nickname; Sadie compared him to a stray calf.

"Okay, my little dogie," Sadie said, "you've been gunning for the top spot for years. Here's your chance. You also have one year, serving under Wil, to learn the ins and outs of the job. At the end of your trial period, Wil decides whether to recommend you permanently as CEO or to toss you out on your ear." She waggled a finger a second time. "I believe you can do this, Mikey, but try not to incite a riot in my employees. I love them more than a bear loves honey."

Michael relaxed against his chair, and Sarah immediately understood that her own position at the company had changed and not in a good way. He was going to be her boss. Her cousin had never understood Sarah's role as the single person in the customer relations area. It wasn't about answering phones or resolving complaints; Sarah and Sadie had brainstormed ways to keep her connected to her fans. Sarah's job had been about building strong relationships through appearances, social media posts, special fan messages and big and small ways to draw people to Sadie Hearst for recipes, advice and entertainment.

When Sadie continued on without addressing her position within the business, Sarah started to worry.

"Everybody study that wall. Those are my mountains, remember?" On the video, Sadie pointed to the right. There in the boardroom, a large painting filled the wall exactly where Sadie had ordered it to be put, no doubt, showing soaring mountains covered in tall trees and with white-capped peaks.

Sarah noticed everyone in the room followed her great-aunt's directions and stared hard at the painting. They'd all learned not to ignore her wishes. Sarah didn't have to. She had the painting memorized. It had hung behind her great-aunt's desk in her messy office until today.

"Home. Where I grew up. Some of you might even remember before I was the Cookie Queen, when I was only a local talent on public broadcasting, that I lived in a place called Prospect. My daddy's fishing lodge, grandly titled the Majestic Prospect Lodge, you recall? We used to get together during the summer, fish and swim and generally enjoy every blessing Mother Nature has tucked away in the prettiest locale in creation. Been a long time since I've been there, but the memories are sweet." Sadie cleared her throat. "Sarah, Jordan and Brooke…well, you might have hoped for something less troublesome, but I know you'll figure out what to do. After fifteen years, the Majestic may be nothing but weathered wood and cobwebs, but it's all

yours. Renovate it and run it, sell it as quick as you can or
let the mountains claim it again after the buildings turn
to dust. You girls decide. But do it together and remember
this legacy we've built.

"We all had such good times there. When I think of
your mama, I picture her in the old hammock by the lake,
remember? Place never was the same after she was gone,
was it? That lovely girl could bake like a dream, too. I despair that not a sorry one of you children caught the bug,
but those days sure were special. I could never let the lodge
go myself, but it's a puzzle that needs a solution. You girls
were always my favorite troublemakers, and that is saying quite a lot with this crowd. I couldn't trust the Majestic to anyone else."

Sadie cupped a hand over her ear. "What's that? Can't
be complaints, not from this lot. A bunch of questions?
Well, my time is up. I love you all. Don't forget to miss
me but not too much."

The screen went dark.

Howard Marshall stacked his papers efficiently and
waited. "May I answer any questions?"

Stunned silence filled the room. Not even Sarah could
recover quickly enough to get her mouth in gear.

Eventually, Jordan asked, "Is there more information
about the fishing lodge? A budget or…"

Sarah understood why Jordan trailed off. The questions were too big to chew unless they bit off small pieces
at first.

The lawyer slid a second folder down the table. Heads
turned as it slipped past to land in front of Sarah. "Instructions are here. There are funds to cover this year's
taxes and any minor incidentals, but the rest of the funds
will come after the sale of all other assets are final and
distributed among the heirs. Nothing additional has been

set aside for upkeep. The property manager in town has only secured the physical building, so the repairs may be extensive and all utilities will need to be restored before improvements begin." His lips were a tight line, as if he expected this to present a problem.

He could be right. Without upkeep, what state would the lodge be in after all this time?

The longer Sarah and her sisters took to decide about this remote piece of land they hadn't seen in years, the greater the threat of losing the lodge or their own savings to hold it.

"When should we expect to see the rest?" Brooke asked. "The funds..."

"The sales won't be rushed. Sadie had particular wishes." Howard Marshall sniffed. "My office will see to the disposition of any assets. Make sure your current address is on file with my assistant. We'll be in further contact when funds are ready to be disbursed." Howard Marshall stood. He didn't wave them toward the door, but his expression suggested he was ready for them to clear the boardroom. "If the new members of the board could remain, I have paperwork for you to sign."

Sarah and her sisters moved out into the hallway and followed the silent pack of Hearsts to the elevator. They waited for the next car to go down.

"Well, Sarah, not sure how you managed to get the family land," Michael said, sidling up next to her. "You and Sadie spent a lot of time together at the end, I guess." He shoved his hands in his pockets and jingled his change.

The urge to return a snarky comment about worming his way into the top position burned, but Sarah shoved it down.

"Congratulations, Michael," Sarah said, holding on to her position as the peacemaker with a tight grip. "I know you'll do a great job as CFO." Did she, though? Maybe not. She was certain he expected her to say so and there would be trouble if she didn't. Since Sadie hadn't done anything to protect Sarah's job, making nice with the new boss seemed prudent.

"Sarah worked with Sadie, the same as you did," Jordan snapped, ready to step in front and go to war as usual.

"Not exactly like I did." Michael ran his hand down his tie. "I worked all the way up to the head of marketing. Sadie had to create the customer relations director role, which..." Michael tapped Sarah's shoulder. "That's marketing, isn't it?"

It was more than that but explaining it to him again would be a waste of time.

Jordan's exasperated gust of air was enough of an answer that Sarah let the whole thing go.

"Good thing your position isn't essential day to day," he said. "You'll have plenty of time to sort out the lodge. Not sure there's much of a decision, though. You three have the money to reopen it? Lack of experience wouldn't stop you from trying."

"What's it to you, cousin?" Jordan drawled.

"Nothing, I guess." Michael jingled his coins again. "I look forward to your decision on what to do with the lodge and Sadie's legacy in Prospect. Sarah, when you're back at your desk, let me know. I'm going to make a presentation to the new board, a realignment of staffing and duties that makes good sense now, and I'd like to include your position in my plans."

He walked away before she could demand any details.

"Does that mean you'll still have your job or..." Brooke asked, her forehead wrinkled in concern. It was a valid question. His tone made Sarah think she wouldn't survive any personnel changes.

"Let's stop at Lark's on the way to the airport," Brooke muttered. "We need to talk."

Since her sister was right and she'd finally stopped harping about not missing her flight back to New York, Sarah was happy to agree. They were seated around a cramped table with the pizza they'd ordered ahead of time before anyone spoke.

"How quickly do you think we can sell?" Brooke asked before she took a bite.

The fact that Jordan paused and chose not to fire back convinced Sarah that both of her sisters were on the same page. "We won't know until we see what shape it's in," she said. "Since my job is apparently...open-ended now, I'll head up to Prospect this weekend." She wiped her fingers on her napkin. "We could make it a girls' trip, go together and make the decision as one."

They hadn't successfully traveled together ever, but certainly not after the summer her mother had died. Sarah had spent every family trip in the middle of the backseat, the wall preventing her sisters from brawling and her father from turning the car around.

"It could be fun," she added.

Both of her sisters sucked in air, ready to explain how wrong she was, when her father pulled out the fourth seat at the table. He wrapped his arms around her before hugging Jordan and Brooke. "The Everything Pizza. My favorite." He immediately pulled the mushrooms off a slice and took a bite. "What's the plan?"

Sarah rubbed her temple. "We got here fifteen minutes before you, Dad. We're good, but we aren't that good."

He nodded and waved his hand to tell her to go on.

"I'm heading to Prospect. Brooke has to get home. Jordan..." Sarah raised her eyebrows.

"I've got a project to wrap up, but I could make it...

next week? Do you want to wait that long?" she asked. "My guess is that the internet service in Prospect may not be up to running high-speed cybersecurity tests and tech firms want everything finished yesterday. My boss will complain if I extend this unexpected break." Jordan's guilty expression was so familiar that Sarah immediately winced. Her middle sister had always worried so much about doing enough that she overcompensated. Not joining Sarah weighed her down.

"No rush, I guess. Once the taxes are paid, you should have a year or so." Her father frowned. "But I'm not sure how many buyers there are for a run-down fishing lodge. It could take a while to get a decent price." Her father made a good point. Since he and his art supply store scraped by, he wasn't known for giving financial advice.

"But the proceeds from the sale of Sadie's assets will help if we have to hold it longer," Sarah said.

"Unless we need those for…life." Brooke closed her eyes before forcing a smile on her face. "Sarah, when you go, be sure to take some pictures. Then we can all see the place and decide on how to go about listing it for sale."

Jordan wanted to argue; the urge was written on her face, but it was a valid suggestion.

"What if we don't want to sell?" Jordan asked. "I mean, what if we can't agree?"

"Why would we want to keep a fishing lodge in a town in the mountains hours away from anywhere?" Brooke asked slowly and loudly. Before Jordan could reply, Brooke's cell phone rang. Brooke snatched it off the table and scowled down at the number on the display. "I have to take this." She was shaking her head as she stood and marched toward the door.

They watched Brooke pace in front of the window of Lark Street Pizza, the hole-in-the-wall pizza place that had kept their whole family alive after Beth Hearst had died and their father had moved them to this modest, albeit neighborly neighborhood. Leaving Denver had been hard, but Lark's had always hit the spot.

"That was Paul's number, I think." Jordan chewed her bottom lip. "It was definitely New York."

Sarah knew Jordan was worried about Brooke. They all were. Talking to her on the phone only kept her up to date with the big events in her youngest sister's life. Seeing the circles under her eyes and the way the fancy suit hung on her thinner frame was enough evidence to support their concern.

If it was Brooke's husband on the other end of the call, were they having trouble? What should she do about it?

"I'm going to run to the restroom so we can hit the road," Jordan mumbled before walking away.

Sarah met her father's stare.

"Good thing Sadie lumped you three together, isn't it? No better way for her to leave chaos in her wake, and she loved chaos." He squeezed Sarah's hand. "You'll work it all out, Sarah. They'll follow you."

Sarah sipped her water and wondered if it was worth mentioning to her father that Brooke was losing too much weight and Jordan was shorter tempered than usual. His sunny disposition had always made him better at celebration than problem-solving. That was her job.

"Ever notice how often they disappear when the bill hits the table?" he asked with a grin. He plopped his credit card down and handed it and the bill back to the waiter. "Like they have honed a sixth sense about it somehow."

The tension headache forming in her temples was going to be a problem.

"Listen, don't worry about your job. We've got a board meeting planned for two weeks from Friday. We'll all sit down and discuss any major changes before they're set in stone." Her father squeezed her shoulder. "Try to enjoy this trip back to Prospect. Sadie was always one with ulterior motives. It wouldn't surprise me if she planned this for you to take a break and have the chance to revisit old haunts in Colorado."

While also saddling her with her sisters' futures, too. Maybe. Maybe not.

"Dad, why do you think Sadie didn't make a place for me? At the company. I work hard there." That worried Sarah more than this lodge problem. When she got to Prospect, the problem about what to do with their inheritance would be answered, no doubt.

But what about her career and her life and all the rest? If she wasn't working for her aunt, then…

He sighed. "Hard to say. I wish she'd been the kind of person who made her plans clear, but there is one thing I am certain of." He bent his head to meet her stare. "My daughters are equal to whatever Sadie dreamed up for them. She knew that, too."

Sarah nodded to reassure him. He was right, of course. Finding another job wouldn't be difficult.

Finding anyone else like Sadie, though, would be impossible.

Stretching her neck slowly from side to side as she followed her father and sisters out of Lark's didn't do a lot to ease the headache. For now, all Sarah could do was take the next step: find her way back to Prospect.

LET'S TALK ABOUT BOOKS!

JOIN THE CONVERSATION

**MILLSANDBOON
AUSTRALIA**

@MILLSANDBOONAUS

ESCAPE THE EVERY DAY AT
MILLSANDBOON.COM.AU